The VEGAN Cookbook

300 RECIPES FOR ANY OCCASION

JOLINDA HACKETT
WITH LORENA NOVAK BULL, RD

New York

For my angel, Adrienne. She knows why.

FALL RIVER PRESS

New York

An Imprint of Sterling Publishing Co., Inc.
1166 Avenue of the Americas
New York, NY 10036

ISBN 978-1-4351-6745-2

For information about custom editions, special sales, and premium and corporate purchases,
please contact Sterling Special Sales at 800-805-5489 or specialsales@sterlingpublishing.com.

Manufactured in China

2 4 6 8 10 9 7 5 3 1

sterlingpublishing.com

Contents

Acknowledgments

With thanks to Rhonda Parkinson and Linda Larsen for mentoring me; Lia Belardo for her inspiration and urban insights; Joey, Ray, German, Shell, Daisy, and Lindsay for keeping me sane; and especially to Donald Watson, who humbly and quietly started a revolution.

Introduction

AFTER WITNESSING THE ABUSE of dairy cows firsthand, a shy British farm boy decided to stop drinking milk. Already a vegetarian and a conscientious war objector, young Donald Watson couldn't reconcile his philosophical pacifism with what he had seen. Though the idea of avoiding animal foods goes back to ancient times, it was Watson who first created the word *vegan* (the beginning and end of "vegetarian," he reasoned). In 1944, he joined together a handful of like-minded people into the first vegan society in the UK, corresponding and spreading ideas via old-fashioned mail. Four years later, the first vegan association was born in the United States. Watson went on to live a mostly quiet life as a solitary craftsman and an organic farmer. Determined to outlive those who would criticize his ideas, he regularly hiked through the British countryside hills until his death at ninety-five years of age. He had been vegan for sixty-one years, and vegetarian for more than eighty.

Religious ascetics and philosophers have dabbled with vegetarian and mostly vegan diets throughout history. Among the ancient Greeks, mathematician and philosopher Pythagoras mentored a group of vegetarians in the sixth century b.c., and at the same time in India, the ancient Jains were already practicing *ahimsa*, pledging not to kill by avoiding animal flesh and eggs. More recent philosophers, such as Jeremy Bentham and Peter Singer, have shaped the modern face of veganism, and many religious groups, from the Rastafarians to the Eastern Orthodox Church, continue to promote the merits of veganism in achieving physical and spiritual purity.

But it is mostly thanks to Donald Watson, an unlikely and modest revolutionary, that veganism today thrives around the world. Nearly all major cities, and many smaller ones, boast one or more vegan restaurants, and hundreds of businesses proudly stamp their wares—from mock caviar to cruelty-free condoms—with a vegan certification.

So what does it mean?

While a vegetarian diet excludes the consumption of all animals, including pigs, cows, birds, fish, and all other sea animals, a vegan diet avoids the meat of animals as well as foods that come from animals, including milk and all other dairy products (butter, cheese, ice cream) and eggs. The many processed foods such as mayonnaise and baked goods that include eggs or dairy are also eliminated. Many packaged and premade goods contain hidden animal ingredients that vegans also avoid. The most common of these are dairy derivatives such as whey, lactose, casein, caseinate, and sodium caseinate, albumen from eggs, and gelatin, which is derived from animal collagens.

Some vegans take it a step further, avoiding foods that may have used animals in their production, such as some white sugars and wines. A few foods, primarily honey, cause debate as to whether they may be called vegan or not. Though honey can easily be substituted by agave nectar or brown rice syrup, other questionable foods such as civet coffee and truffles sniffed by pigs may give pause to vegan gourmands.

Without fatty meats and rich creams, vegan chefs are some of the most inspired artists on the planet, drawing upon an international array of herbs and spices to create naturally nourishing and cholesterol-free dishes. With a bit of experimentation and a few good substitutes, you'll soon be on your way to exploring the many incarnations of vegan cuisine: from heirloom produce and exotic treasures to down-home traditional comfort foods and the most indulgent cavity-inducing desserts a sweet tooth could dream of.

Chapter 1
The Vegan Revolution

Cook some dim sum topped off with hoisin sauce and your friends will think you're a talented Chinese food chef. Perhaps even a connoisseur. But when you create a vegan meal, you are literally changing the world. Call it gastronomical activism at the tip of your fork. Just by eating vegan, you become an eco-activist and a healthier person. Veganism is not just a diet, and not just the food on your plate: it is an active stance against environmental inefficiencies, a boycott against animal cruelty, and a method of preventive medicine. Yes, all that comes just from trading in milk and meat for mushrooms and marinara. One small bite for you is one giant leap toward a healthier planet and a healthier body.

What Are Vegan Foods?

If you're used to eating eggs for breakfast and steak for dinner, you may be wondering, what's left? Rest assured that with a little ingenuity, a plant-centered diet will bring more color, spice, and variety to your plate than ever before.

As a matter of habit, most people reach for the same few foods day after day, but all that stops now! A nearly infinite array of grains, herbs, fruits, vegetables, beans, and legumes from around the world is at your fingertips. There are dozens of varieties of beans alone—navy, cannellini, kidney beans, black beans—and many other pulses, such as chickpeas and lentils, each with its own distinct flavors and textures. There's no need to ever ask "What do vegans eat?" It's simpler to question what vegans don't eat, as the list is much shorter!

Instead of packaged and processed foods, vegans eat mostly whole foods (fruits, vegetables, beans, nuts, grains) and dairy- and egg-free versions of traditional favorites (cheeseless pizza, bean burritos minus the cheese) flavored with herbs and spices from around the world. Vegans today can savor hundreds of vegan substitute products, including nondairy cream cheese, "beef" jerky, and vegan white chocolate.

> ### Can I eat . . . ?
> Of course you *can*! Vegans *can* eat anything, but *choose* not to eat certain foods. When thinking about what to include and exclude in your diet, consider your reasons and values for choosing a vegan diet. Does eating a particular food align or conflict with these values? Whatever your diet may be, stick with your personal values and goals rather than dictionary definitions.

Whatever comfort food you crave has a vegan version. There are dozens of brands of the more common substitutes, such as soy milk and vegan meats and cheeses, each with their own texture and taste. Some will fool even the most ardent wrangler, and others, well, won't. You'll also find ways to duplicate many of your favorite comfort foods in this book, without eggs and dairy.

Why Eat Vegan?

Ask 100 vegans why they pass on animal foods and you may get 100 different answers. Animal suffering, environmental waste, and personal health usually top the list. But global poverty, food safety and sanitation, or food allergies are valid reasons to reduce reliance on animal foods. People of Western faiths may cite the biblical order for "stewardship" over creation, while others commit to the Eastern spiritual principle of *ahimsa*—that is, nonviolence and harmlessness. Call it the vegan Hippocratic oath.

So then, what's the harm with eating eggs and dairy?

For the Animals

Concerns over animal suffering understandably lead to a vegetarian diet, but the suffering and killing of animals in dairy and egg production inspires many well-intentioned vegetarians who learn of such practices to quickly go vegan.

Gone are the days of Old MacDonald's happily mooing dairy cows and clucking chickens. Today's cows are relentlessly milked by machines, not cheery, freckle-faced men in overalls. Females must be kept constantly pregnant in order to lactate, but the dairy industry has little use for their male offspring. Sent to slaughter at a few months old for veal, male calves are just leftovers, the collateral damage of dairy production. When her ability to produce milk naturally slows at five or six years of age (think of it as a sort of cow menopause), a dairy cow's final destination is the slaughterhouse.

Egg-laying hens are tightly packed into filthy cages, stacked floor to ceiling in huge warehouses called CAFOs, or Concentrated Animal Feeding Operations, within the industry. The Occupational Safety and Health Administration (OSHA) recommends that workers only enter when suited up with goggles and respirators, as the air is hazardously putrid with feces. Here, chickens struggle for space to move and air to breathe. Imagine sharing a portable toilet all summer long with three of your closest friends for a spatial approximation. Under these circumstances, deaths from dehydration and suffocation are common. To avoid pecking conflicts, baby chicks have their beaks sliced off at birth, and the industry has discovered that although a hen's egg-laying ability eventually slows, it can be kick-started through "forced molting," which involves weeks of starvation.

Such are the lives of animals used for industrialized food production. Not a pleasant life. It's no wonder that more and more people are refusing to support these practices, voting with their stomachs and pocketbooks in favor of tofu scramble over eggs from tortured hens.

> Despite marketing ploys, eggs labeled "free-range" or "cage-free" are no better for your health or the environment than regular eggs, and they're not much better for the chickens. With little regulation, "free-range" hens may still never once see sunlight and still suffer debeaking, and when productivity wanes, they end up in the same place as conventional hens. There's simply no such thing as a "free-range" slaughterhouse.

For many vegans, inspired by philosophers Jeremy Bentham and Peter Singer, the atrocities of food production are a concern, but dominance, use, and exploitation of some creatures (animals) by another (humans) is the real underlying issue. Agree or disagree, the words of novelist, feminist, and vegan Alice Walker summarize this sentiment: "The animals of the world exist for their own reasons. They were not made for humans any more than black people were made for white, or women created for men." This is the idea of animal rights; that animals may lead their own lives, completely unencumbered by humans.

Many social justice activists, including notable heroes Coretta Scott King and Cesar Chavez, reject animal exploitation as a logical extension of their belief in equality. In the words of Albert Einstein, they have "widened the circle of compassion" to include all victims of oppression and injustice—animals and humans alike.

Some concerned human rights and civil rights activists eat vegan to boycott the sweatshop treatment of slaughterhouse workers, many of whom are illegal immigrants exploited by big businesses to do the dirtiest work. Without basic protections, illegal workers don't object when USDA and OSHA safety violations inevitably occur, and, without health insurance, they are a cheap source of labor that can be ignored when injured performing their dangerous duties.

For the Earth

Modern food production is no friend to local environments, as anyone who has lived near a large death factory can tell you. Neighbors of industrialized farms are constantly complaining of the air and water pollution caused by the concentrated waste of these poor animals. And the larger global environment suffers as well. Everyone from environmental groups to the United Nations agrees that animal agriculture is one of the largest contributors to global warming and environmental devastation. Because exponentially more water, energy, land, and resources are needed to raise and feed animals than to support a plant-based diet, one simply can't call oneself an environmentalist while still consuming animal products.

The problem of disposing of the waste produced by the approximately 10 billion animals raised for food in the United States is minor in comparison to the very real threat of global climate change. The UN estimates that 20 percent of all greenhouse gases come from the food animal industry; much more than is caused by private jets, SUVs, and all forms of transport worldwide combined. Red meat and dairy are the biggest culprits, closely followed by pigs, chickens, and egg production.

> Just one individual switching from a meat-based to a plant-based diet reduces carbon emissions by about one and a half tons a year. That's more than eating locally grown food and trading in your SUV for a hybrid.

With an increasing global population, land and water availability is a concern. More than three-fourths of all agricultural land in the United States is used not to grow food for humans, but rather feed for farm animals or as grazing land. This is a shameful waste of resources that could be redistributed to alleviate hunger worldwide. Yet it's still not enough to feed the selfish American desire for meat. Clear-cutting for grazing land has claimed hundreds of millions of forest acres in the United States, and South American rain forests are now losing timber to provide wealthier nations with imported beef.

A single half-ton cow consumes thousands of pounds of grain, soy, or corn over its short lifetime, yet produces only a few hundred hamburgers. Water used to grow that grain (about half of all water used in the United States goes toward raising animals) and the chemicals and herbicides used to quicken its growth are just more environmental casualties of an animal-based diet. Raising animals for food is a tragically inefficient squandering of water, food, land, chemical fertilizers, and energy.

For Personal and Global Health

Along with humane and environmental concerns, personal health is a strong motivator to eat vegan. From significantly reduced rates of hypertension, arterial hardening, stroke, type 2 diabetes, obesity, heart disease, and several types of cancer (prostate and breast cancer being the best documented), a plant-based diet helps prevent the vast majority of life-threatening diseases that plague modernity.

Medical research and the American Dietetic Association affirm that a plant-based diet prevents many ailments, helps reverse some, and eases the symptoms of others. Veganism isn't a bulletproof vest in protecting against these killers, but it just may be the best bet.

Hormone use is a major concern in much of the world, though the American public and lawmakers are less aware of the dangers. In quest of the almighty dollar, U.S. dairy cows are fed a tasty-sounding drug called "recombinant bovine growth hormone" (rBGH), which increases milk production up to 20 percent. Because this powerful hormone ends up in consumers' stomachs, Japan, Australia, Canada, and the European Union have banned the use of rBGH, and the EU bans the import of American beef because of it. Medical studies implicate these hormones in the connection between diet and cancer, particularly breast, prostate, and testicular cancers. The unnatural and unsanitary conditions of production are increasingly convincing the health conscious to reduce their animal-based food consumption, not only to avoid these hormones, but also to avoid exposure to E. coli and the other common pathogens originating in animal feces and contaminating animal products.

The number of children afflicted with one or more food sensitivities has inexplicably grown in recent years, though some people theorize this may be related to the increasing number of unnatural hormones and additives in commonly consumed foods. Trigger foods are more easily avoided on a whole-foods diet, and eating vegan or mostly vegan makes this easier. Some food allergy sufferers have even reported the reversal of their sensitivities on a healthy plant-based diet.

Whatever your reasons for exploring the vegan lifestyle, keep them in mind when confronted with the inevitable naysayers, and remember that they are your reasons alone. Others may have different motivating factors. Committing yourself 100 percent to your goals will help you in the face of adversity when your deer-hunting uncle cackles at your Thanksgiving tofu turkey.

Vegan Nutrition

Despite a national obsession with protein, most Americans eat much more than recommended, and deficiency in vegans is rare. Professional body-builders and pregnant women aside, most vegans easily meet their daily requirement of protein (and most omnivores exceed it exponentially), but beware of your zinc, vitamin D, iron, and calcium intake, and foremost, vitamin B_{12}.

If you are pregnant, you'll need to plan adequately to obtain all the nutrients you need—not just protein—and have likely already consulted with your doctor about this. If not, please do. And, as most bodybuilders already know, the timing of protein consumption coupled with the stress of lifts is more important than whether that protein is plant or animal based.

Though not readily supplied by a vegan diet, vitamin D is easily obtained from sunlight. Step outside for a few minutes a day and you're set for vitamin D. Make sure your vegan kids do the same. If you happen to be a vegan living in Antarctica or the Arctic circle, best to rely on a supplement or fortified foods, such as fortified orange juice or soy milk.

Similarly, many soy foods are fortified with calcium, another important nutrient for dairy-free folks, and broccoli, tofu, tahini, almonds, and dark leafy greens provide a good natural source. But to build strong bones, you need exercise as well as calcium, so vegan or not, diet is only half the equation.

When it comes to iron, most vegans and vegetarians actually get more than omnivores, but to be on the safe side, lentils, chickpeas, tahini, and once again, those dark leafy greens like spinach and kale are good vegan sources.

Before you pour that glass of orange juice or soy milk, shake it up! The calcium in these drinks tends to settle to the bottom of the carton, so to get the best bone-boosting effect, shake before you drink. If you're a heavy smoker or coffee drinker, consider taking a supplement, as these inhibit absorption of several nutrients.

Noticing a pattern? Dark leafy green vegetables are one of the most nutrient-rich foods on the planet. Find ways to include kale, spinach, or other greens in your diet by snipping them into pasta sauces and casseroles, or include a few spinach leaves along with your other salad greens.

Fish oils and fish such as salmon are often touted as a source of healthy omega-3 fatty acids, but vegetarians and vegans can obtain these from flaxseeds and flax oil, as well as walnuts or hempseeds.

Flaxseed oil is rich in omega-3s, and has a sweet and nutty flavor. Never use flax as a cooking oil, however, as the heat destroys the healthy fats and creates unhealthy free radicals. Instead, add a teaspoonful of flax oil to your favorite salad dressing, or drizzle over already cooked dishes for your daily omega-3s. Look for a brand that is cold-pressed and stored chilled to keep it fresh.

Vitamin B_{12} cannot reliably be obtained from vegan foods. Deficiencies of this important nutrient are admittedly rare, and, if you're eating vegan meals only occasionally, you don't need to worry. Vegetarians will absorb B_{12} from food sources, but long-term vegans, and pregnant and breastfeeding women, in particular, need a reliable source. Take a supplement and eat fortified foods, such as nutritional yeast. Because the body needs very little B_{12}, and it can be stored for years, some people claim a supplement is not needed, or suggest that omnivores are more likely to be deficient in a variety of nutrients, and thus the B_{12} issue for vegans is grossly overblown. While this last argument may be true, the bottom line, according to most experts, is to take a supplement. Better safe than sorry.

The Truth about Protein

In 1971 Frances Moore Lappé wrote a book that revolutionized the relationship thousands of Americans had with their plates, effectively launching vegetarianism into the public consciousness. *Diet for a Small Planet* continues to be a widely read and cited book today. Much to the chagrin of generations of vegetarians, however, it was the beginning of a myth still often retold, including by some nutritionists who ought to know better. This is the myth of "protein combining," or the idea that plant sources provide "incomplete" proteins while meats provide "complete" proteins.

Lappé theorized that in order to digest all nine of the essential amino acids that the human body needs to build protein, vegetarians needed to combine foods so as to consume each essential amino acid in one sitting. Whole grains needed to be consumed at the same time as nuts, for example.

The truth is, by eating a variety of foods, you'll have nothing to worry about. Although you do need a full range of amino acids, and plant-based foods contain varying amounts of the essentials, Lappé's error was to assume these nine essentials needed to be consumed at the same meal. Nutritionists, including the American Dietetic Association and the USDA, have since refuted this claim, and even Lappe herself revised her stance in later editions of the book. Your body will store and combine proteins on its own. Just so this point is not missed: protein combining is a complete myth.

> Quinoa, soy, and hempseeds are vegan powerhouses when it comes to protein, as they contain the highest amount of all nine essential amino acids. Hempseeds are also high in omega-3 and omega-6 essential fatty acids.

If, however, you tend to go weeks eating nothing but bananas and soda, you'll quickly find yourself deficient in more than just protein. But eat a relatively healthy diet and you'll be just fine. From the American Dietetic Association: "Plant sources of protein alone can provide adequate amounts of the essential and nonessential amino acids, assuming that dietary protein sources from plants are reasonably varied."

Vegan Health Advantages

While B_{12} is a genuine concern, the health advantages of a plant-based diet are endless. The average vegan gets twice as much fiber as most omnivores. A vegan diet is naturally cholesterol free, and is almost guaranteed to lead to marked decreases in cholesterol levels in just two weeks. If lowering your cholesterol naturally is one of your goals, test your levels before and again a few weeks into a vegan diet, and gamble with your skeptical friends, just for fun.

But this is just the tip of the iceberg.

Blood pressure, too, is shown to decrease drastically in a short period of time on a plant-based diet. High blood pressure is rarely a concern for vegans, and making the switch can decrease your blood pressure in less than two months. No need to give up salt as conventional wisdom dictates—just get rid of the meat and dairy!

As an added bonus for men (and for women too, really), it's possible that vegans really do make better lovers. High blood pressure, high cholesterol, and particularly the decreased blood flow associated with blocked arteries are common causes leading to erectile dysfunction, and vegans certainly have fewer instances of these symptoms. Sure, a little purple pill can help out for the night, but a vegan diet can help forever!

The fountain of youth may not flow with water after all—it may be full of fruits and veggies.

You do need to eat a balanced diet in order to reap these benefits. After all, French fries and potato chips are animal free, but that doesn't make them healthy. When it comes to vegan nutrition, variety is key. Make sure your protein sources are varied, rather than from just one food group. Eat a rainbow of fruits and veggies, and include green leafy vegetables as often as possible.

But the health benefits of reduced animal consumption go beyond your blood pressure and your bedroom; it's a global concern.

The powerful cocktail of hormones and antibiotics pumped into cows and chickens by today's food industry ends up right back in local water supplies and affects everyone, even vegans. All these antibiotics, combined with the cramped conditions of modern farms, lead to dangerous new drug-resistant pathogens and bacterial strains. Swine flu, bird flu, SARS, and mad-cow disease are all traced back to intense animal agriculture practices. Because of our rapidly shrinking planet, the "butterfly effect" is a very real phenomenon: a pig in Mexico sneezed, and a child in Bangkok died.

Getting Started

There's no need to toss out all your old cookbooks and family recipes, as many of them can provide inspiration for fabulous vegan meals after a few minor tweaks, of course. Most recipes for cookies, muffins, and cakes can be made with nondairy milk, vegan margarine, and a commercial egg replacer. For recipes calling for honey, try an equivalent amount of agave nectar, which is equally lovely in tea and drizzled over vegan pancakes. Store-bought mock ground beef is surprisingly tasty, and TVP (textured vegetable protein) granules provide a meaty texture in dishes like tacos or chili.

Take a look at some of your favorite meals. Like spaghetti with meatballs? Try a vegetable marinara instead, grab some ready-made vegetarian meatballs from your grocery store, or try the recipe on page 159. Try your favorite chicken noodle soup recipe without the chicken, and omit the beef from your Chinese beef and broccoli, or use seitan as a beef substitute instead. Often, it's the spices, flavors, and textures that make a meal satisfying and nostalgic, not the actual meat.

> Cooking for omnivores? If your family still insists on eating a bit of meat, no need to cook two separate meals. Prepare a bit of meat separately, and add it into a portion of an otherwise vegan soup, pasta, or casserole.

For the novice chef, restaurants can offer a tasty introduction to new foods. Check your phonebook or the Internet for vegetarian and vegan restaurants in your area. Thai and Chinese restaurants serve up vegan curries and stir-fries, many with an array of mock meats. As a general rule, ethnic restaurants including Mexican (just hold the cheese), Indian, and Middle Eastern offer more options for vegetarians and vegans than American chains and diners, which may offer little more than a veggie burger as an afterthought.

Creating Amazing Meals

When eating at restaurants, the flavors often come from an overdose of salt, fat, and sometimes MSG. But when cooking at home, you're better off enhancing your foods with flavors that come from nature.

One flavor enhancer unique to vegan cuisine is the almighty nutritional yeast. It's a yellowish powder universally loved by vegans for its nutty and cheesy taste and ability to add that *je ne sais quoi* to just about any savory dish.

> Watch out for brewer's yeast, which many well-meaning people insist is the same as nutritional yeast. It's not. Depending on where you live, nutritional yeast may be called "savory yeast flakes" or "nutritional food yeast," but brewer's yeast is something altogether different.

Most chefs agree that sea salt has a superior taste to table salt. Once you've tried sea salt, you'll never go back to regular refined salt, and the trace minerals in sea salt are an added bonus. Similarly, freshly cracked black pepper is always best. Use vegetable broth instead of water whenever possible, stock up on vegetarian bouillon or powdered vegetable broth, and don't be afraid to use it with a heavy hand in stir-fries, soups, gravies, and casseroles—just about anything savory or spicy.

Fresh herbs and spices are an obvious choice for adding flavor, but their true power comes in their variety and combination. No matter how many spices are on your spice rack, there's always room for one or two more! Most of the spices called for in this book are commonly found, but don't let that limit you. Add garam masala to Indian dishes and smoked Spanish paprika to paellas. Same with fresh herbs. If you can find them, add lemongrass and kaffir lime leaves to your Thai curries!

One or two gourmet or unusual ingredients can add pizzazz to an otherwise standard dish. A salad drizzled with champagne vinegar and avocado oil trumps regular vinaigrette any day, and a meatless pasta salad enhanced with sun-dried tomatoes, dried blueberries, or artichoke hearts, for example, is more exciting than a pasta salad with ordinary grilled chicken. The difference between a simple meal versus a culinary affair to remember may be just a handful of wasabi-coated macadamia nuts.

Got a big bunch of basil? Make your fresh herbs last longer by giving them a quick rinse. Then, wrap your lightly damp herbs in a paper towel. Place the paper towel in a ziplock bag and store in your refrigerator's crisper. They'll keep about ten days this way.

Vegan Machines and Coddled Cooks

The equipment and utensils needed in a vegan kitchen vary little from what any other home cook might need. A blender and food processor are essential. Rather than working up a sweat grating carrots, a food processor will do the trick in ten seconds. Quality chopping knives and a cutting board are standard for any cook, as are a large skillet or sauté pan, a stock pot for soups, and some oven basics, such as a casserole dish and a baking pan. With these few items, you'll be prepared to create almost all of the recipes in this book.

Get rid of your microwave, and force yourself to heat and eat healthier foods, rather than packaged meals. Leftovers are just as easy to reheat stovetop or in the oven. In a healthy whole-foods kitchen, the only thing a microwave is good for is lightly cooking vegetables. But a steamer basket and some water is almost as quick.

A few convenient luxuries can enliven your whole-foods vegan kitchen. Though not an essential, a rice steamer means one less pot on the stove to worry about. After adding liquid and just about any grain (not just rice), you can walk away without worry.

The difference between one stock pot and another is minimal (both the $10 one and the $50 one boil water equally), but splurge for a quality piece when purchasing a nonstick pan. It's essential for making vegan crepes and comes in handy for pancakes and French toast. But the real value of a nonstick pan is in reducing the oil needed to sauté veggies or scramble tofu. If lowering dietary fat is a concern, shop for a quality nonstick pan.

To slash the fat in the many vegan recipes that call for sautéing onions, garlic, or veggies in oil, use half oil and half vegetable broth; soy sauce; or even cooking wine, sherry, or another liquid. Some chefs call this technique "steam-frying."

For feeding a large family or baking in quantity, a soy-milk maker is a cost cutter in the long run. Unless the label says "unsweetened," store-bought soy milk is packed with sugar, so homemade is better for you as well. Making soy milk is a bit of an effort by hand, but with a machine, it's a snap. If you're feeding a large family, it's a convenient investment.

Shopping Tips

Health-food stores and gourmet grocers stock vegan specialty goods, but these days, even most regular chain supermarkets carry mock meats and dairy substitutes. Some stores have a separate "natural foods" aisle, while others stock the veggie burgers with the other frozen foods. Most health-food stores and co-ops are happy to place special orders, so don't be afraid to ask.

Browse farmers' markets and farm stands for good deals and environmental karma and seek out ethnic and import grocers for hidden treasures. Kosher stores stock enough dairy substitutes to fill a vegan's dreams; Asian grocery stores are a paradise of exotic meatless "meats," sauces, and spices; and Middle Eastern and Mexican grocers supply unusual ingredients and flavors.

Insiders know that the Seventh Day Adventist religion has a long history of vegetarianism and even their own brand of veggie "meats." If you're lucky enough to have one in your area, check out Adventist book supply stores for a bounty of veggie hams, fish, and sausages.

Do I need to read labels to make sure I'm buying animal-free foods?

By avoiding foods that contain trace amounts of animal by-products, you're sending a message to companies to use non-animal sources. Then again, standing in supermarket aisles meticulously reading labels may seem wacky and obsessive, rather than healthy and compassionate, the latter being the more exemplary image for vegans to cultivate. Your choice.

If you live in Manhattan, you'll find vegan foods on literally every corner, but even if you reside in the middle of Mayberry, you can still enjoy a tasty and nutritious vegan diet based on the bounty of grains, beans, fruits, and vegetables that are available anywhere on the planet.

But seriously. Find some nutritional yeast. That stuff is good.

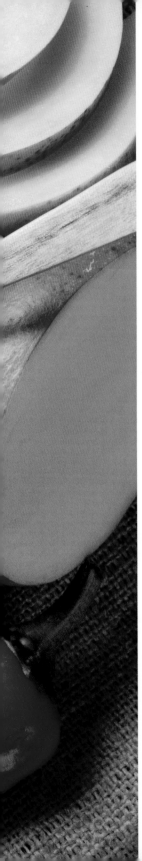

Chapter 2

Appetizers, Sauces, and Dips

Green and Black Olive Tapenade

Mediterranean olive tapenade can be used as a spread or dip for baguettes or crackers. If you don't have a food processor, you could also mash the ingredients together with a mortar and pestle or a large fork.

INGREDIENTS | YIELDS 1 CUP

½ cup green olives
¾ cup black olives
2 cloves garlic
1 tablespoon capers (optional)
2 tablespoons lemon juice
2 tablespoons olive oil
¼ teaspoon oregano
¼ teaspoon black pepper

Process all ingredients in a food processor until almost smooth.

PER TABLESPOON Calories: 29 | Fat: 3g | Sodium: 116mg | Fiber: 0g | Protein: 0g

Roasted Red Pepper Hummus

You'll rarely meet a vegan who doesn't love hummus in one form or another. As a veggie dip or sandwich spread, hummus is always a favorite. Up the garlic in this recipe, if that's your thing, and don't be ashamed to lick the spoons or spatula.

INGREDIENTS | YIELDS 1½ CUPS

1 15-ounce can chickpeas, drained
⅓ cup tahini
⅔ cup chopped roasted red peppers
3 tablespoons lemon juice
2 tablespoons olive oil
2 cloves garlic
½ teaspoon cumin
⅓ teaspoon salt
¼ teaspoon cayenne pepper (optional)

Process all ingredients together in a blender or food processor until smooth, scraping the sides down as needed.

Do-It-Yourself Roasted Red Peppers
Sure, you can buy them from a jar, but it's easy to roast your own. Here's how: Fire up your oven to 450°F (or use the broiler setting) and drizzle a few whole peppers with olive oil. Bake for 30 minutes, turning over once. Direct heat will also work, if you have a gas stove. Hold the peppers with tongs over the flame until lightly charred. Let your peppers cool, then remove the skin before making hummus.

PER TABLESPOON Calories: 53 | Fat: 3g | Sodium: 110mg | Fiber: 1g | Protein: 1g

Eggplant Baba Ghanoush

*Whip up a batch of Eggplant Baba Ghanoush, Roasted Red Pepper Hummus (p. 18),
and some Vegan Tzatziki (p. 29) and make a Mediterranean appetizer spread.
Don't forget some vegan pita bread to dip into your Baba.*

INGREDIENTS | YIELDS 1½ CUPS

2 medium eggplants
3 tablespoons olive oil, divided
2 tablespoons lemon juice
¼ cup tahini
3 cloves garlic
½ teaspoon cumin
½ teaspoon chili powder (optional)
¼ teaspoon salt
1 tablespoon chopped fresh parsley

1. Preheat oven to 400°F. Slice eggplants in half and prick several times with a fork.

2. Place on a baking sheet and drizzle with 1 tablespoon olive oil. Bake for 30 minutes, or until soft. Allow to cool slightly.

3. Remove inner flesh and place in a bowl.

4. Using a large fork or potato masher, mash eggplant together with remaining ingredients until almost smooth.

5. Adjust seasonings to taste.

PER ¼ CUP Calories: 161 | Fat: 13g | Sodium: 113mg | Fiber: 6g | Protein: 3g

Black Bean Guacamole

*Sneaking some extra fiber and protein into a traditional Mexican guacamole
makes this dip a more nutritious appetizer.*

INGREDIENTS | YIELDS 2 CUPS

1 15-ounce can black beans
3 avocados, pitted
1 tablespoon lime juice
3 scallions, chopped
1 large tomato, diced
2 cloves garlic, minced
½ teaspoon chili powder
¼ teaspoon salt
1 tablespoon chopped fresh cilantro

1. Using a fork or a potato masher, mash the beans in a medium-sized bowl just until they are halfway mashed, leaving some texture.

2. Combine all the remaining ingredients, and mash together until mixed.

3. Adjust seasonings to taste.

4. Allow to sit for at least 10 minutes before serving to allow the flavors to set.

5. Gently mix again just before serving.

PER ¼ CUP Calories: 198 | Fat: 11g | Sodium: 206mg | Fiber: 10g | Protein: 7g

Fresh Basil Bruschetta with Balsamic Reduction

Your guests will be so delighted by the rich flavors of the balsamic reduction sauce that they won't even notice that the cheese is missing from this vegan bruschetta. Use a fresh artisan bread, if you can, for extra flavor.

INGREDIENTS | SERVES 4

8–10 slices French bread
¾ cup balsamic vinegar
1 tablespoon sugar
2 large tomatoes, diced small
3 cloves garlic, minced
2 tablespoons olive oil
¼ cup chopped fresh basil
Salt and pepper to taste

A Tuscan Tradition

A true Italian chef will prepare the bread for bruschetta by toasting homemade bread over hot coals, then quickly rubbing a sliced clove of garlic over both sides of the bread before drizzling with just a touch of the finest olive oil. In lieu of hot coals, a toaster or 5 minutes in the oven at 350°F will work just fine.

1. Toast bread in toaster or for 5 minutes in the oven at 350°F.

2. Whisk together the balsamic vinegar and sugar in a small saucepan. Bring to a boil; then reduce to a slow simmer. Allow to cook for 6–8 minutes until almost thickened. Remove from heat.

3. Combine the tomatoes, garlic, olive oil, basil, salt, and pepper in a large bowl. Gently toss with balsamic sauce.

4. Spoon tomato and balsamic mixture over bread slices and serve immediately.

PER SERVING Calories: 321 | Fat: 8g | Sodium: 434mg | Fiber: 3g | Protein: 9g

Hot Artichoke Spinach Dip

Serve this creamy dip hot with some baguette slices, crackers, pita bread, or sliced bell peppers and jicama. If you want to get fancy, you can carve out a bread bowl for an edible serving dish.

INGREDIENTS | SERVES 8

1 12-ounce package frozen spinach, thawed
1 14-ounce can artichoke hearts, drained
¼ cup vegan margarine
¼ cup flour
2 cups soy milk
½ cup nutritional yeast
1 teaspoon garlic powder
1½ teaspoons onion powder
¼ teaspoon salt

1. Preheat oven to 350°F. Purée spinach and artichokes together until almost smooth and set aside.

2. In a small saucepan, melt the vegan margarine over low heat. Slowly whisk in flour, 1 tablespoon at a time, stirring constantly to avoid lumps, until thick.

3. Remove from heat and add spinach and artichoke mixture, stirring to combine. Add remaining ingredients.

4. Transfer to an oven-proof casserole dish or bowl and bake for 20 minutes. Serve hot.

PER SERVING Calories: 134 | Fat: 7g | Sodium: 378mg | Fiber: 4g | Protein: 6g

Homemade Tahini

If you're serving this as a Middle Eastern dip or spread, use the paprika for extra flavor, but leave it out if your tahini will be the basis for a salad dressing or a noodle dish.

INGREDIENTS | YIELDS 1 CUP

2 cups sesame seeds
½ cup olive oil
½ teaspoon paprika (optional)

1. Heat oven to 350°F. Once oven is hot, spread sesame seeds in a thin layer on a baking sheet and toast for 5 minutes in the oven, shaking the sheet once to mix.

2. Allow sesame seeds to cool, then process with oil in a food processor or blender until thick and creamy. You may need a little more or less than ½ cup oil. Garnish with paprika, if desired. Tahini will keep for up to one month in the refrigerator in a tightly sealed container, or store your tahini in the freezer and thaw before using.

PER TABLESPOON Calories: 163 | Fat: 16g | Sodium: 2mg | Fiber: 2g | Protein: 3g

Fresh Mint Spring Rolls

Wrapping spring rolls is a balance between getting them tight enough to hold together, but not so tight the thin wrappers break! It's like riding a bike: once you've got it, you've got it, and then spring rolls can be very quick and fun to make.

INGREDIENTS | SERVES 4

1 3-ounce package clear bean thread noodles
1 cup hot water
1 tablespoon soy sauce
½ teaspoon powdered ginger
1 teaspoon sesame oil
¼ cup shiitake mushrooms, diced
1 carrot, grated
10–12 spring roll wrappers
Warm water
½ head green leaf lettuce, chopped
1 cucumber, sliced thin
1 bunch fresh mint

To Dip, or Not to Dip?

Store-bought sweet chili sauce, spicy sriracha sauce, or a Japanese salad dressing or marinade will work in a pinch, but a simple homemade dip is best. Try Thai Orange Peanut Dressing (p. 62) or Easy Asian Dipping Sauce (p. 23).

1. Break noodles in half to make smaller pieces, then submerge in 1 cup hot water until soft, about 6–7 minutes. Drain.

2. In a large bowl, toss together the hot noodles with the soy sauce, ginger, sesame oil, mushrooms, and carrots, tossing well to combine.

3. In a large shallow pan, carefully submerge spring roll wrappers, one at a time, in warm water until just barely soft. Remove from water and place a bit of lettuce in the center of the wrapper. Add about 2 tablespoons of noodle mixture, a few slices of cucumber, and place 2–3 mint leaves on top.

4. Fold the bottom of the wrapper over the filling, fold in each side, then roll.

PER SERVING Calories: 216 | Fat: 1g | Sodium: 262mg | Fiber: 2g | Protein: 4g

Easy Asian Dipping Sauce

Tangy, salty, spicy, and a bit sour—this easy dipping sauce has it all!
Use it for dipping vegetarian sushi or Fresh Mint Spring Rolls (p. 22).
It would also make an excellent marinade for a baked tofu dish.

INGREDIENTS | YIELDS ⅓ CUP

¼ cup soy sauce
2 tablespoons rice vinegar
2 teaspoons sesame oil
1 teaspoon sugar
1 teaspoon fresh ginger, minced
2 cloves garlic, minced and crushed
¼ teaspoon crushed red pepper flakes,
or to taste

Whisk together all ingredients.

PER TABLESPOON Calories: 29 | Fat: 2g | Sodium: 719mg |
Fiber: 0g | Protein: 1g

Vegan Mayonnaise

The secret to getting a really creamy homemade vegan mayonnaise is to
add the oil very, very slowly—literally just a few drops at a time—and use
the highest available speed on your food processor.

INGREDIENTS | YIELDS 1 CUP

1 12-ounce block silken tofu
1½ tablespoons lemon juice
1 teaspoon prepared mustard
1½ teaspoons vinegar (apple cider or
white)
1 teaspoon sugar
¾ teaspoon onion powder
½ teaspoon salt
⅓ cup canola or safflower oil

1. Process all ingredients, except oil, in a food processor until smooth.

2. On high speed, slowly incorporate the oil just a few drops at a time until smooth and creamy.

3. Chill for at least 1 hour before serving to allow flavors to blend. Mayonnaise will also thicken as it sits.

From Aioli Sauce to Thousand Island Dressing

Mayonnaise is used in so many comfort foods that you'll really want to have a good one on hand most of the time. If you prefer to try a store-bought vegan mayo, shop around or try a couple different types, as there's a vast range of brands and flavors available.

PER TABLESPOON Calories: 54 | Fat: 5g | Sodium: 77mg |
Fiber: 0g | Protein: 1g

Mango Citrus Salsa

Salsa has a variety of uses, and this recipe adds color and variety to your usual chips and dip or Mexican dishes.

INGREDIENTS | YIELDS 2 CUPS

1 mango, chopped
2 tangerines, chopped
½ red bell pepper, chopped
½ red onion, minced
3 cloves garlic, minced
½ jalapeño pepper, minced
2 tablespoons lime juice
½ teaspoon salt
¼ teaspoon black pepper
3 tablespoons chopped fresh cilantro

1. Gently toss together all ingredients.

2. Allow to sit for at least 15 minutes before serving, to allow flavors to mingle.

PER ¼ CUP Calories: 37 | Fat: 0g | Sodium: 147mg | Fiber: 1g | Protein: 1g

Vegan "Pigs" in a Blanket

Use store-bought vegetarian hot dogs to make this great little appetizer that kids and adults both love. Serve with ketchup or hot mustard.

INGREDIENTS | MAKES 16 "PIGS"

1 batch Quick and Easy Vegan Biscuit dough (p. 49)
8 vegan hot dogs, sliced in half

Party Pigs

Head to enough vegan parties, and you'll inevitably run into a variation of this recipe sooner or later—it's an old vegan favorite. If you're short on time, roll out some store-bought vegan crescent roll dough, and to try something a bit different, add a thin slice of vegan cheese or a generous sprinkle of red pepper flakes before wrapping.

1. Preheat oven to 400°F and lightly grease a baking sheet.

2. Divide dough into sections and roll into ovals.

3. Place each hot dog piece on the edge of each dough circle and wrap. Place on baking sheet.

4. Bake for 10–12 minutes or until lightly golden brown.

PER 1 "PIG" Calories: 119 | Fat: 4g | Sodium: 358mg | Fiber: 1g | Protein: 7g

Nacho "Cheese" Dip

Peanut butter in cheese sauce? No, that's not a typo! Just a touch of peanut butter creates a creamy and nutty layer of flavor to this sauce, and helps it to thicken nicely. Use this sauce to dress plain steamed veggies or make homemade nachos.

INGREDIENTS | YIELDS ABOUT 1 CUP

3 tablespoons vegan margarine
1 cup unsweetened soy milk
¾ teaspoon garlic powder
½ teaspoon salt
½ teaspoon onion powder
1 tablespoon peanut butter
¼ cup flour
¼ cup nutritional yeast
¾ cup salsa
2 tablespoons chopped canned jalapeño peppers (optional)

Chili Cheese
Add a can of store-bought vegetarian chili for a chili cheese dip, or smother some French fries to make chili cheese fries.

1. Heat margarine and soy milk together in a pan over low heat. Add garlic powder, salt, and onion powder, stirring to combine. Add peanut butter and stir until melted.

2. Whisk in flour, 1 tablespoon at a time, until smooth. Heat until thickened, about 5–6 minutes.

3. Stir in nutritional yeast, salsa, and jalapeño peppers.

4. Allow to cool slightly before serving, as cheese sauce will thicken as it cools.

PER ¼ CUP Calories: 184 | Fat: 12g | Sodium: 725mg | Fiber: 3g | Protein: 6g

Mushroom Gravy

Stir, stir, stir! Just like regular gravy, the secret to perfect vegan gravy is in the stirring, to prevent those pesky lumps. That, and all the added flavors!

INGREDIENTS | YIELDS 1½ CUPS

¼ cup vegan margarine
¾ cup sliced mushrooms
2½ cups vegetable broth
1 teaspoon garlic powder
1 teaspoon onion powder
½ teaspoon sage
½ teaspoon thyme
¼ teaspoon marjoram (optional)
3 tablespoons flour
2 tablespoons nutritional yeast (optional)
Salt and pepper to taste

1. Heat the vegan margarine in a large skillet over medium heat and add mushrooms. Sauté for 2–3 minutes.

2. Reduce heat to medium low and add vegetable broth, garlic powder, onion powder, sage, thyme, and marjoram, stirring well to combine.

3. Add flour, 1 tablespoon at a time, whisking constantly to combine well and prevent lumps. Allow to cook for 2–3 minutes before adding the next tablespoon of flour. Continue simmering over low heat until thick.

4. Remove from heat and stir in nutritional yeast. Taste, and add a bit of salt and pepper, as needed. Gravy will thicken as it cools.

PER ¼ CUP Calories: 104 | Fat: 7g | Sodium: 129mg | Fiber: 0g | Protein: 2g

Tropical Cashew Nut Butter

You can make a homemade cashew nut butter with any kind of oil, so feel free to substitute using whatever you have on hand, but you're in for a real treat when you use coconut oil in this recipe!

INGREDIENTS | YIELDS ¾ CUP

2 cups roasted cashews
½ teaspoon sugar (optional)
¼ teaspoon salt (optional)
3–4 tablespoons coconut oil or other vegetable oil

Making Nut Butters

Nut butters can be very expensive to purchase, but are so easy to make at home! Try making almond, walnut, or macadamia nut butter for a delicious alternative to store-bought peanut butter. Roasted nuts work best, so heat them in the oven at 400°F for 6–8 minutes or toast them on the stove top in a dry skillet for a few minutes.

1. Process the cashews, sugar, and salt in a food processor on high speed until finely ground. Continue processing until cashews form a thick paste.

2. Slowly add coconut oil until smooth and creamy, scraping down sides and adding a little more oil as needed.

PER 2 TABLESPOONS Calories: 320 | Fat: 28g | Sodium: 7mg | Fiber: 1g | Protein: 7g

Fried Zucchini Sticks

You don't have to deep-fry these zucchini sticks, just sauté them in a bit of oil if you prefer. This is a great appetizer or snack for kids!

INGREDIENTS | SERVES 4

¾ cup flour
½ teaspoon garlic powder
¾ teaspoon Italian seasoning
¼ teaspoon salt
4 zucchini, cut into strips
Oil for frying
Vegan ranch dressing or ketchup for dipping

1. In a large bowl or pan, combine the flour, garlic powder, Italian seasoning, and salt.

2. Lightly toss the zucchini strips with the flour mixture, coating well.

3. Heat oil in a large skillet or frying pan. When oil is hot, gently add zucchini strips to pan.

4. Fry until lightly golden brown on all sides. Serve with vegan ranch dressing or ketchup.

PER SERVING Calories: 178 | Fat: 7g | Sodium: 166mg | Fiber: 3g | Protein: 5g

Sun-Dried Tomato Pesto

Nutritional yeast lends a strong cheesy flavor to this vegan pesto, and the sun-dried tomatoes add another layer of flavor to the traditional basil. Don't tell anyone it's vegan, and they might never know!

INGREDIENTS | YIELDS 1 CUP

⅓ cup sun-dried tomatoes

2 cups fresh basil leaves

½ cup pine nuts or walnuts

3 cloves garlic

¼ cup nutritional yeast

½ teaspoon salt

¼ teaspoon black pepper

¼ cup olive oil

1. If using dehydrated sun-dried tomatoes, reconstitute in water until soft and pliable, about 15 minutes.

2. Purée together all ingredients, adding oil last to achieve desired consistency.

PER 2 TABLESPOONS Calories: 133 | Fat: 13g | Sodium: 193mg | Fiber: 1g | Protein: 3g

Beyond Pesto Pasta

Pesto makes everything better, doesn't it? It's a simple sauce, but it just sounds so elegant! Toss it with pasta, of course, or, create a vegan pesto pizza, serve it with whole-grain crackers as an appetizer, or use it as a sandwich spread. To turn it into a creamy veggie dip, combine one batch of Sun-Dried Tomato Pesto with a container of nondairy sour cream.

Vegan Tzatziki

Use a vegan soy yogurt to make this classic Greek dip, which is best served very cold.
A nondairy sour cream may be used instead of the soy yogurt, if you prefer.

INGREDIENTS | YIELDS 1½ CUPS

1½ cups vegan soy yogurt, plain or lemon flavored
1 tablespoon olive oil
1 tablespoon lemon juice
4 cloves garlic, minced
2 cucumbers, grated or chopped fine
1 tablespoon chopped fresh mint or fresh dill

1. Whisk together yogurt with olive oil and lemon juice until well combined.

2. Combine with remaining ingredients.

3. Chill for at least 1 hour before serving to allow flavors to mingle. Serve cold.

PER ¼ CUP Calories: 76 | Fat: 3g | Sodium: 10mg | Fiber: 1g | Protein: 2g

Avocado and Shiitake Pot Stickers

Once you try these California-fusion pot stickers, you'll wish you had made
a double batch! These little dumplings don't need to be enhanced with
a complex dipping sauce, so serve them plain or with soy sauce.

INGREDIENTS | YIELDS 12–15 POT STICKERS

1 avocado, diced small
½ cup shiitake mushrooms, diced
½ block silken tofu, crumbled
1 clove garlic, minced
2 teaspoons balsamic vinegar
1 teaspoon soy sauce
12–15 vegan dumpling wrappers
Water for steaming or oil for pan frying

Whether Steamed or Fried . . .

In dumpling houses across East Asia, dumplings are served with a little bowl of freshly grated ginger, and diners create a simple dipping sauce from the various condiments on the table. To try it, pour some rice vinegar and a touch of soy sauce over a bit of ginger and add hot chili oil to taste.

1. In a small bowl, gently mash together all ingredients, except wrappers, just until mixed and crumbly.

2. Place about 1½ teaspoons of the filling in the middle of each wrapper. Fold in half and pinch closed, forming little pleats. You may want to dip your fingertips in water to help the dumplings stay sealed if needed.

3. To pan fry: Heat a thin layer of oil in a large skillet. Carefully add dumplings and cook for just 1 minute. Add about ½ cup water, cover, and cook for 3–4 minutes.

4. To steam: Carefully place a layer of dumplings in a steamer, being sure the dumplings don't touch. Place steamer above boiling water and allow to cook, covered, for 3–4 minutes.

PER 2 POT STICKERS (STEAMED) Calories: 304 | Fat: 6g | Sodium: 356mg | Fiber: 4g | Protein: 9g

Mushroom Fondue

Nutritional yeast lends a rich flavor to this fun party fondue. If you don't have a fondue pot, you can mix the ingredients over low heat and serve hot. Don't forget plenty of dippers—French bread, mushrooms, or lightly cooked baby potatoes would work well. Long live the '70s!

INGREDIENTS | SERVES 4

2 tablespoons vegan margarine

2 cups sliced mushrooms

½ cup soy milk or soy cream

1 teaspoon onion powder

½ teaspoon garlic powder

½ teaspoon celery salt

2 tablespoons flour

3 tablespoons nutritional yeast

Dust Off Your Disco Ball . . .

What could be more fun than a vegan fondue–themed party? The retro trend is in! Melt some vegan chocolate with soy cream, or try a wine reduction with fresh herbs. A Nacho "Cheese" Dip (p. 25) can be warmed in a fondue pot. Get together with friends for some Saturday night fun, and don't double-dip! Fondue sets also make a fun gift for the vegan cook who has everything.

1. Melt the vegan margarine over low heat and add mushrooms. Allow to cook for 5 minutes, then add soy milk or soy cream, onion powder, garlic powder, and celery salt. Cook over low heat for 8–10 minutes until mushrooms are soft.

2. Allow mixture to cool slightly, then purée in a blender.

3. Place puréed mushrooms in a fondue pot and add soy milk. Over medium heat, whisk in flour and heat until thickened. Stir in nutritional yeast and serve immediately.

PER SERVING Calories: 99 | Fat: 6g | Sodium: 163mg | Fiber: 1g | Protein: 4g

Vegan Cheese Ball

Use this recipe to make one impressive-looking large cheese ball, a cheese log, or make individual bite-sized servings for a party or the holidays. Everyone will be asking you for the recipe!

INGREDIENTS | MAKES 1 LARGE CHEESE BALL OR 12–14 BITE-SIZED CHEESE BALLS

1 block vegan nacho or Cheddar cheese, room temperature
1 container vegan cream cheese, room temperature
1 teaspoon garlic powder
½ teaspoon hot sauce
¼ teaspoon salt
1 teaspoon paprika
¼ cup nuts, finely chopped

1. Grate vegan cheese into a large bowl, or process in a food processor until finely minced. Using a large fork, mash the vegan cheese together with the cream cheese, garlic powder, hot sauce, and salt until well mixed. (You may need to use your hands for this.)

2. Chill until firm, at least 1 hour, then shape into ball or log shape, pressing firmly. Sprinkle with paprika and carefully roll in nuts. Serve with crackers.

PER 1 BITE-SIZED CHEESE BALL Calories: 132 | Fat: 10g | Sodium: 285mg | Fiber: 2g | Protein: 2g

Vegan Chocolate Hazelnut Spread

*Treat yourself or your family with this rich, sticky chocolate spread.
This one will have you dancing around the kitchen and licking your spoons!*

INGREDIENTS | YIELDS 1 CUP

2 cups hazelnuts, chopped
½ cup cocoa powder
¾ cup powdered sugar
½ teaspoon vanilla
4–5 tablespoons vegetable oil

Besides Just Licking the Spoons . . .

Europeans spread it on toast, Asian teenagers spread it on pancakes and stuff it inside waffles, but you can use it however you want, perhaps to top Vegan Crepes (p. 52) for dessert, spread over apple slices for the kids, or, go ahead, just eat it plain. No one will know! If you can't find hazelnuts, cashews will lend a similar creamy consistency.

1. Process hazelnuts in a food processor until very finely ground, about 3–4 minutes.

2. Add cocoa powder, sugar, and vanilla, and process to combine.

3. Add oil, just a little bit at a time, until mixture is soft and creamy and desired consistency is reached. You may need to add a bit more or less than 4–5 tablespoons.

PER TABLESPOON Calories: 164 | Fat: 14g | Sodium: 1mg | Fiber: 3g | Protein: 3g

Simple Scallion Pancakes

Whether you eat them as an accompaniment to a Chinese feast, or just as a snack or appetizer, these salty fried pancakes are a popular street food snack served up hot in East Asia. Plain soy sauce is the perfect dip.

INGREDIENTS | YIELDS 6 LARGE PANCAKES

2 cups flour
½ teaspoon salt
2 teaspoons sesame oil
¾ cup hot water
6 scallions, chopped (green parts only)
Oil for frying
Soy sauce for dipping

1. In a large bowl, combine flour and salt. Slowly add sesame oil and water, mixing, just until a dough forms. You may need a little bit less than ¾ cup water.

2. Knead dough for a few minutes, then let sit for 30 minutes.

3. Divide dough into six 2-inch balls. Roll out each ball on a lightly floured surface. Brush with sesame oil and cover with scallions. Roll up dough and twist to form a ball. Roll out again ¼ inch thick.

4. Fry each pancake in hot oil 1–2 minutes on each side. Slice into squares or wedges and serve with soy sauce.

PER 1 PANCAKE Calories: 232 | Fat: 9g | Sodium: 198mg | Fiber: 2g | Protein: 5g

Walnut Asparagus "Egg" Rolls

It's not traditional, but it's certainly delicious. Spring roll wrappers or wonton wrappers are just fine if you can't find eggless egg roll wraps.

INGREDIENTS | YIELDS 15 EGG ROLLS

1 bunch asparagus
2 avocados, pitted
½ onion, minced
1 teaspoon lime juice
1 tablespoon soy sauce
1 teaspoon chipotle powder
½ cup walnuts, finely chopped
¼ cup chopped fresh cilantro
15 vegan egg roll wrappers
Oil for frying

1. Steam the asparagus until crisp-tender, then chop into ½-inch slices.

2. Mash together the asparagus with the avocados, onion, lime juice, soy sauce, chipotle, walnuts, and cilantro.

3. Place 2–3 tablespoons of filling in each wrapper. Fold the bottom up, then fold the sides in, and roll, wetting the edges with water to help it stick together.

4. Fry in hot oil for 1–2 minutes on each side.

PER 1 EGG ROLL Calories: 219 | Fat: 10g | Sodium: 209mg | Fiber: 3g | Protein: 5g

Parsley and Onion Dip

*If you like packaged onion dip mixes, try this tofu-based version
with fresh parsley and chives. Perfect for carrots or crackers.*

INGREDIENTS | SERVES 6

1 onion, chopped
3 cloves garlic, minced
1 tablespoon olive oil
1 block firm tofu, well pressed
½ teaspoon onion powder
3 teaspoons lemon juice
¼ cup chopped fresh parsley
2 tablespoons chopped fresh chives
¼ teaspoon salt

1. Sauté onions and garlic in oil for 3–4 minutes until onions are soft. Remove from heat and allow to cool slightly.

2. Process the onion and garlic with the tofu, onion powder, and lemon juice in a food processor or blender until onion is minced and tofu is almost smooth.

3. Mash together with remaining ingredients by hand.

PER SERVING Calories: 68 | Fat: 5g | Sodium: 104mg | Fiber: 1g | Protein: 5g

Roasted Cashew and Spicy Basil Pesto

*The combination of spicy purple Thai basil or holy basil instead of Italian sweet
basil and the bite of the garlic creates an electrifying vegan pesto.*

INGREDIENTS | SERVES 3

4 cloves garlic
1 cup Thai basil or holy basil, packed
⅔ cup roasted cashews
½ cup nutritional yeast
¾ teaspoon salt
½ teaspoon black pepper
⅓–½ cup olive oil

1. Process all ingredients except olive oil in a blender or food processor just until coarse and combined.

2. Slowly incorporate olive oil until desired consistency is reached.

PER SERVING Calories: 435 | Fat: 38g | Sodium: 779mg | Fiber: 4g | Protein: 10g

Traditional Pesto

For a more traditional Italian pesto, you can, of course, use regular Italian basil. In this case, cut back on the garlic a bit, and use pine nuts or walnuts instead of roasted cashews.

Quick Hollandaise Sauce

A classic Hollandaise sauce is made from raw eggs, but this vegan cheater's version uses prepared vegan mayonnaise with a bit of turmeric for a yellow hue. Pour over steamed asparagus, artichokes, or cauliflower for an easy side dish, or make a Tofu Florentine (p. 54) or "eggs" Benedict.

INGREDIENTS | YIELDS ½ CUP SAUCE

⅓ cup vegan mayonnaise

¼ cup lemon juice

3 tablespoons unsweetened soy milk

1½ tablespoons Dijon mustard

¼ teaspoon turmeric

1 tablespoon nutritional yeast (optional)

½ teaspoon salt

¼ teaspoon black pepper

¼ teaspoon hot sauce, or to taste (optional)

Whisk together all ingredients and heat over low heat before serving. Adjust seasonings to taste.

PER TABLESPOON Calories: 66 | Fat: 6g | Sodium: 163mg | Fiber: 0g | Protein: 0g

Soy, Almond, and Rice Milks

Though soy milk is the most common, vegans can also choose from almond and rice milk substitutes. Rice milk is thinner and sweeter than soy milk, and almond milk has a grainier texture. For baking, soy or almond milk is best, and in savory casseroles and sauces such as this one, use soy milk for its neutral flavor. Choose brands fortified with vitamin D, B_{12}, and calcium, particularly if you've got kids.

Tomato and Dill–Stuffed Grape Leaves (Dolmas)

*Little Middle Eastern dolmas overflow with flavors and travel well in lunch boxes.
Look for canned or jarred grape leaves in the ethnic aisle of your grocery store.*

**INGREDIENTS | YIELDS APPROX.
2 DOZEN DOLMAS**

3 scallions, chopped
1 tomato, diced small
¼ cup olive oil, divided
1 cup uncooked rice
½ cup water
½ teaspoon salt
1 tablespoon chopped fresh dill
1 teaspoon dried parsley
1 tablespoon chopped fresh mint (optional)
Approx. 40 grape leaves
Water for boiling
2 tablespoons lemon juice

In a Hurry?
Mix together some leftover rice with vegan pesto for the filling. Wrap, simmer just a few minutes, and eat!

1. Heat scallions and tomato in 2 tablespoons of olive oil for 2 minutes, then add rice, water, salt, dill, parsley, and mint. Cover and cook for 5 minutes. Remove from heat and cool.

2. Place about 2 teaspoons of the rice filling in the center of a grape leaf near the stem. Fold the bottom of the leaf over the filling, then fold in the sides, and roll. Continue with each grape leaf.

3. Line the bottom of a pan with extra or torn grape leaves to prevent burning. Add wrapped and filled leaves and add enough water just to cover the dolmas. Add remaining 2 tablespoons of olive oil and bring to a slow simmer.

4. Cook for 20 minutes. Drizzle with lemon juice just before serving.

PER 1 STUFFED GRAPE LEAF Calories: 25 | Fat: 2g | Sodium: 163mg | Fiber: 0g | Protein: 0g

Chapter 3

Vegan Breakfasts

Chili Masala Tofu Scramble

Tofu scramble is an easy and versatile vegan breakfast. This version adds chili and curry for subcontinental flavor. Toss in whatever veggies you have on hand—tomatoes, spinach, or diced broccoli would work well.

INGREDIENTS | SERVES 2

1 block firm or extra-firm tofu, pressed
1 small onion, diced
2 cloves garlic, minced
2 tablespoons olive oil
1 small red chili pepper, minced
1 green bell pepper, chopped
¾ cup sliced mushrooms
1 tablespoon soy sauce
1 teaspoon curry powder
½ teaspoon cumin
¼ teaspoon turmeric
1 teaspoon nutritional yeast (optional)

The Next Day

Leftover tofu scramble makes an excellent lunch. You can also wrap leftovers (or planned-overs!) in a warmed flour tortilla to make breakfast-style burritos, perhaps with some salsa or beans. Why isn't it called "scrambled tofu" instead of "tofu scramble" if it's a substitute for scrambled eggs? This is one of the great conundrums of veganism.

1. Cut or crumble pressed tofu into 1-inch cubes.

2. Sauté onion and garlic in olive oil for a minute or 2 until onions are soft.

3. Add tofu, chili pepper, bell pepper, and mushrooms, stirring well to combine.

4. Add remaining ingredients, except nutritional yeast, and combine well. Allow to cook until tofu is lightly browned, about 6–8 minutes.

5. Remove from heat and stir in nutritional yeast if desired.

PER SERVING Calories: 288 | Fat: 21g | Sodium: 479mg | Fiber: 4g | Protein: 16g

Carob Peanut Butter Banana Smoothie

Yummy enough for a dessert, but healthy enough for breakfast, this smoothie is also a great protein boost after a sweaty workout at the gym. Use cocoa powder if you don't have any carob.

INGREDIENTS | SERVES 2

7–8 ice cubes
2 bananas
2 tablespoons peanut butter
2 tablespoons carob powder
1 cup soy milk

Blend together all ingredients until smooth.

PER SERVING Calories: 262 | Fat: 10g | Sodium: 136mg | Fiber: 6g | Protein: 9g

Vegan Pancakes

A touch of sugar and hint of sweet banana flavor more than make up for the lack of eggs and butter in this pancake recipe.

INGREDIENTS | YIELDS 1 DOZEN PANCAKES

1 cup flour
1 tablespoon sugar
1¾ teaspoons baking powder
¼ teaspoon salt
½ banana
1 teaspoon vanilla
1 cup soy milk

Don't Overmix!

When it comes to mixing pancake batter, less is more! Pancakes should be light and fluffy, but overmixing the batter will make them tough and rubbery. Gently combine the wet ingredients with the dry ones and don't be afraid of a few lumps; they'll sort themselves out when heated. If you let the batter sit for about 5 minutes, you'll need to stir even less.

1. Mix together flour, sugar, baking powder, and salt in a large bowl.

2. In a separate small bowl, mash banana with a fork. Add vanilla and whisk until smooth and fluffy. Add soy milk and stir to combine well.

3. Add soy milk mixture to the flour and dry ingredients, stirring just until combined.

4. Heat a lightly greased griddle or large frying pan over medium heat. Drop batter about 3 tablespoons at a time and heat until bubbles appear on surface, about 2–3 minutes. Flip and cook other side until lightly golden brown, another minute or 2.

PER 1 PANCAKE Calories: 56 | Fat: 0g | Sodium: 128mg | Fiber: 0g | Protein: 2g

Sweet Potato Apple Latkes

Use your food processor to process the potatoes, apples, and onion to a fine grate and cut the preparation time in half for this recipe. Serve topped with No-Sugar Apricot Applesauce (p. 47) or nondairy sour cream.

INGREDIENTS | YIELDS 1 DOZEN LATKES

3 large sweet potatoes, grated
1 apple, grated
1 small yellow onion, grated
Egg replacer for 2 eggs
3 tablespoons flour
1 teaspoon baking powder
½ teaspoon cinnamon
½ teaspoon nutmeg
½ teaspoon salt
Oil for frying

1. Using a cloth or paper towel, gently squeeze out excess moisture from potatoes and apples, and combine with onions in a large bowl.

2. Mix together remaining ingredients, except for oil, and combine with potato mixture.

3. Heat a few tablespoons of oil in a skillet or frying pan. Drop potato mixture in the hot oil a scant ¼ cup at a time, and use a spatula to flatten, forming a pancake. Cook for 3–4 minutes on each side until lightly crisped.

PER 1 LATKE Calories: 89 | Fat: 4g | Sodium: 162mg | Fiber: 2g | Protein: 1g

Super Green Quiche

Get your greens in before noon with this veggie quiche.
To avoid a crumbly mess, you'll have to be patient and let it cool before slicing.

INGREDIENTS | SERVES 4

1 10-ounce package frozen chopped spinach, thawed and drained
½ cup broccoli, diced small
1 block firm or extra-firm tofu
1 tablespoon soy sauce
¼ cup soy milk
1 teaspoon mustard
2 tablespoons nutritional yeast
½ teaspoon garlic powder
1 teaspoon parsley
½ teaspoon rosemary
¾ teaspoon salt
¼ teaspoon pepper
Prepared vegan crust (see sidebar)

An Easy Whole-Wheat Crust

Combine ¾ cup whole-wheat flour with ¾ cup all-purpose flour, and a teaspoon of salt. Cut in ⅓ cup vegan margarine until it's crumbly, then add ice-cold water, a few tablespoons at a time, until you can form a dough. You'll need about ½ cup. Roll out the dough and press it into your pie pan and you're ready to fill it up!

1. Preheat oven to 350°F.

2. Steam the spinach and broccoli until just lightly cooked, then set aside to cool. Press as much moisture as possible out of the spinach.

3. In a blender or food processor, combine the tofu with the remaining ingredients, except crust, until well mixed. Mix in the spinach and broccoli by hand until combined.

4. Spread mixture evenly in prepared pie crust.

5. Bake for 35–40 minutes, or until firm. Allow to cool for at least 10 minutes before serving. Quiche will firm up a bit more as it cools.

PER SERVING Calories: 403 | Fat: 20g | Sodium: 1,560mg | Fiber: 7g | Protein: 17g

Quick Tofu Breakfast Burrito

Toss in a fresh diced chili if you need something to really wake you up in the morning. There's no reason you can't enjoy these burritos for lunch, either!

INGREDIENTS | SERVES 2

1 block firm or extra-firm tofu, well pressed
2 tablespoons olive oil
½ cup salsa
½ teaspoon chili powder
Salt and pepper to taste
2 flour tortillas, warmed
Ketchup or hot sauce, to taste
2 slices vegan cheese
½ avocado, sliced

1. Cube or crumble the tofu into 1-inch chunks. Sauté in olive oil over medium heat for 2–3 minutes.

2. Add salsa and chili powder, and cook for 2–3 more minutes, stirring frequently. Season generously with salt and pepper.

3. Layer each warmed flour tortilla with half of the tofu and salsa mix and drizzle with ketchup or hot sauce.

4. Add vegan cheese and avocado slices and wrap like a burrito.

PER SERVING Calories: 607 | Fat: 38g | Sodium: 983mg | Fiber: 10g | Protein: 22g

Vanilla Date Breakfast Smoothie

Adding dates to a basic soy milk and fruit smoothie adds a blast of unexpected sweetness. A healthy breakfast treat or a cooling summer snack.

INGREDIENTS | SERVES 1

4 dates
Water
¾ cup soy milk
2 bananas
6–7 ice cubes
¼ teaspoon vanilla

1. Cover the dates with water and allow to soak for at least 10 minutes. This makes them softer and easier to blend.

2. Discard the soaking water and add the dates and all other ingredients to the blender.

3. Process until smooth, about 1 minute on medium speed.

PER SERVING Calories: 439 | Fat: 4g | Sodium: 93mg | Fiber: 11g | Protein: 9g

For a Smoother Smoothie

Soaking your dates first will help them process a little quicker and results in a smoother consistency. Place dates in a small bowl and cover with water. Let them sit for about 10 minutes, then drain.

Morning Cereal Bars

Store-bought breakfast bars are often loaded with artificial sugars, and most homemade recipes require corn syrup. This healthier method makes a sweet and filling snack or breakfast to munch on the run.

INGREDIENTS | YIELDS 12–14 BARS

3 cups breakfast cereal, any kind
1 cup peanut butter
⅓ cup tahini
1 cup maple syrup
½ teaspoon vanilla
2 cups muesli
½ cup flax meal or wheat germ
½ cup diced dried fruit or raisins

1. Lightly grease a baking pan or two casserole pans.

2. Place cereal in a sealable bag and crush partially with a rolling pin. If you're using a smaller cereal, you can skip this step. Set aside.

3. Combine peanut butter, tahini, and maple syrup in a large saucepan over low heat, stirring well to combine.

4. Remove from heat and stir in the vanilla, and then the cereal, muesli, flax meal or wheat germ, and dried fruit or raisins.

5. Press firmly into greased baking pan and chill until firm, about 45 minutes, then slice into bars.

PER 1 BAR Calories: 326 | Fat: 15g | Sodium: 194mg | Fiber: 3g | Protein: 8g

Strawberry Protein Smoothie

Add silken tofu to a simple fruit smoothie for a creamy protein boost.

INGREDIENTS | SERVES 2

½ cup frozen strawberries (or other berries)
½ block silken tofu
1 banana
¾ cup orange juice
3–4 ice cubes
1 tablespoon agave nectar (optional)

Blend together all ingredients until smooth and creamy.

Protein Shakes

If you're tempted by those rows of fancy-looking dairy and egg–based protein powders sold at your gym, try a vegan version! Well-stocked natural-foods stores sell a variety of naturally vegan protein powders that you can add to a smoothie for all your muscle-building needs. Look for hemp protein powder or flax-meal blends and don't be afraid of the green proteins—some of them are quite tasty!

PER SERVING Calories: 154 | Fat: 3g | Sodium: 6mg | Fiber: 3g | Protein: 5g

Vanilla Flax Granola

Making your own granola allows you to create whatever flavors you desire. Crystallized ginger, chopped dates, a sprinkle of cinnamon, coconut flakes, dried papaya—the possibilities are endless!

INGREDIENTS | YIELDS 2½ CUPS

⅔ cup maple syrup
⅓ cup vegan margarine
1½ teaspoons vanilla
2 cups oats
½ cup flax meal or wheat germ
¾ cup dried fruit, small dices

1. Preheat oven to 325°F.

2. Melt and whisk together maple syrup, vegan margarine, and vanilla over low heat until margarine is melted.

3. Toss together oats, flax meal, and dried fruit on a large baking tray in a single layer (you may need to use two trays).

4. Drizzle maple-syrup mixture over oats and fruit, gently tossing to combine as needed.

5. Bake for 25–30 minutes, carefully tossing once during cooking. Granola will harden as it cools.

PER ½ CUP Calories: 340 | Fat: 15g | Sodium: 148mg | Fiber: 6g | Protein: 6g

Apple Cinnamon Waffles

For perfect vegan waffles, make sure your waffle iron is hot and very well greased, as vegan waffles tend to be stickier than regular waffles.

INGREDIENTS | SERVES 4

1¼ cups flour
2 teaspoons baking powder
½ teaspoon cinnamon
2 teaspoons sugar
1 cup soy milk
½ cup applesauce
1 teaspoon vanilla
1 tablespoon vegetable oil

1. In a large bowl, combine the flour, baking powder, cinnamon, and sugar. Set aside.

2. In a separate bowl, combine soy milk, applesauce, vanilla, and oil.

3. Add the soy milk mixture to the dry ingredients, stirring just until combined; do not overmix.

4. Carefully drop about ¼ cup batter onto preheated waffle iron for each waffle, and cook until done.

PER SERVING Calories: 230 | Fat: 5g | Sodium: 270mg | Fiber: 2g | Protein: 6g

Peanut Butter Granola Wrap

Eating on the go? This wrap has all you need for a healthy breakfast, including whole grains, fresh fruit, and protein. It's the perfect breakfast for the busy health nut!

INGREDIENTS | SERVES 1

2 tablespoons peanut butter (or other nut butter)

1 whole-wheat flour tortilla

2 tablespoons granola (or any vegan breakfast cereal)

½ banana, sliced thin

¼ teaspoon cinnamon

1 tablespoon raisins

1 teaspoon agave nectar (optional)

1. Spread peanut butter down the center of the tortilla and layer granola and banana on top.

2. Sprinkle with cinnamon and raisins, and drizzle with agave nectar if desired.

3. Warm in the microwave for 10–15 seconds to slightly melt peanut butter.

PER SERVING Calories: 423 | Fat: 21g | Sodium: 368mg | Fiber: 8g | Protein: 13g

Exploring Nut Butters

Peanut butter is a great source of protein and kids love it, but shop around for other nut butters for variety. Cashew nut butter is a rich and creamy treat, and soy nut butter is similar to peanut butter but with an earthy taste. If you've got a food processor, mix and match your favorites to make your own homemade nut butters (p. 27).

Granola Breakfast Parfait

Sneak some healthy flax meal or wheat germ into your morning meal by adding it to a layered soy yogurt and granola parfait. If you don't have fresh fruit on hand, try adding some dried fruit, such as chopped dried apricots or pineapple. Serve in glass bowls or cups for presentation.

INGREDIENTS | SERVES 2

¼ cup flax meal or wheat germ
2 containers soy yogurt, any flavor
2 tablespoons maple syrup or agave nectar (optional)
½ cup granola
½ cup sliced fruit

1. In a small bowl, combine the flax meal or wheat germ, yogurt, and maple syrup.

2. In two serving bowls, place a few spoonfuls of granola, then a layer of soy yogurt. Top with a layer of fresh fruit, and continue layering until ingredients are used up. Serve immediately.

PER SERVING Calories: 354 | Fat: 10g | Sodium: 40mg | Fiber: 8g | Protein: 10g

Homemade Nut Milk

Homemade nut milk is delicious in breakfast cereal or oatmeal, smoothies, or to use in baking. If you don't have a sieve or cheesecloth, you can still enjoy this recipe, but it will be a bit grainy.

INGREDIENTS | YIELDS 4 CUPS

1 cup raw almonds or cashews
Water for soaking
4 cups water
½ teaspoon salt
½ teaspoon vanilla
1 teaspoon sugar (optional)

1. In a large bowl, cover nuts with plenty of water and allow to soak for at least 1 hour, or overnight. Drain.

2. Blend together soaked nuts with 4 cups water and purée on high until smooth.

3. Strain through a cheesecloth or sieve.

4. Stir in salt, vanilla, and sugar, and adjust to taste.

PER 1 CUP Calories: 189 | Fat: 16g | Sodium: 296mg | Fiber: 0g | Protein: 8g

Does It Taste Different than What You Expected?

If you read the label of most nondairy milks, you'll find them loaded with sugar! The first few times you make a homemade batch, you may need to add extra sugar to replicate the store-bought taste. Or, try using a healthier sweetener, such as maple syrup or agave nectar.

No-Sugar Apricot Applesauce

You don't really need to peel the apples if you're short on time, but it only takes about 5 minutes and will give you a smoother sauce. Try adding a touch of nutmeg or pumpkin pie spice for extra flavor.

INGREDIENTS | YIELDS 4 CUPS

6 apples
⅓ cup water
½ cup dried apricots, chopped
4 dates, chopped
Cinnamon to taste (optional)

1. Peel, core, and chop apples. Add apples and water to a large soup or stock pot and bring to a low boil. Simmer, covered, for 15 minutes, stirring occasionally.

2. Add chopped apricots and dates and simmer for another 10–15 minutes.

3. Mash with a large fork until desired consistency is reached, or allow to cool slightly and purée in a blender until smooth.

4. Sprinkle with cinnamon to taste.

PER ½ CUP Calories: 109 | Fat: 0g | Sodium: 1mg | Fiber: 2g | Protein: 1g

Whole-Wheat Blueberry Muffins

Because these muffins have very little fat, they'll want to stick to the papers or the muffin tin. Letting them cool before removing them will help prevent this, and be sure to grease your muffin tin well.

INGREDIENTS | YIELDS APPROX. 1½ DOZEN MUFFINS

2 cups whole-wheat flour
1 cup all-purpose flour
1¼ cups sugar
1 tablespoon baking powder
1 teaspoon salt
1½ cups soy milk
½ cup applesauce
½ teaspoon vanilla
2 cups blueberries

Making Vegan Muffins

Got a favorite muffin recipe? Try making it vegan! Use a commercial egg replacer brand in place of the eggs, and substitute a vegan soy margarine and soy milk for the butter and milk. Voilà!

1. Preheat oven to 400°F.

2. In a large bowl, combine the flours, sugar, baking powder, and salt. Set aside.

3. In a separate small bowl, whisk together the soy milk, applesauce, and vanilla until well mixed.

4. Combine the wet ingredients with the dry ingredients, stirring just until mixed. Gently fold in half of the blueberries.

5. Spoon batter into lined or greased muffin tins, filling each tin about ⅔ full. Sprinkle remaining blueberries on top of muffins.

6. Bake for 20–25 minutes, or until lightly golden brown on top.

PER 1 MUFFIN Calories: 147 | Fat: 1g | Sodium: 220mg | Fiber: 2g | Protein: 3g

Quick and Easy Vegan Biscuits

Use these vegan biscuits to mop up your Mushroom Gravy (p. 26), to make Vegan "Pigs" in a Blanket (p. 24), or top with vegan margarine or jam, pour some Earl Grey tea, and enjoy a British afternoon tea.

INGREDIENTS | YIELDS 12–14 BISCUITS

2 cups flour
1 tablespoon baking powder
½ teaspoon onion powder
½ teaspoon garlic powder
½ teaspoon salt
5 tablespoons cold vegan margarine
⅔ cup unsweetened soy milk

1. Preheat oven to 425°F.

2. Combine flour, baking powder, onion powder, garlic powder, and salt in a large bowl. Add margarine.

3. Using a fork, mash the margarine with the dry ingredients until crumbly.

4. Add soy milk a few tablespoons at a time and combine just until dough forms. You may need to add a little more or less than ⅔ cup.

5. Knead a few times on a floured surface, then roll out to ¾ inch thick. Cut into 3-inch rounds.

6. Bake for 12–14 minutes, or until done.

PER 1 BISCUIT Calories: 125 | Fat: 5g | Sodium: 211mg | Fiber: 1g | Protein: 3g

Easy Vegan French Toast

Kids love golden fried French toast drowning in powdered sugar and maple syrup,
but a fruit compote or some agave nectar would be just as sweet.

INGREDIENTS | SERVES 4

2 bananas

½ cup soy milk

1 tablespoon orange juice

1 tablespoon maple syrup

¾ teaspoon vanilla

1 tablespoon flour

1 teaspoon cinnamon

½ teaspoon nutmeg

Oil or vegan margarine for frying

12 thick slices bread

The Perfect Vegan French Toast

Creating an eggless French toast is a true art. Is your French toast too soggy or too dry? Thickly sliced bread lightly toasted will be more absorbent. Too mushy, or the mixture doesn't want to stick? Try spooning it onto your bread, rather than dipping.

1. Using a blender or mixer, mix together the bananas, soy milk, orange juice, maple syrup, and vanilla until smooth and creamy.

2. Whisk in flour, cinnamon, and nutmeg, and pour into a pie plate or shallow pan.

3. Heat 1–2 tablespoons of vegan margarine or oil in a large skillet.

4. Dip or spoon mixture over each bread slice on both sides, and fry in hot oil until lightly golden brown on both sides, about 2–3 minutes.

PER SERVING Calories: 391 | Fat: 11g | Sodium: 629mg | Fiber: 4g | Protein: 9g

Fat-Free Banana Bread

You can add ½ cup chopped walnuts to this simple banana bread, but then, of course, it won't be fat free. If you want a bit of texture and crunch without the fat, try adding chopped dates or raisins instead.

INGREDIENTS | YIELDS 1 LOAF

4 ripe bananas
⅓ cup soy milk
⅔ cup sugar
1 teaspoon vanilla
2 cups all-purpose flour
1 teaspoon baking powder
½ teaspoon baking soda
½ teaspoon salt
¾ teaspoon cinnamon

1. Preheat oven to 350°F. Lightly grease a loaf pan.

2. Mix together the bananas, soy milk, sugar, and vanilla until smooth and creamy.

3. In a separate bowl, combine the flour, baking powder, baking soda, and salt.

4. Combine the flour mixture with the banana mixture just until smooth.

5. Spread batter in loaf pan and sprinkle the top with cinnamon. Bake for 55 minutes, or until a toothpick inserted in the middle comes out clean.

PER ⅛ LOAF Calories: 237 | Fat: 0g | Sodium: 288mg | Fiber: 3g | Protein: 4g

Vegan Crepes

Crepes make a lovely brunch or even dessert, depending on what you fill them with!

INGREDIENTS | SERVES 4

1 cup flour
¾ cup soy milk
¼ cup water
2 teaspoons sugar
1 teaspoon vanilla
¼ cup vegan margarine, melted
¼ teaspoon salt

It's All in the Wrist

Don't worry if the first one or two turn out less than perfect; it always seems to happen. As you master the swirl technique, you'll soon be churning out perfect crepes every time. If you've never tried, you may want to make a double batch so you can practice. Be sure to use a nonstick pan!

1. Whisk together all ingredients. Chill for at least 1 hour. Remove from fridge and remix.

2. Lightly grease a nonstick pan and heat over medium-high heat.

3. Place about ¼ cup batter in pan and swirl to coat. Cook for just a minute, until set, then carefully flip, using a spatula or even your hands. Heat for just 1 more minute, then transfer to a plate.

PER SERVING Calories: 221 | Fat: 12g | Sodium: 336mg | Fiber: 1g | Protein: 4g

Baked "Sausage" and Mushroom Frittata

Baked tofu frittatas are an easy brunch or weekend breakfast. Once you've got the technique down, it's easy to adjust the ingredients to your liking. With tofu and mock meat, this one packs a super protein punch!

INGREDIENTS | SERVES 4

½ yellow onion, diced
3 cloves garlic, minced
½ cup sliced mushrooms
1 12-ounce package vegetarian sausage substitute or vegetarian "beef" crumbles
2 tablespoons olive oil
¾ teaspoon salt
¼ teaspoon black pepper
1 block firm or extra-firm tofu
1 block silken tofu
1 tablespoon soy sauce
2 tablespoons nutritional yeast
¼ teaspoon turmeric (optional)
1 tomato, sliced thin (optional)

1. Preheat oven to 325°F and lightly grease a glass pie pan.

2. Heat onion, garlic, mushrooms, and vegetarian sausage in olive oil in a large skillet for 3–4 minutes until sausage is browned and mushrooms are soft. Season with salt and pepper and set aside.

3. Combine firm tofu, silken tofu, soy sauce, nutritional yeast, and turmeric in a blender, and process until mixed. Combine tofu with sausage mixture and spread into pan. Layer slices of tomato on top (optional).

4. Bake in oven for about 45 minutes, or until firm. Allow to cool for 5–10 minutes before serving, as frittata will set as it cools.

PER SERVING Calories: 301 | Fat: 17g | Sodium: 1,037mg | Fiber: 4g | Protein: 25g

Tofu Florentine

Satisfy your comfort food cravings with this "eggy" tofu and spinach mixture drowning in a creamy Quick Hollandaise Sauce (p. 35) on toast.

INGREDIENTS | SERVES 2

1 block firm or extra-firm tofu, well pressed
2 tablespoons flour
1 teaspoon nutritional yeast
1 teaspoon garlic powder
2 tablespoons canola or safflower oil
1 10-ounce box frozen spinach, thawed and drained
½ cup Quick Hollandaise Sauce (p. 35)
2 slices bread, lightly toasted (or English muffins or bagels)

Benedict vs. Florentine

For a variation on this classic brunch recipe, skip the spinach and add a layer of lightly browned store-bought vegan bacon for Tofu Benedict instead of Florentine.

1. Slice tofu into ½-inch-thick slabs.

2. In a small bowl, combine the flour, nutritional yeast, and garlic powder. Dredge tofu in this mixture, then fry in oil for 2–3 minutes on each side until lightly browned.

3. Reduce heat and add spinach and 2 tablespoons of hollandaise sauce, gently coating tofu. Cook for just a minute or 2 over low heat until spinach is heated through.

4. Stack spinach and 2 strips of tofu mixture on each piece of toasted bread and cover with remaining sauce.

PER SERVING Calories: 436 | Fat: 26g | Sodium: 412mg | Fiber: 7g | Protein: 23g

Potato Poblano Breakfast Burritos

With or without the optional ingredients, this is a filling breakfast. Plan on two servings without the vegetarian ground beef, and stretch it to three servings with the mock meat.

INGREDIENTS | SERVES 2–3

2 tablespoons olive oil

2 small potatoes, diced small

2 poblano or Anaheim chilies, diced

1 teaspoon chili powder

Salt and pepper to taste

1 tomato, diced

⅔ cup vegetarian ground beef or sausage substitute (optional)

2–3 flour tortillas, warmed

Grated vegan cheese (optional)

Ketchup or hot sauce (optional)

1. Heat olive oil in a pan and add potatoes and chilies, sautéing until potatoes are almost soft, about 6–7 minutes.

2. Add chili powder, salt and pepper, tomato, and meat substitute, and stir well to combine.

3. Continue cooking until potatoes and tomatoes are soft and meat substitute is cooked, another 4–5 minutes.

4. Wrap in warmed flour tortillas with vegan cheese and ketchup or a bit of hot sauce, if desired.

PER SERVING Calories: 353 | Fat: 9g | Sodium: 322mg | Fiber: 8g | Protein: 9g

Homemade Rice Milk

When blending, add a bit more water to get the consistency you prefer. If you don't have cheesecloth, you can pour the milk into a new container, leaving most of the grainy bits at the bottom of the first container.

INGREDIENTS | YIELDS 1 QUART

½ cup long-grain rice

6½ cups water

½ teaspoon vanilla

2 tablespoons maple syrup

Dash salt, to taste

How to Use Rice Milk

Though it's not as thick and creamy as dairy milk, rice milk is sweet and delicious in its own right. Use rice milk in your morning cereal and in smoothies or tea.

1. Slowly simmer rice in water, covered, for 1 hour. Remove from heat, add vanilla, stir to combine, then cover and allow rice and water to cool.

2. Transfer to a blender and purée until smooth, working in batches as needed. Chill for at least 30 minutes.

3. Strain through cheesecloth and add maple syrup and salt, to taste.

PER 1 CUP Calories: 112 | Fat: 0g | Sodium: 34mg | Fiber: 0g | Protein: 2g

Chapter 4

Salads and Salad Dressings

Spicy Southwestern Two-Bean Salad

This cold bean salad with Tex-Mex flavors is even better the next day—if it lasts that long!

INGREDIENTS | SERVES 6

1 15-ounce can black beans, drained and rinsed

1 15-ounce can kidney beans, drained and rinsed

1 red or yellow bell pepper, chopped

1 large tomato, diced

⅔ cup corn (fresh, canned, or frozen)

1 red onion, diced

⅓ cup olive oil

¼ cup lime juice

½ teaspoon chili powder

½ teaspoon garlic powder

¼ teaspoon cayenne pepper

½ teaspoon salt

¼ cup chopped fresh cilantro

1 avocado, diced

1. In a large bowl, combine the black beans, kidney beans, bell pepper, tomato, corn, and onion.

2. In a separate small bowl, whisk together the olive oil, lime juice, chili powder, garlic powder, cayenne, and salt.

3. Pour over bean mixture, tossing to coat. Stir in fresh cilantro.

4. Chill for at least 1 hour before serving to allow flavors to mingle.

5. Add avocado and gently toss again just before serving.

PER SERVING Calories: 320 | Fat: 18g | Sodium: 573mg | Fiber: 13g | Protein: 11g

Make It a Pasta Salad

Omit the avocado and add some cooked pasta and extra dressing to turn it into a high-protein Tex-Mex pasta salad!

Sesame and Soy Coleslaw Salad

You don't need mayonnaise to make a coleslaw! Make it a full meal by adding some Sesame Baked Tofu (p. 242).

INGREDIENTS | SERVES 4

1 head Napa cabbage, shredded
1 carrot, grated
2 green onions, chopped
1 red bell pepper, sliced thin
2 tablespoons olive oil
2 tablespoons apple cider vinegar
2 teaspoons soy sauce
½ teaspoon sesame oil
2 tablespoons maple syrup
2 tablespoons sesame seeds (optional)

1. Toss together the cabbage, carrot, green onions, and bell pepper in a large bowl.

2. In a separate small bowl, whisk together the olive oil, vinegar, soy sauce, sesame oil, and maple syrup until well combined.

3. Drizzle dressing over cabbage and veggies, add sesame seeds, and toss well to combine.

PER SERVING Calories: 168 | Fat: 8g | Sodium: 203mg | Fiber: 7g | Protein: 4g

Raspberry Vinaigrette

Create a colorful and inviting salad with this purplish dressing. Dress up a plain fruit salad, or toss some cranberries, pine nuts, and baby spinach with this vinaigrette for a gourmet touch.

INGREDIENTS | YIELDS 1¼ CUP

¼ cup balsamic or raspberry vinegar
2 tablespoons lime juice
¼ cup raspberry preserves
2 tablespoons Dijon mustard
½ teaspoon sugar
¾ cup olive oil
Salt and pepper to taste

1. Process together vinegar, lime juice, raspberry preserves, mustard, and sugar in a food processor or blender until smooth.

2. Slowly add olive oil, just a few drops at a time, processing on high speed to allow oil to emulsify.

3. Season generously with salt and pepper.

PER TABLESPOON Calories: 87 | Fat: 8g | Sodium: 19mg | Fiber: 0g | Protein: 0g

No-Mayo Apple Coleslaw

There's nothing wrong with grabbing a store-bought preshredded coleslaw mix from the produce section to make this vegan salad—just double the dressing if you find it's not enough.

INGREDIENTS | SERVES 4

1 head cabbage, shredded

1 apple, diced small

1 15-ounce can pineapple, drained (reserve 2 tablespoon of juice)

1 tablespoon apple cider vinegar

2 tablespoons olive oil

1 tablespoon tahini

2 tablespoons agave nectar or 1 teaspoon sugar

2 tablespoons sunflower seeds (optional)

Make It Vegan!

If you have a favorite family coleslaw recipe, there's no need to give it up when eating vegan. Just use a store-bought or homemade Vegan Mayonnaise (p. 23) or dressing. Whatever recipe you use, coleslaw works best if it sits for several hours to soften up the cabbage, so make this recipe in advance if possible. The night before would be best.

1. In a large bowl, combine the cabbage, apple, and pineapple.

2. In a separate small bowl, whisk together 2 tablespoons of the pineapple juice with the cider vinegar, olive oil, and tahini. Pour over cabbage and apples, tossing gently to coat.

3. Drizzle with agave nectar, again tossing to coat.

4. Chill for at least 30 minutes before serving, and toss with sunflower seeds.

PER SERVING Calories: 196 | Fat: 2g | Sodium: 47mg | Fiber: 8g | Protein: 4g

Dairy-Free Ranch Dressing

An all-American creamy homemade ranch dressing, without the buttermilk. Get those baby carrots ready to dip!

INGREDIENTS | YIELDS 1 CUP

1 cup Vegan Mayonnaise (p. 23)
¼ cup soy milk
1 teaspoon Dijon mustard
1 tablespoon lemon juice
1 teaspoon onion powder
¾ teaspoon garlic powder
1 tablespoon minced fresh chives

1. Whisk or blend together all ingredients, except chives, until smooth.

2. Stir in chives until well combined.

PER TABLESPOON Calories: 57 | Fat: 5g | Sodium: 83mg | Fiber: 0g | Protein: 1g

Creamy Miso Sesame Dressing

A creamy and tangy Japanese-inspired salad dressing. A bit of minced fresh ginger would add another layer of flavor if you happened to have some on hand.

INGREDIENTS | YIELDS 1 CUP

¼ cup miso
2 tablespoons rice wine vinegar
¼ cup soy sauce
2 tablespoons sesame oil
½ cup soy milk
2 tablespoons lime juice

Process all ingredients together in a blender or food processor until smooth.

PER TABLESPOON Calories: 30 | Fat: 2g | Sodium: 389mg | Fiber: 0g | Protein: 1g

Miso Trivia

Miso is available in a variety of interchangeable flavors and colors; red, white, and barley miso being the most common. It's really a personal preference which type you use. Asian grocers stock miso at about one-third the price of natural-foods stores, so if you're lucky enough to have one in your neighborhood, it's worth a trip.

Asian Ranch Dressing

An Asian combination of flavors fuses with all-American mayonnaise for a twist on the usual ranch dressing.

INGREDIENTS | YIELDS ⅔ CUP

½ cup Vegan Mayonnaise (p. 23)

⅓ cup rice vinegar

¼ cup soy sauce

2 tablespoons sesame oil

2 teaspoons sugar

½ teaspoon powdered ginger

¾ teaspoon garlic powder

1 tablespoon chopped fresh chives

Combine all ingredients except chives in a blender or food processor, and process until smooth and creamy. Stir in chives by hand.

PER TABLESPOON Calories: 69 | Fat: 6g | Sodium: 383mg | Fiber: 0g | Protein: 1g

Thai Orange Peanut Dressing

A sweet and spicy take on traditional Thai and Indonesian peanut and satay sauce. Add a bit less liquid to use this salad dressing as a dip for veggies.

INGREDIENTS | YIELDS ¾ CUP

¼ cup peanut butter at room temperature

¼ cup orange juice

2 tablespoons soy sauce

2 tablespoons rice vinegar

2 tablespoons water

½ teaspoon garlic powder

½ teaspoon sugar

¼ teaspoon crushed red chili flakes (optional)

Whisk together all ingredients until smooth and creamy, adding more or less liquid to achieve desired consistency.

PER TABLESPOON Calories: 36 | Fat: 3g | Sodium: 176mg | Fiber: 0g | Protein: 1g

Deli-Style Macaroni Salad

A classic creamy pasta salad with vegan mayonnaise.
Add a can of kidney beans or chickpeas for a protein boost.

INGREDIENTS | SERVES 6

3 cups cooked macaroni
1 carrot, diced small
½ cup green peas
½ cup corn
1 rib celery, diced
½ cup Vegan Mayonnaise (p. 23)
1½ tablespoons prepared mustard
2 tablespoons white or apple cider vinegar
2 teaspoons sugar
2 tablespoons pickle relish
1 tablespoon chopped fresh dill (optional)
Salt and pepper to taste

1. Combine the macaroni, carrot, peas, corn, and celery in a large bowl.

2. In a separate small bowl, whisk together the mayonnaise, mustard, vinegar, sugar, and relish. Combine with macaroni.

3. Stir in the fresh dill and season with salt and pepper, to taste.

4. Chill for at least 2 hours before serving, to allow flavors to combine and to soften veggies.

PER SERVING Calories: 220 | Fat: 8g | Sodium: 183mg | Fiber: 3g | Protein: 7g

Pasta Salad Secrets

One secret to making flavorful vegan pasta salads is to use heavily salted water when boiling the pasta. So go ahead, dump in a full tablespoon (or even two!) of salt to the cooking water.

Tempeh Dill "Chicken" Salad

Turn it into a sandwich, or slice up some tomatoes and serve on a bed of lettuce.

INGREDIENTS | SERVES 3

1 8-ounce package tempeh, diced small
Water for boiling
3 tablespoons Vegan Mayonnaise (p. 23)
2 teaspoons lemon juice
½ teaspoon garlic powder
1 teaspoon Dijon mustard
2 tablespoons sweet pickle relish
½ cup green peas
2 stalks celery, diced small
1 tablespoon chopped fresh dill
(optional)

Curried Chicken Tempeh

For curried chicken salad, omit the dill and add ½ teaspoon curry powder and a dash cayenne and black pepper. If you don't feel up to dicing and simmering tempeh, try combining the dressing with store-bought mock chicken, or even veggie turkey or deli slices.

1. Cover tempeh with water and simmer for 10 minutes, until tempeh is soft. Drain and allow to cool completely.

2. Whisk together mayonnaise, lemon juice, garlic powder, mustard, and relish.

3. Combine tempeh, mayonnaise mixture, peas, celery, and dill and gently toss to combine.

4. Chill for at least 1 hour before serving to allow flavors to combine.

PER SERVING Calories: 237 | Fat: 14g | Sodium: 233mg | Fiber: 2g | Protein: 16g

Kidney Bean and Chickpea Salad

This marinated two-bean salad is perfect for summer picnics or as a side for outdoor barbecues or potlucks.

INGREDIENTS | SERVES 6

¼ cup olive oil
¼ cup red wine vinegar
½ teaspoon paprika
2 tablespoons lemon juice
1 14-ounce can chickpeas, drained
1 14-ounce can kidney beans, drained
½ cup sliced black olives
1 8-ounce can corn, drained
½ red onion, chopped
1 tablespoon chopped fresh parsley
Salt and pepper to taste

1. Whisk together olive oil, vinegar, paprika, and lemon juice.

2. In a large bowl, combine the chickpeas, beans, olives, corn, red onion, and parsley. Pour the olive oil dressing over the bean mixture and toss well to combine.

3. Season generously with salt and pepper, to taste.

4. Chill for at least 1 hour before serving to allow flavors to mingle.

PER SERVING Calories: 252 | Fat: 12g | Sodium: 569mg | Fiber: 8g | Protein: 7g

Cucumber Cilantro Salad

Cooling cucumbers and cold creamy yogurt are coupled with a dash of cayenne pepper for a salad that keeps you guessing.

INGREDIENTS | SERVES 3

4 cucumbers, diced
2 tomatoes, chopped
½ red onion, diced small
1 cup soy yogurt, plain or lemon flavored
1 tablespoon lemon juice
2 tablespoons chopped fresh cilantro
Salt and pepper to taste
¼ teaspoon cayenne pepper (optional)

1. Toss together all ingredients, stirring well to combine.

2. Chill for at least 2 hours before serving, to allow flavors to marinate. Toss again just before serving.

PER SERVING Calories: 134 | Fat: 2g | Sodium: 23mg | Fiber: 4g | Protein: 6g

Hot German Dijon Potato Salad

Tangy deli-style German potato salad requires potatoes that are thinly sliced and not overcooked. This vegan version is just as good—if not better—than any other recipe you'll find.

INGREDIENTS | SERVES 4

4 large potatoes, precooked and cooled
½ yellow onion, sliced thin
2 tablespoons olive oil
⅓ cup water
⅓ cup white or apple cider vinegar
1 tablespoon Dijon mustard
1 tablespoon flour
1 teaspoon sugar
2 scallions, chopped
3 tablespoons vegetarian bacon bits (optional)
Salt and pepper, to taste

1. Slice potatoes into thin coins and set aside.

2. In a large skillet, heat onions in olive oil over medium heat and cook until just barely soft, about 2–3 minutes.

3. Reduce heat and add water, vinegar, mustard, flour, and sugar, stirring to combine. Bring to a simmer and cook until thickened, just a minute or 2.

4. Reduce heat and stir in potatoes, scallions, and bacon bits. Season with salt and pepper to taste.

PER SERVING Calories: 390 | Fat: 7g | Sodium: 71mg | Fiber: 7g | Protein: 9g

Perfect Potatoes

To prepare your potatoes for a potato salad, give them a quick scrub. Peeling is an aesthetic preference entirely up to you. Either way, chop them into chunks (or thin coins, for a German-style salad), then simmer just until soft, about 15 minutes or less. Drain and rinse your potatoes immediately under cold water to stop them from cooking further and getting too soft.

Lemon Cumin Potato Salad

A mayonnaise-free potato salad with exotic flavors,
this one is delicious either hot or cold.

INGREDIENTS | SERVES 4

1 small yellow onion, diced
2 tablespoons olive oil
1½ teaspoons cumin
4 large cooked potatoes, chopped
3 tablespoons lemon juice
2 teaspoons Dijon mustard
1 scallion, chopped
¼ teaspoon cayenne pepper
2 tablespoons chopped fresh cilantro
(optional)

1. Heat onions in olive oil just until soft. Add cumin and potatoes, and cook for just 1 minute, stirring well to combine. Remove from heat.

2. Whisk together the lemon juice and Dijon mustard and pour over potatoes, tossing gently to coat. Add scallions, cayenne pepper, and cilantro and combine well.

3. Chill before serving.

PER SERVING Calories: 360 | Fat: 7g | Sodium: 53mg | Fiber: 9g | Protein: 8g

The Family Recipe

Traditional American potato salads are easy to veganize, so if you've got a family favorite, take a look at the ingredients. Substitute vegan mayonnaise or sour cream for regular, omit the eggs, and use mock meats in place of the bacon bits or other meats.

Basic Balsamic Vinaigrette

No need to purchase expensive and sugar-laden salad dressings at the grocery store!
This simple vinaigrette will serve you well for a last-minute salad dressing.

INGREDIENTS | YIELDS 1 CUP

¼ cup balsamic vinegar
¾ cup olive oil
1 tablespoon Dijon mustard
¼ teaspoon salt
⅛ teaspoon black pepper
½ teaspoon dried basil
½ teaspoon dried parsley

Whisk together all ingredients with a fork until well combined.

PER TABLESPOON Calories: 94 | Fat: 10g | Sodium: 48mg | Fiber: 0g | Protein: 0g

You Are a Goddess Dressing

Turn this zesty salad dressing into a dip for veggies or a sandwich spread
by reducing the amount of liquids.

INGREDIENTS | YIELDS 1½ CUPS

⅔ cup tahini
¼ cup apple cider vinegar
⅓ cup soy sauce
2 teaspoons lemon juice
1 clove garlic
¾ teaspoon sugar (optional)
⅓ cup olive oil

1. Process all the ingredients, except olive oil, together in a blender or food processor until blended.

2. With the blender or food processor on high speed, slowly add in the olive oil, blending for another full minute, allowing the oil to emulsify.

3. Chill in the refrigerator for at least 10 minutes before serving; dressing will thicken as it chills.

PER TABLESPOON Calories: 70 | Fat: 7g | Sodium: 208mg | Fiber: 1g | Protein: 1g

In Search of Tahini

Tahini is a sesame seed paste native to Middle Eastern cuisine with a thinner consistency and milder flavor than peanut butter. You'll find a jarred or canned version in the ethnic foods aisle of large grocery stores, or a fresh version chilling next to the hummus if you're lucky. Check the bulk bins at co-ops and natural-foods stores for powdered tahini, which can be rehydrated with a bit of water, or, try the recipe on p. 21.

Italian White Bean and Fresh Herb Salad

Don't let the simplicity of this bean salad fool you! The fresh herbs marinate the beans to flavorful perfection, so there's no need to add anything else!

INGREDIENTS | SERVES 4

2 14.5-ounce cans cannellini or great northern beans, drained and rinsed

2 ribs celery, diced

¼ cup chopped fresh parsley

¼ cup chopped fresh basil

3 tablespoons olive oil

3 large tomatoes, chopped

½ cup sliced black olives

2 tablespoons lemon juice

Salt and pepper to taste

¼ teaspoon crushed red pepper flakes (optional)

1. In a large skillet, combine the beans, celery, parsley, and basil with olive oil. Heat, stirring frequently, over low heat for 3 minutes, until herbs are softened but not cooked.

2. Remove from heat and stir in remaining ingredients, gently tossing to combine. Chill for at least 1 hour before serving.

PER SERVING Calories: 377 | Fat: 14g | Sodium: 279mg | Fiber: 12g | Protein: 16g

Vegan Pesto Vinaigrette

Turn your Sun-Dried Tomato Pesto (p. 28) into a flavorful salad dressing. Perfect on a green salad with red onions, black olives, and diced avocado. You may need a little more or less liquid, depending on how thick your pesto is.

INGREDIENTS | YIELDS 1¼ CUP

⅔ cup vegan pesto such as Sun-Dried Tomato Pesto (p. 28)

¼ cup red wine vinegar

1 tablespoon lemon juice

⅓ cup olive oil

1 tablespoon Dijon mustard

Whisk together all ingredients until well combined.

PER TABLESPOON Calories: 68 | Fat: 7g | Sodium: 60mg | Fiber: 0g | Protein: 1g

Messy Taco Salad

If you're bored with the usual salads but still want something light and green, try this taco salad. The taste and texture is best with iceberg lettuce, but if you want something more nutritious, use a blend of half iceberg and half romaine. Top with a handful of shredded vegan cheese if you'd like.

INGREDIENTS | SERVES 4

2 heads iceberg lettuce, chopped

½ cup sliced black olives

½ cup corn

1 jalapeño pepper, seeded and sliced, or 2 tablespoons canned green chilies (optional)

1 can refried black beans

2 tablespoons taco sauce or 1 teaspoon hot sauce

¼ cup salsa

¼ cup vegan mayonnaise

10–12 tortilla chips, crumbled

1 avocado, diced (optional)

Baked Tortilla Chips

Why not make your own tortilla chips! Slice whole-wheat tortillas into strips or triangles, and arrange in a single layer on a baking sheet. Drizzle with olive oil for a crispier chip, and season with a bit of salt and garlic powder if you want, or just bake them plain. It'll take about 5–6 minutes on each side in a 300°F oven.

1. Combine the lettuce, olives, corn, and jalapeño peppers in a large bowl.

2. Warm the beans slightly over the stove or in the microwave, just until softened. Combine beans with taco sauce, salsa, and mayonnaise, breaking up the beans and mixing to form a thick sauce.

3. Combine bean mixture with lettuce, stirring to combine as much as possible. Add tortilla chips and avocado, and stir gently to combine. Add a dash or two of extra hot sauce, to taste.

PER SERVING Calories: 307 | Fat: 13g | Sodium: 965mg | Fiber: 10g | Protein: 11g

Spicy Sweet Cucumber Salad

Japanese cucumber salad is cool and refreshing, but with a bit of spice.
Enjoy it as a healthy afternoon snack, or as a fresh accompaniment to take-out.

INGREDIENTS | SERVES 2

2 cucumbers, thinly sliced
¾ teaspoon salt
¼ cup rice wine vinegar
1 teaspoon sugar or 1 tablespoon agave nectar
1 teaspoon sesame oil
¼ teaspoon red pepper flakes
½ onion, thinly sliced

1. In a large shallow container or baking sheet, spread the cucumbers in a single layer and sprinkle with salt. Allow to sit at least 10 minutes.

2. Drain any excess water from the cucumbers.

3. Whisk together the rice wine vinegar, sugar or agave nectar, oil, and red pepper flakes.

4. Pour dressing over the cucumbers, add onions, and toss gently.

5. Allow to sit at least 10 minutes before serving to allow flavors to mingle.

PER SERVING Calories: 90 | Fat: 3g | Sodium: 880mg | Fiber: 2g | Protein: 2g

Tangerine and Mint Salad

Fennel and mint are a wonderful combination, but the sweet tangerines will carry the salad if you can't find fennel. A small drizzle of gourmet oil, if you have some, would kick up the flavor even more. Try walnut or even truffle oil.

INGREDIENTS | SERVES 2

1 head green lettuce, chopped
2 tablespoons chopped fresh mint
2 tangerines or oranges (Clementine or Satsuma), sectioned
⅓ cup chopped walnuts
1 bulb fennel, sliced thin (optional)
2 tablespoons olive oil
Salt and pepper to taste

1. Gently toss together the lettuce, mint, tangerines, walnuts, and sliced fennel.

2. Drizzle with olive oil, salt, and pepper.

PER SERVING Calories: 322 | Fat: 27g | Sodium: 55mg | Fiber: 6g | Protein: 6g

Homemade Flavored Oils

A flavored oil will beautify your kitchen and add flavor to your food. Simply combine several of your favorite herbs, whole garlic cloves, peppercorns, dried lemon or orange zest, or dried chilies with a quality olive oil. For safety's sake, avoid fresh herbs and zests, and always use dried. Oils infused with dried herbs will keep for up to one year, while fresh herbs can cause spoilage after less than a week.

Carrot and Date Salad

If you're used to carrot and raisin salads with pineapple and drowning in mayonnaise, this lighter version with tahini, dates, and mandarin oranges will be a welcome change.

INGREDIENTS | SERVES 4

⅓ cup tahini

1 tablespoon olive oil

2 tablespoons agave nectar (or 2 teaspoons sugar)

3 tablespoons lemon juice

¼ teaspoon salt

4 large carrots, grated

½ cup chopped dates

3 Satsuma or mandarin oranges, sectioned

⅓ cup coconut flakes (optional)

1. In a small bowl, whisk together the tahini, olive oil, agave nectar, lemon juice, and salt.

2. Place grated carrots in a large bowl, and toss well with tahini mixture. Add dates, oranges, and coconut flakes and combine well.

3. Allow to sit for at least 1 hour before serving to soften carrots and dates. Toss again before serving.

PER SERVING Calories: 307 | Fat: 15g | Sodium: 220mg | Fiber: 7g | Protein: 5g

Edamame Salad

If you can't find shelled edamame, try this recipe with lima beans instead.

INGREDIENTS | SERVES 4

2 cups frozen shelled edamame, thawed and drained

1 red or yellow bell pepper, diced

¾ cup corn kernels

3 tablespoons chopped fresh cilantro (optional)

3 tablespoons olive oil

2 tablespoons red wine vinegar

1 teaspoon soy sauce

1 teaspoon chili powder

2 teaspoons lemon or lime juice

Salt and pepper to taste

1. Combine edamame, bell pepper, corn, and cilantro in a large bowl.

2. Whisk together the olive oil, vinegar, soy sauce, chili powder, and lemon or lime juice, and combine with the edamame. Add salt and pepper to taste.

3. Chill for at least 1 hour before serving.

Eda-What?

You're probably familiar with the lightly steamed and salted edamame served as an appetizer at Japanese restaurants, but many grocers sell shelled edamame in the frozen foods section. Edamame, baby green soybeans, are a great source of unprocessed soy protein.

PER SERVING Calories: 246 | Fat: 16g | Sodium: 133mg | Fiber: 9g | Protein: 10g

Sweet Red Salad with Strawberries and Beets

Colorful and nutritious, this vibrant red salad can be made with roasted or canned beets, or even raw grated beets if you prefer.

INGREDIENTS | SERVES 4

3–4 small beets, peeled and chopped
Water for boiling
Spinach or other green lettuce
1 cup sliced strawberries
½ cup chopped pecans
¼ cup olive oil
2 tablespoons red wine vinegar
2 tablespoons agave nectar
2 tablespoons orange juice
Salt and pepper to taste

1. Boil beets in water until soft, about 20 minutes. Allow to cool completely.

2. In a large bowl, combine spinach, strawberries, pecans, and cooled beets.

3. In a separate small bowl, whisk together the olive oil, vinegar, agave nectar, and orange juice and pour over salad, tossing well to coat.

4. Season generously with salt and pepper, to taste.

PER SERVING Calories: 295 | Fat: 24g | Sodium: 73mg | Fiber: 5g | Protein: 3g

Pesto and New Potato Salad

A simple side dish if served hot, or potato salad if served cold, these creamy pesto potatoes are a lively and creative way to use an elegant ingredient.

INGREDIENTS | SERVES 4

½ cup vegan pesto such as Sun-Dried Tomato Pesto (p. 28)
¼ cup Vegan Mayonnaise (p. 23)
2 pounds new potatoes, chopped and cooked
3 scallions, chopped
⅓ cup sliced black olives
Salt and pepper, to taste

1. Whisk together pesto and mayonnaise, and toss with potatoes and remaining ingredients.

2. Season generously with salt and pepper, to taste.

PER SERVING Calories: 448 | Fat: 20g | Sodium: 453mg | Fiber: 7g | Protein: 10g

Chapter 5

Soups

Kidney Bean and Zucchini Gumbo

This vegetable gumbo uses zucchini instead of okra. Traditional gumbo always calls for filé powder, but if you can't find this anywhere, increase the amounts of the other spices.

INGREDIENTS | SERVES 5

1 onion, diced
1 red or green bell pepper, chopped
3 stalks celery, chopped
2 tablespoons olive oil
1 zucchini, sliced
1 14-ounce can diced tomatoes
3 cups vegetable broth
1 teaspoon hot sauce
1 teaspoon filé powder (optional)
¾ teaspoon thyme
1 teaspoon Cajun seasoning
2 bay leaves
1 15-ounce can kidney beans, drained
1½ cups rice, cooked

1. In a large soup or stock pot, sauté the onion, bell pepper, and celery in olive oil for just a minute or 2. Reduce heat and add zucchini, tomatoes, vegetable broth, and remaining ingredients, except rice and beans.

2. Bring to a simmer, cover, and allow to cook for 30 minutes.

3. Uncover, add beans, and stir to combine. Heat for 5 more minutes. Remove bay leaves before serving. Serve over cooked rice.

PER SERVING Calories: 227 | Fat: 6g | Sodium: 1,128mg | Fiber: 7g | Protein: 7g

Gumbo on the Go

If you don't have some precooked rice on hand, add ⅔ cup instant rice and an extra cup vegetable broth during the last 10 minutes of cooking. For a "meatier" texture, quickly brown some vegetarian sausage or ground beef substitute and toss it in the mix.

Ten-Minute Cheater's Chili

No time? No problem! This is a quick and easy way to get some veggies and protein on the table with no hassle. Instead of veggie burgers, you could toss in a handful of TVP flakes, if you'd like, or any other mock meat you happen to have on hand.

INGREDIENTS | SERVES 4

1 12-ounce jar salsa
1 14-ounce can diced tomatoes
2 14-ounce cans kidney beans or black beans, drained
1½ cups frozen veggies
4 veggie burgers, crumbled (optional)
2 tablespoons chili powder
1 teaspoon cumin
½ cup water

In a large pot, combine all ingredients together. Simmer for 10 minutes, stirring frequently.

PER SERVING Calories: 271 | Fat: 3g | Sodium: 1,154mg | Fiber: 17g | Protein: 15g

Cream of Carrot Soup with Coconut

This carrot soup will knock your socks off! The addition of coconut milk transforms an ordinary carrot and ginger soup into an unexpected treat.

INGREDIENTS | SERVES 6

3 medium carrots, chopped
1 sweet potato, chopped
1 yellow onion, chopped
3½ cups vegetable broth
3 cloves garlic, minced
2 teaspoons minced fresh ginger
1 14-ounce can coconut milk
1 teaspoon salt
¾ teaspoon cinnamon (optional)

1. In a large soup or stock pot, bring the carrots, sweet potato, and onion to a simmer in the vegetable broth. Add garlic and ginger, cover, and heat for 20–25 minutes until carrots and potatoes are soft.

2. Allow to cool slightly, then transfer to a blender, and purée until smooth.

3. Return soup to pot. Over very low heat, stir in the coconut milk and salt, stirring well to combine. Heat just until heated through, another 3–4 minutes.

4. Garnish with cinnamon just before serving.

PER SERVING Calories: 177 | Fat: 14g | Sodium: 978mg | Fiber: 2g | Protein: 2g

Cashew Cream of Asparagus Soup

A dairy-free and soy-free asparagus soup with a rich cashew base brings out the natural flavors of the asparagus without relying on other enhancers.

INGREDIENTS | SERVES 4

1 onion, chopped

4 cloves garlic, minced

2 tablespoons olive oil

2 pounds asparagus, trimmed and chopped

4 cups vegetable broth

¾ cup raw cashews

¾ cup water

¼ teaspoon sage

½ teaspoon salt

¼ teaspoon black pepper

2 teaspoons lemon juice

2 tablespoons nutritional yeast (optional)

1. In a large soup or stock pot, sauté onion and garlic in olive oil for 2–3 minutes until onion is soft. Reduce heat and carefully add asparagus and vegetable broth.

2. Bring to a simmer, cover, and cook for 20 minutes. Cool slightly, then purée in a blender, working in batches as needed until almost smooth. Return to pot over low heat.

3. Purée together cashews and water until smooth and add to soup. Add sage, salt, and pepper and heat for a few more minutes, stirring to combine.

4. Stir in lemon juice and nutritional yeast just before serving, and adjust seasonings to taste.

PER SERVING Calories: 271 | Fat: 18g | Sodium: 1,241mg | Fiber: 6g | Protein: 10g

Varieties of Veggie Broths

A basic vegetable broth is made by simmering vegetables, potatoes, and a bay leaf or two in water for at least 30 minutes. While you may be familiar with the canned and boxed stocks available at the grocery store, vegan chefs have a few other tricks up their sleeves to impart extra flavor to recipes calling for vegetable broth. Check your natural grocer for specialty flavored bouillon cubes such as vegetarian "chicken" or "beef" flavor, or shop the bulk bins for powdered vegetable broth mix.

Thai Tom Kha Coconut Soup

In Thailand, this soup is a full meal, served alongside a large plate of steamed rice, and the vegetables vary with the season and whim of the chef—broccoli, bell peppers, or mild chilies are common. Don't worry if you can't find lemongrass or galangal, as lime and ginger add a similar flavor.

INGREDIENTS | SERVES 4

1 14-ounce can coconut milk
2 cups vegetable broth
1 tablespoon soy sauce
3 cloves garlic, minced
5 slices fresh ginger or galangal
1 stalk lemongrass, chopped (optional)
1 tablespoon lime juice
1–2 small chilies, chopped
½ teaspoon red pepper flakes, or to taste
1 onion, chopped
2 tomatoes, chopped
1 carrot, sliced thin
½ cup sliced mushrooms, any kind
¼ cup chopped fresh cilantro

1. Combine the coconut milk and vegetable broth over medium-low heat. Add soy sauce, garlic, ginger, lemongrass, lime juice, chilies, and red pepper flakes. Heat, but do not boil.

2. When broth is hot, add onion, tomatoes, carrot, and mushrooms. Cover and cook on low heat for 10–15 minutes.

3. Remove from heat and top with chopped fresh cilantro.

PER SERVING Calories: 240 | Fat: 21g | Sodium: 725mg | Fiber: 2g | Protein: 4g

Shiitake and Garlic Broth

Shiitake mushrooms transform ordinary broth into a rich stock with a deep flavor.

INGREDIENTS | YIELDS 6 CUPS BROTH

⅓ cup dried shiitake mushrooms
6 cups water
2 cloves garlic, smashed
1 bay leaf
½ teaspoon thyme
½ onion, chopped

1. Combine all ingredients in a large soup or stock pot and bring to a slow simmer.

2. Cover and allow to cook for at least 30–40 minutes.

3. Strain before using.

PER 1 CUP Calories: 8 | Fat: 0g | Sodium: 5mg | Fiber: 0g | Protein: 0g

Vegetarian Dashi

To turn this into a Japanese dashi stock for miso and noodle soups, omit the bay leaf and thyme and add a generous amount of seaweed, preferably kombu, if you can find it!

Cold Spanish Gazpacho with Avocado

Best enjoyed on an outdoor patio just after sunset on a warm summer evening. But really, anytime you want a simple light starter soup will do, no matter the weather. Add some crunch by topping with homemade croutons.

INGREDIENTS | SERVES 6

2 cucumbers, diced

½ red onion, diced

2 large tomatoes, diced

¼ cup fresh chopped cilantro

2 avocados, diced

4 cloves garlic

2 tablespoons lime juice

1 tablespoon red wine vinegar

¾ cup vegetable broth

1 chili pepper (jalapeño, serrano, or cayenne) or 1 teaspoon hot sauce

Salt and pepper to taste

1. Mix together the cucumbers, red onion, tomatoes, cilantro, and avocado. Set half of the mixture aside. Take the other half and mix in a blender. Add the garlic, lime juice, vinegar, vegetable broth, and chili pepper or hot sauce and process until smooth.

2. Transfer to serving bowl and add remaining diced cucumbers, onion, tomatoes, cilantro, and avocado, stirring gently to combine.

3. Season generously with salt and pepper, to taste.

PER SERVING Calories: 149 | Fat: 10g | Sodium: 130mg | Fiber: 7g | Protein: 3g

Crunchy Croutons

Slice your favorite vegan artisan bread, focaccia, or whatever you've got into 1-inch cubes. Toss them in a large bowl with a generous coating of olive oil or a flavored oil, a bit of salt, and some Italian seasonings, garlic powder, a dash of cayenne, or whatever you prefer; then transfer to a baking sheet and bake 15–20 minutes at 275°F, tossing once or twice.

Indian Curried Lentil Soup

Similar to a traditional Indian lentil dal recipe but with added vegetables to make it into an entrée, this lentil soup is perfect as is or paired with rice or some warmed Indian flatbread.

INGREDIENTS | SERVES 4

1 onion, diced
1 carrot, sliced
3 whole cloves
2 tablespoons vegan margarine
1 teaspoon cumin
1 teaspoon turmeric
1 cup yellow or green lentils, uncooked
2¾ cups vegetable broth
2 large tomatoes, chopped
1 teaspoon salt
¼ teaspoon black pepper
1 teaspoon lemon juice

1. In a large soup or stock pot, sauté the onion, carrot, and cloves in margarine until onions are just turning soft, about 3 minutes. Add cumin and turmeric and toast for 1 minute, stirring constantly to avoid burning.

2. Reduce heat to medium low and add lentils, vegetable broth, tomatoes, and salt. Bring to a simmer, cover, and cook for 35–40 minutes, or until lentils are done.

3. Season with black pepper and lemon juice just before serving.

PER SERVING Calories: 265 | Fat: 6g | Sodium: 1,328mg | Fiber: 17g | Protein: 14g

Cannellini Bean and Corn Chowder

This is a filling and textured soup that could easily be a main dish. Some chopped collards or a dash of hot sauce would be a welcome addition. For a lower-fat version, skip the initial sauté and add about 5 minutes to the cooking time.

INGREDIENTS | SERVES 4

1 potato, chopped small
1 onion, chopped
2 tablespoons olive oil
3 cups vegetable broth
2 ears of corn, kernels cut off, or
1½ cups frozen or canned corn
1 14-ounce can cannellini or great northern beans
½ teaspoon thyme
¼ teaspoon black pepper
1 tablespoon flour
1½ cups soy milk

1. In a large soup or stock pot, sauté potato and onion in olive oil for 3–5 minutes.

2. Reduce heat and add vegetable broth. Bring to a slow simmer, cover, and allow to cook for 15–20 minutes.

3. Uncover and add corn, beans, thyme, and pepper.

4. Whisk together flour and soy milk, and add to the pot, stirring well to prevent lumps. Reduce heat to prevent soy milk from curdling, and cook, uncovered, for 5–6 more minutes, stirring frequently.

5. Allow to cool slightly before serving, as soup will thicken as it cools.

PER SERVING Calories: 322 | Fat: 9g | Sodium: 761mg | Fiber: 8g | Protein: 13g

Fresh Is Always Best

Cans are convenient, but dried beans are cheaper, need less packaging, and add a fresher flavor. And if you plan in advance, they aren't much work at all to prepare. Place beans in a large pot, cover with water (more than you think you'll need), and allow to sit for at least 2 hours or overnight. Drain the water and simmer in fresh water for about an hour, then you're good to go! One cup dried beans yields about 3 cups cooked.

Barley Vegetable Soup

Barley Vegetable Soup is an excellent "kitchen sink" recipe, meaning that you can toss in just about any fresh or frozen vegetables or spices you happen to have on hand.

INGREDIENTS | SERVES 6

1 onion, chopped
2 carrots, sliced
2 ribs celery, chopped
2 tablespoons olive oil
8 cups vegetable broth
1 cup barley, uncooked
1½ cups frozen mixed vegetables
1 14-ounce can crushed or diced tomatoes
½ teaspoon parsley
½ teaspoon thyme
2 bay leaves
Salt and pepper to taste

1. In a large soup or stock pot, sauté the onion, carrots, and celery in olive oil for 3–5 minutes, just until onions are almost soft.

2. Reduce heat to medium low, and add remaining ingredients, except salt and pepper.

3. Bring to a simmer, cover, and allow to cook for at least 45 minutes, stirring occasionally.

4. Remove cover and allow to cook for 10 more minutes.

5. Remove bay leaves; season with salt and pepper to taste.

PER SERVING Calories: 228 | Fat: 5g | Sodium: 1,380mg | Fiber: 9g | Protein: 6g

Super "Meaty" Chili with TVP

Any mock meat will work well in a vegetarian chili, but TVP is easy to keep on hand and very inexpensive. This is more of a thick, "meaty" Texas chili than a vegetable chili, but chili is easy and forgiving, so if you want to toss in some zucchini, broccoli, or diced carrots, by all means, do!

INGREDIENTS | SERVES 6

1½ cups TVP granules

1 cup hot vegetable broth

1 tablespoon soy sauce

1 yellow onion, chopped

5 cloves garlic, minced

2 tablespoons olive oil

1 cup corn kernels (fresh, frozen, or canned)

1 bell pepper, any color, chopped

2 15-ounce cans beans (black, kidney, or pinto)

1 15-ounce can diced tomatoes

1 jalapeño pepper, minced, or ½ teaspoon cayenne pepper (optional)

1 teaspoon cumin

2 tablespoons chili powder

Salt and pepper to taste

1. Cover the TVP with hot vegetable broth and soy sauce. Allow to sit for 3–4 minutes only, then drain.

2. In a large soup or stock pot, sauté the onion and garlic in olive oil until onions are soft, about 3–4 minutes.

3. Add remaining ingredients and TVP, stirring well to combine. Cover, and allow to simmer over low heat for at least 30 minutes, stirring occasionally.

4. Adjust seasonings to taste.

PER SERVING Calories: 272 | Fat: 6g | Sodium: 603mg | Fiber: 13g | Protein: 20g

Rehydrating TVP

Most of the time, TVP needs to be rehydrated in hot water for 8–10 minutes, unless it will be hydrated when cooking, such as in a soup with extra liquid. But the secret in this recipe is to only partially rehydrate the TVP, so that it absorbs some of the spices from the chili and the liquid from the tomatoes.

Easy Roasted Tomato Soup

Use the freshest, ripest, juiciest red tomatoes you can find for this super-easy recipe, as there are few other added flavors. If you find that you need a bit more spice, add a spoonful of nutritional yeast, a dash of cayenne pepper, or an extra shake of salt and pepper.

INGREDIENTS | SERVES 4

6 large tomatoes
1 small onion
4 cloves garlic
2 tablespoons olive oil
1¼ cups soy milk
2 tablespoons chopped fresh basil
1½ teaspoons balsamic vinegar
¾ teaspoon salt
¼ teaspoon black pepper

1. Preheat oven to 425°F.

2. Slice tomatoes in half and chop onion into quarters. Place tomatoes, onion, and garlic on baking sheet and drizzle with olive oil.

3. Roast in the oven for 45 minutes to 1 hour.

4. Carefully transfer tomatoes, onion, and garlic to a blender, including any juices on the baking sheet. Add remaining ingredients and purée until almost smooth.

5. Reheat over low heat for just a minute or 2 if needed, and adjust seasonings to taste.

PER SERVING Calories: 153 | Fat: 9g | Sodium: 488mg | Fiber: 4g | Protein: 5g

Udon Noodle Buddha Bowl

Say that five times fast! This is a nutritious full meal in a bowl, which might be particularly comforting on the edge of a cold or after an early-morning zazen meditation. For an authentic Japanese flavor, add a large piece of kombu seaweed to the broth or use a vegetarian dashi stock (p. 81).

INGREDIENTS | SERVES 4

2 8-ounce packages udon noodles
3½ cups Shiitake and Garlic Broth (p. 81)
1½ teaspoons fresh minced ginger
1 tablespoon sugar
1 tablespoon soy sauce
1 tablespoon rice vinegar
¼ teaspoon red pepper flakes, or to taste
1 baby bok choy, sliced
1 cup mushrooms, any kind, sliced
1 block silken tofu, cubed
¼ cup bean sprouts
1 cup fresh spinach
1 teaspoon sesame oil or hot chili oil

1. Cook noodles in boiling water until soft, about 5 minutes. Drain and divide into four serving bowls and set aside.

2. In a large pot, combine the Shiitake and Garlic Broth, ginger, sugar, soy sauce, vinegar, and red pepper flakes and bring to a simmer. Add bok choy, mushrooms, and tofu and cook just until veggies are soft, about 10 minutes.

3. Add bean sprouts and spinach and simmer for 1 more minute until spinach has wilted. Remove from heat and drizzle with sesame oil or chili oil.

4. Divide soup into the four bowls containing cooked noodles and serve immediately.

PER SERVING Calories: 240 | Fat: 4g | Sodium: 453mg | Fiber: 1g | Protein: 12g

Know Your Noodles: Udon, Somen, Soba, Shirataki

Udon noodles have a thick and chewy texture, but you can try this recipe with any noodle you like. Noodles cook quicker than pasta, so they're great when you're super hungry or in a hurry. Many grocery stores even stock shirataki noodles—a high-protein, low-carb noodle that doesn't need to be cooked—perfect for hungry vegans to slurp! Check the refrigerator section for these.

Winter Seitan Stew

If you're used to a "meat and potatoes" kind of diet, this hearty seitan and potato stew ought to become a favorite.

INGREDIENTS | SERVES 6

2 cups chopped seitan
1 onion, chopped
2 carrots, chopped
2 stalks celery, chopped
2 tablespoons olive oil
4 cups vegetable broth
2 potatoes, chopped
½ teaspoon sage
½ teaspoon rosemary
½ teaspoon thyme
2 tablespoons cornstarch
⅓ cup water
Salt and pepper to taste

1. In a large soup pot, heat seitan, onion, carrots, and celery in olive oil for 4–5 minutes, stirring frequently, until seitan is lightly browned.

2. Add vegetable broth and potatoes and bring to a boil. Reduce to a simmer, add herbs, and cover. Allow to cook for 25–30 minutes until potatoes are soft.

3. In a small bowl, whisk together cornstarch and water. Add to soup, stirring to combine.

4. Cook, uncovered, for another 5–7 minutes until stew has thickened.

5. Season generously with salt and pepper to taste.

PER SERVING Calories: 213 | Fat: 6g | Sodium: 974mg | Fiber: 4g | Protein: 17g

Potato and Leek Soup

With simple earthy flavors, this classic soup is a comforting starter.

INGREDIENTS | SERVES 6

1 yellow onion, diced
2 cloves garlic, minced
2 tablespoons olive oil
6 cups vegetable broth
3 leeks, sliced
2 large potatoes, chopped
2 bay leaves
1 cup soy milk
2 tablespoons vegan margarine
¾ teaspoon salt
⅓ teaspoon black pepper
½ teaspoon sage
½ teaspoon thyme
2 tablespoons nutritional yeast (optional)

Get Your Leeks Ready

Fresh leeks impart an oniony root flavor. To prepare your leeks, chop off the inedible dark green leaves, and use only the white and soft light green stem. Leeks tend to hide bits of dirt inside, so rinse or submerge well, chop, then rinse again, using a colander or salad spinner. Got extras? Toss any leftover bits into a vegetable broth.

1. Sauté onions and garlic in olive oil for a few minutes until onions are soft.

2. Add vegetable broth, leeks, potatoes, and bay leaves and bring to a slow simmer.

3. Allow to cook, partially covered, for 30 minutes until potatoes are soft.

4. Remove bay leaves. Working in batches as needed, purée soup in a blender until almost smooth, or desired consistency.

5. Return soup to pot and stir in remaining ingredients. Adjust seasonings and reheat as needed.

PER SERVING Calories: 223 | Fat: 9g | Sodium: 1,321mg | Fiber: 4g | Protein: 4g

African Peanut and Greens Soup

*Cut back on the red pepper flakes to make this soup for kids, or
reduce the liquids to turn it into a thick and chunky curry to pour over rice.
Although the ingredients are all familiar, this is definitely not a boring meal!*

INGREDIENTS | SERVES 4

1 onion, diced
3 tomatoes, chopped
2 tablespoons olive oil
2 cups vegetable broth
1 cup coconut milk
⅓ cup peanut butter
1 15-ounce can chickpeas, drained
½ teaspoon salt
1 teaspoon curry powder
1 teaspoon sugar
⅓ teaspoon red pepper flakes
1 bunch fresh spinach

1. Sauté the onions and tomatoes in olive oil until onions are soft, about 2–3 minutes.

2. Reduce heat to medium low and add remaining ingredients, except spinach, stirring well to combine.

3. Allow to simmer on low heat, uncovered, stirring occasionally for 8–10 minutes.

4. Add spinach and allow to cook for another minute or 2, just until spinach is wilted.

5. Remove from heat and adjust seasonings to taste. Soup will thicken as it cools.

PER SERVING Calories: 408 | Fat: 24g | Sodium: 1,202mg | Fiber: 8g | Protein: 13g

"Chicken" Noodle Soup

If you're sick in bed, this brothy soup is just as comforting and nutritious as the real thing.

INGREDIENTS | SERVES 6

6 cups vegetable broth
1 carrot, diced
2 ribs celery, diced
1 onion, chopped
½ cup TVP
2 bay leaves
1½ teaspoons Italian seasonings
Salt and pepper to taste
1 cup vegan noodles, or small pasta

Combine all ingredients in a large soup or stock pot. Cover and simmer for 15–20 minutes.

To Get That Chicken Flavor

Several brands make a vegetarian chicken-flavored broth and vegetarian chicken-flavored bouillon cubes if you want a more genuine flavor. Just about any natural-foods store will stock these products. Rarely spotted is the elusive chicken-flavored TVP, so if you can find some, stock up!

PER SERVING Calories: 123 | Fat: 0g | Sodium: 960mg | Fiber: 3g | Protein: 7g

Curried Pumpkin Soup

You don't have to wait for fall to make this pumpkin soup, as canned pumpkin purée will work just fine. It's also excellent with coconut milk instead of soy milk.

INGREDIENTS | SERVES 4

1 yellow onion, diced
3 cloves garlic, minced
2 tablespoons vegan margarine
1 15-ounce can pumpkin purée
3 cups vegetable broth
2 bay leaves
1 tablespoon curry powder
1 teaspoon cumin
½ teaspoon ground ginger
1 cup soy milk
¼ teaspoon salt

Ditch the Can

If you've got the time, there's nothing like fresh roasted pumpkin! Make your own purée to substitute for canned. Carefully chop your pumpkin in half, remove the seeds (save and toast those later!), and roast for 45 minutes to an hour in a 375°F oven. Cool, then peel off the skin, and mash or purée until smooth. Whatever you don't use will keep in the freezer for next time.

1. In a large soup or stock pot, heat onion and garlic in margarine until onion is soft, about 4–5 minutes.

2. Add pumpkin and vegetable broth and stir well to combine. Add bay leaves, curry powder, cumin, and ginger and bring to a slow simmer.

3. Cover and allow to cook for 15 minutes.

4. Reduce heat to low and add soy milk, stirring to combine. Heat for just another minute or 2 until heated through.

5. Season with salt to taste and remove bay leaves before serving.

PER SERVING Calories: 136 | Fat: 7g | Sodium: 1,112mg | Fiber: 4g | Protein: 3g

Garlic Miso and Onion Soup

Boiling miso destroys some of its beneficial enzymes, so be sure to heat this soup to just below a simmer. Use a soft hand when slicing the silken tofu, so it doesn't crumble.

INGREDIENTS | SERVES 4

5 cups water or dashi stock (p. 81)
½ cup sliced shiitake mushrooms
3 scallions, chopped
½ onion, chopped
4 cloves garlic, minced
¾ teaspoon garlic powder
2 tablespoons soy sauce
1 teaspoon sesame oil
1 block silken tofu, diced
⅓ cup miso
1 tablespoon chopped seaweed, any kind (optional)

1. Combine all ingredients except for miso and seaweed in a large soup or stock pot and bring to a slow simmer. Cook, uncovered, for 10–12 minutes.

2. Reduce heat and stir in miso and seaweed, being careful not to boil.

3. Heat, stirring to dissolve miso, for another 5 minutes until onions and mushrooms are soft.

PER SERVING Calories: 133 | Fat: 5g | Sodium: 1336mg | Fiber: 2g | Protein: 10g

Cream Cheese and Butternut Squash Soup

This isn't a healthy hippie vegetable soup—it's a rich, decadent, stick-to-your-thighs soup. Nonetheless, it's absolutely delicious. Top with a mountain of homemade croutons or serve with crusty French bread.

INGREDIENTS | SERVES 4

2 cloves garlic, minced
½ yellow onion, diced
2 tablespoons olive oil
3½ cups vegetable broth
1 medium butternut squash, peeled, seeded, and chopped into cubes
1 teaspoon curry powder
¼ teaspoon nutmeg
½ 8-ounce container vegan cream cheese
¼ teaspoon salt

1. In a large skillet or stock pot, sauté garlic and onions in olive oil until soft, about 3–4 minutes.

2. Reduce heat to medium low and add vegetable broth, squash, curry powder, and nutmeg. Simmer for 25 minutes until squash is soft.

3. Working in batches, purée until almost smooth, or to desired consistency. Or, if squash is soft enough, mash smooth with a large fork.

4. Return soup to very low heat and stir in vegan cream cheese until melted, combined, and heated through. Add salt and adjust seasonings to taste.

PER SERVING Calories: 212 | Fat: 12g | Sodium: 1,133mg | Fiber: 3g | Protein: 2g

Chinese Hot and Sour Soup

*If you can't get enough of traditional Chinese cuisine,
this delicious soup is for you.*

INGREDIENTS | SERVES 6

2 cups seitan, diced small (or other meat substitute)
2 tablespoons vegetable oil
1½ teaspoons hot sauce
6 cups vegetable broth
½ head Napa cabbage, shredded
¾ cup sliced shiitake mushrooms
1 small can bamboo shoots, drained
2 tablespoons soy sauce
2 tablespoons white vinegar
¾ teaspoon crushed red pepper flakes
¾ teaspoon salt
2 tablespoons cornstarch
¼ cup water
3 scallions, sliced
2 teaspoons sesame oil

Traditional Ingredients

If this Americanized version of hot and sour soup just doesn't satisfy your Szechuan cravings, hit up a specialty Asian grocery store for some exotic ingredients. Replace the cabbage with ½ cup dried lily buds and substitute half of the shiitake with wood ear fungus and add a healthy shake of white pepper and chili oil.

1. Brown seitan in vegetable oil for 2–3 minutes until cooked. Reduce heat to low and add hot sauce, stirring well to coat. Cook over low heat for 1 more minute, then remove from heat and set aside.

2. In a large soup or stock pot, combine vegetable broth, cabbage, mushrooms, bamboo, soy sauce, vinegar, red pepper, and salt. Bring to a slow simmer and cover. Simmer for at least 15 minutes.

3. In a separate small bowl, whisk together the cornstarch and water, then slowly stir into soup. Heat just until soup thickens.

4. Portion into serving bowls, then top each serving with scallions and drizzle with sesame oil.

PER SERVING Calories: 195 | Fat: 7g | Sodium: 1,927mg | Fiber: 3g | Protein: 18g

White Bean and Orzo Minestrone

Italian minestrone is a simple and universally loved soup.
This version uses tiny orzo pasta, cannellini beans, and plenty of veggies.

INGREDIENTS | SERVES 6

3 cloves garlic, minced
1 onion, chopped
2 ribs celery, chopped
2 tablespoons olive oil
5 cups vegetable broth
1 carrot, diced
1 cup green beans, chopped
2 small potatoes, chopped small
2 tomatoes, chopped
1 15-ounce can cannellini beans, drained
1 teaspoon basil
½ teaspoon oregano
¾ cup orzo
Salt and pepper to taste

1. In a large soup pot, heat garlic, onion, and celery in olive oil until just soft, about 3–4 minutes.

2. Add vegetable broth, carrot, green beans, potatoes, tomatoes, beans, basil, and oregano and bring to a simmer. Cover, and cook on medium-low heat for 20–25 minutes.

3. Add orzo and heat another 10 minutes, just until orzo is cooked. Season well with salt and pepper.

PER SERVING Calories: 304 | Fat: 5g | Sodium: 814mg | Fiber: 8g | Protein: 11g

Chapter 6

Vegetables, Stir-Fries, and Sides

Orange and Ginger Mixed-Veggie Stir-Fry

*Rice vinegar can be substituted for the apple cider vinegar, if you prefer.
As with most stir-fry recipes, the vegetables are merely a suggestion; use
your favorites or whatever looks like it's been sitting too long in your crisper.*

INGREDIENTS | SERVES 4

3 tablespoons orange juice
1 tablespoon apple cider vinegar
2 tablespoons soy sauce
2 tablespoons water
1 tablespoon maple syrup
1 teaspoon powdered ginger
2 cloves garlic, minced
2 tablespoons oil
1 bunch broccoli, chopped
½ cup sliced mushrooms
½ cup snap peas, chopped
1 carrot, sliced
1 cup chopped cabbage or bok choy

1. Whisk together the orange juice, vinegar, soy sauce, water, maple syrup, and ginger.

2. Heat garlic in oil and add veggies. Allow to cook, stirring frequently, over high heat for 2–3 minutes until just starting to get tender.

3. Add sauce and reduce heat. Simmer, stirring frequently, for another 3–4 minutes, or until veggies are cooked.

PER SERVING Calories: 117 | Fat: 3g | Sodium: 518mg | Fiber: 6g | Protein: 6g

Oodles of Noodles

When stir-frying a saucy veggie dish, you can add quick-cooking Asian-style noodles right into the pan. Add some extra sauce ingredients and ¼ to ⅓ cup of water. Add the noodles, stir up the sauce, reduce the heat so the veggies don't scald, and keep covered for just a few minutes.

Creamed Spinach and Mushrooms

The combination of greens and nutritional yeast is simply delicious and provides an excellent jolt of nutrients that vegans need. Don't forget that spinach will shrink when cooked, so use lots!

INGREDIENTS | SERVES 4

½ onion, diced
2 cloves garlic, minced
1½ cups sliced mushrooms
2 tablespoons olive oil
1 tablespoon flour
2 bunches fresh spinach, trimmed
1 cup soy milk
1 tablespoon vegan margarine
¼ teaspoon nutmeg (optional)
2 tablespoons nutritional yeast (optional)
Salt and pepper, to taste

1. Sauté onion, garlic, and mushrooms in olive oil for 3–4 minutes. Add flour and cook, stirring constantly, for 1 minute.

2. Reduce heat to medium low and add spinach and soy milk. Cook uncovered for 8–10 minutes until spinach is soft and liquid has reduced.

3. Stir in remaining ingredients and season with salt and pepper to taste.

PER SERVING Calories: 169 | Fat: 11g | Sodium: 206mg | Fiber: 5g | Protein: 8g

Roasted-Garlic Mashed Potatoes

In the absence of milk and butter, load up your mashed potatoes with a full head of roasted garlic for a flavor blast.

INGREDIENTS | SERVES 4

1 whole head garlic
2 tablespoons olive oil
6 potatoes, cooked
¼ cup vegan margarine
½ cup soy creamer or soy milk
Sea salt and pepper to taste

Vegan Mashed Potato Tricks

There's nothing wrong with just switching the butter and milk for vegan versions in your favorite potato recipe, but half a container of nondairy sour cream or cream cheese, a few teaspoons of fresh crumbled sage, or some chopped artichoke hearts will make your spuds come alive. Or simply add a shake of nutmeg or rosemary.

1. Heat oven to 400°F.

2. Remove outer layer of skin from garlic head. Drizzle generously with olive oil, wrap in aluminum foil, and place on a baking sheet. Roast in oven for 30 minutes.

3. Gently press cloves out of the skins, and mash smooth with a fork.

4. Using a mixer or a potato masher, combine roasted garlic with potatoes, margarine, and creamer or soy milk until smooth or desired consistency.

5. Season generously with salt and pepper.

PER SERVING Calories: 367 | Fat: 14g | Sodium: 199mg | Fiber: 8g | Protein: 6g

Indian-Spiced Chickpeas with Spinach (Chana Masala)

This is a mild recipe, suitable for the whole family, but if you want to turn up the heat, toss in some fresh minced chilies or a hearty dash of cayenne pepper. It's enjoyable as is for a side dish or piled on top of rice or another grain for a main meal.

INGREDIENTS | SERVES 3

1 onion, chopped
2 cloves garlic, minced
2 tablespoons vegan margarine
¾ teaspoon coriander
1 teaspoon cumin
1 15-ounce can chickpeas, undrained
3 tomatoes, puréed or ⅔ cup tomato paste
½ teaspoon curry powder
¼ teaspoon turmeric
¼ teaspoon salt
1 tablespoon lemon juice
1 bunch fresh spinach

1. In a large skillet, sauté onions and garlic in margarine until almost soft, about 2 minutes.

2. Reduce heat to medium low and add coriander and cumin. Toast the spices, stirring, for 1 minute.

3. Add the chickpeas with liquid in can, tomatoes, curry powder, turmeric, and salt and bring to a slow simmer. Allow to cook until most of the liquid has been absorbed, about 10–12 minutes, stirring occasionally, then add lemon juice.

4. Add spinach and stir to combine. Cook just until spinach begins to wilt, about 1 minute. Serve immediately.

PER SERVING Calories: 306 | Fat: 10g | Sodium: 818mg | Fiber: 11g | Protein: 12g

Fiery Basil and Eggplant Stir-Fry

Holy basil, called tulsi, *is revered in Vishnu temples across India and is frequently used in Ayurvedic healing. It lends a fantastically spicy flavor, but regular basil will also do.*

INGREDIENTS | SERVES 3

3 cloves garlic, minced

3 small fresh chili peppers, minced

1 block firm or extra-firm tofu, pressed and diced

2 tablespoons olive oil

1 eggplant, chopped

1 red bell pepper, chopped

⅓ cup sliced mushrooms

3 tablespoons water

2 tablespoons soy sauce

1 teaspoon lemon juice

⅓ cup fresh Thai basil or holy basil

1. Sauté the garlic, chili peppers, and tofu in olive oil for 4–6 minutes until tofu is lightly golden.

2. Add eggplant, bell pepper, mushrooms, water, and soy sauce and heat, stirring frequently, for 5–6 minutes, or until eggplant is almost soft.

3. Add lemon juice and basil and cook for another minute or 2, just until basil is wilted.

PER SERVING Calories: 241 | Fat: 14g | Sodium: 624mg | Fiber: 9g | Protein: 13g

Types of Basil

Sweet Italian basil may be the most common, but other varieties can add a layer of sensually enticing flavor. Lemon basil is identifiable by its lighter green color and fresh citrusy scent. For this recipe, look for spicy holy basil or Thai basil with a purplish stem and jagged leaf edge for a delightfully scorching flavor.

Sesame Soy Asparagus and Mushrooms

Fresh asparagus in season has such a vibrant taste, it needs very little enhancement.
If you can't find fresh asparagus, don't bother trying this with the canned variety; it's not the same at all!

INGREDIENTS | SERVES 4

1 pound fresh asparagus, trimmed and chopped
¾ cup chopped mushrooms
2 teaspoons sesame oil
1 teaspoon soy sauce
½ teaspoon sugar
2 tablespoons sesame seeds (optional)

1. Preheat oven to 350°F.

2. Place asparagus and mushrooms on a baking pan and roast for 10 minutes.

3. Remove pan from oven; drizzle with sesame oil, soy sauce, and sugar; and toss gently to coat.

4. Roast in oven for 5–6 more minutes.

5. Remove from oven, and toss with sesame seeds.

PER SERVING Calories: 48 | Fat: 2g | Sodium: 77mg | Fiber: 3g | Protein: 3g

Cajun Collard Greens

Like Brussels sprouts and kimchi, collard greens are one of those foods folks tend to either love or hate. They're highly nutritious, so hopefully this recipe will turn you into a lover, if you're not already.

INGREDIENTS | SERVES 4

1 onion, diced
3 cloves garlic, minced
1 pound collard greens, chopped
2 tablespoons olive oil
¾ cup water or vegetable broth
1 14-ounce can diced tomatoes, drained
1½ teaspoons Cajun seasoning
½ teaspoon hot sauce (or to taste)
¼ teaspoon salt

How to Prepare Collards

Give your collards a good rinse, then tear the leaves off the middle stem. Fold or roll all the leaves together, then run a knife through them to create thin strips, similar to a chiffonade cut used for herbs. The stems can be added to a vegetable broth or your compost pile.

1. In a large skillet, sauté onions, garlic, and collard greens in olive oil for 3–5 minutes until onions are soft.

2. Add water or vegetable broth, tomatoes, and Cajun seasoning. Bring to a simmer, cover, and allow to cook for 20 minutes, or until greens are soft, stirring occasionally.

3. Remove lid, stir in hot sauce and salt, and cook, uncovered, for another minute or 2, to allow excess moisture to evaporate.

PER SERVING Calories: 125 | Fat: 7g | Sodium: 517mg | Fiber: 6g | Protein: 4g

Potatoes "Au Gratin" Casserole

You'll never miss the boxed version after trying these easy potatoes!

INGREDIENTS | SERVES 4

4 potatoes
1 onion, chopped
1 tablespoon vegan margarine
2 tablespoons flour
2 cups unsweetened soy milk
2 teaspoons onion powder
1 teaspoon garlic powder
2 tablespoons nutritional yeast
1 teaspoon lemon juice
½ teaspoon salt
¾ teaspoon paprika
½ teaspoon black pepper
¾ cup bread crumbs or French-fried onions (optional)

1. Preheat oven to 375°F.

2. Slice potatoes into thin coins and arrange half the slices in a casserole or baking dish. Layer half of the onions on top of the potatoes.

3. Melt the margarine over low heat and add flour, stirring to make a paste. Add soy milk, onion powder, garlic powder, nutritional yeast, lemon juice, and salt, stirring to combine. Stir over low heat until sauce has thickened, about 2–3 minutes.

4. Pour half of sauce over potatoes and onions, then layer the remaining potatoes and onions on top of the sauce. Pour the remaining sauce on top.

5. Sprinkle with paprika and black pepper and top with bread crumbs or French-fried onions.

6. Cover and bake for 45 minutes and then an additional 10 minutes uncovered.

PER SERVING Calories: 264 | Fat: 5g | Sodium: 406mg | Fiber: 7g | Protein: 9g

Gingered Bok Choy and Tofu Stir-Fry

Dark leafy bok choy is a highly nutritious vegetable that can be found in well-stocked groceries. Keep an eye out for light green baby bok choy, which are a bit more tender but carry a similar flavor.

INGREDIENTS | SERVES 3

3 tablespoons soy sauce
2 tablespoons lemon or lime juice
1 tablespoon fresh ginger, minced
1 block firm or extra-firm tofu, well pressed
2 tablespoons olive oil
1 head bok choy or 3–4 small baby bok choy, chopped
½ teaspoon sugar
½ teaspoon sesame oil

It's Easy Being Green!

Learn to love your leafy greens! Pound for pound and calorie for calorie, dark leafy green vegetables are the most nutritious food on the planet! Try a variety of greens: bok choy, collard greens, spinach, kale, mustard greens, Swiss chard, or watercress. When you find one or two that you like, sneak them in as many meals as you can!

1. Whisk together soy sauce, lemon or lime juice, and ginger in a shallow pan. Cut tofu into cubes and marinate for at least 1 hour. Drain, reserving marinade.

2. In a large skillet or wok, sauté tofu in olive oil for 3–4 minutes.

3. Carefully add reserved marinade, bok choy, and sugar, stirring well to combine.

4. Cook, stirring, for 3–4 more minutes, or until bok choy is done.

5. Drizzle with sesame oil and serve over rice.

PER SERVING Calories: 213 | Fat: 15g | Sodium: 1,097mg | Fiber: 4g | Protein: 14g

Green Bean Amandine

Fresh green beans are so much tastier than the frozen or canned variety!
Try preparing them with almonds and mushroom, with this easy, rhyming Green Bean Amandine.

INGREDIENTS | SERVES 4

1 pound fresh green beans, trimmed and chopped
2 tablespoons olive oil
⅓ cup sliced almonds
¾ cup sliced mushrooms
½ yellow onion, chopped
½ teaspoon lemon juice

1. Boil green beans in water for just 3–4 minutes; do not overcook. Or steam for 4–5 minutes. Drain and rinse under cold water.

2. In olive oil, sauté almonds, mushrooms, and onion over medium heat for 3–4 minutes, stirring frequently. Add green beans and lemon juice and heat for another minute or 2.

PER SERVING Calories: 147 | Fat: 11g | Sodium: 8mg | Fiber: 5g | Protein: 4g

Roasted Brussels Sprouts with Apples

Brussels sprouts are surprisingly delicious when prepared properly, so if you have bad memories of being force-fed soggy, limp baby cabbages as a child, don't let that stop you from trying this recipe!

INGREDIENTS | SERVES 4

2 cups Brussels sprouts, chopped into quarters
8 whole cloves garlic, peeled
2 tablespoons olive oil
2 tablespoons balsamic vinegar
¾ teaspoon salt
½ teaspoon black pepper
2 apples, cored and chopped

1. Preheat oven to 425°F.

2. Arrange Brussels sprouts and garlic in a single layer on a baking sheet. Drizzle with olive oil and balsamic vinegar and season with salt and pepper. Roast for 10–12 minutes, tossing once.

3. Remove tray from oven and add apples, tossing gently to combine. Roast for 10 more minutes or until apples are soft, tossing once again.

PER SERVING Calories: 143 | Fat: 7g | Sodium: 451mg | Fiber: 4g | Protein: 2g

Reuse and Recycle!

Recycle this basic recipe by adding an extra garnish or two each time you make it: a touch of fresh rosemary, a couple shakes of a vegan Parmesan cheese, some chopped toasted nuts or vegetarian bacon bits for crunch. For a Thanksgiving side dish, toss in some rehydrated dried cranberries.

Saucy Chinese Veggies with Seitan or Tempeh

*This is a simple and basic stir-fry recipe with Asian ingredients,
suitable for a main dish. Serve over noodles or rice.*

INGREDIENTS | SERVES 6

1½ cups vegetable broth
3 tablespoons soy sauce
1 tablespoon rice vinegar
1 teaspoon minced ginger
1 teaspoon sugar
18-ounce block tempeh, cubed, or about
1 cup chopped seitan
2 tablespoons olive oil
1 red bell pepper, chopped
1 cup snow peas
½ cup sliced water chestnuts (optional)
¼ cup sliced bamboo shoots (optional)
2 scallions, sliced
1 tablespoon cornstarch

1. In a small bowl, whisk together the vegetable broth, soy sauce, rice vinegar, ginger, and sugar.

2. In a large skillet, brown the tempeh or seitan in olive oil on all sides, about 3–4 minutes.

3. Add bell pepper, snow peas, water chestnuts, bamboo shoots, and scallions, and heat just until vegetables are almost soft, about 2–3 minutes, stirring constantly.

4. Reduce heat and add vegetable broth mixture. Whisk in cornstarch. Bring to a slow simmer and cook until thickened, stirring to prevent lumps.

PER SERVING Calories: 141 | Fat: 9g | Sodium: 693mg | Fiber: 1g | Protein: 8g

Lemon Mint New Potatoes

Potatoes are an easy standby side that goes with just about any entrée, and this version with fresh mint adds a twist to the usual herb-roasted version.

INGREDIENTS | SERVES 4

10–12 small new potatoes, chopped
4 cloves garlic, minced
1 tablespoon olive oil
¼ cup chopped mint
Salt and pepper to taste
2 teaspoons lemon juice

Got Leftovers?

Make a double batch to have "planned-overs." Turn this into a Greek-inspired potato salad for lunch the next day. Cool the potatoes, then combine with ¼ cup vegan yogurt, green peas, diced red onions or celery, and some extra fresh mint for garnish and flavor.

1. Preheat oven to 350°F. Line or lightly grease a baking sheet.

2. In a large bowl, toss together the potatoes with the garlic, olive oil, and mint, coating potatoes well.

3. Arrange potatoes in a single layer on a baking sheet. Roast for 45 minutes.

4. Season with salt and pepper and drizzle with lemon juice just before serving.

PER SERVING Calories: 330 | Fat: 4g | Sodium: 28mg | Fiber: 11g | Protein: 8g

Coconut Cauliflower Curry

To save time chopping, substitute a bag of mixed frozen veggies or toss in some leftover cooked potatoes to this tropical yellow curry recipe.

INGREDIENTS | SERVES 4

¾ cup vegetable broth

1 cup coconut milk

1½ cups green peas

1 cauliflower, chopped

2 carrots, chopped small

2 teaspoons fresh ginger, minced

3 cloves garlic, minced

2 teaspoons curry powder

½ teaspoon turmeric

1 teaspoon brown sugar

¼ teaspoon salt

¼ teaspoon nutmeg

1 cup diced pineapple

2 tablespoons chopped fresh cilantro (optional)

1. Whisk together the vegetable broth and coconut milk in a large saucepan.

2. Add remaining ingredients except for pineapple and cilantro, stirring well to combine. Bring to a slow simmer, cover, and cook for 8–10 minutes, stirring occasionally. Add pineapple and heat for 2 more minutes.

3. Top with fresh cilantro, if desired, and serve hot over rice or another whole grain.

PER SERVING Calories: 232 | Fat: 13g | Sodium: 449mg | Fiber: 7g | Protein: 7g

Gingered and Pralined Sweet Potatoes

Keep this recipe handy during the holiday season.
Who needs marshmallows anyway?

INGREDIENTS | SERVES 4

4 sweet potatoes, baked
¼ cup soy creamer or soy milk
¼ cup orange juice
½ teaspoon salt
½ cup chopped pecans
2 tablespoons vegan margarine
⅓ cup maple syrup
⅓ cup flour
⅓ cup crystallized (candied) ginger

Why Aren't Marshmallows Vegan?

They aren't even technically vegetarian! Marshmallows contain gelatin, which is extracted from boiled animal bones or hides. Online specialty stores and some natural-foods stores may stock vegan marshmallows, but candied ginger adds an elegant twist to this holiday favorite!

1. Preheat oven to 350°F.

2. Mash together the sweet potatoes, soy creamer or soy milk, orange juice, and salt until smooth and creamy. Transfer to a lightly greased casserole dish.

3. In a small bowl, combine together the remaining ingredients, and spread over the top of the sweet potatoes.

4. Bake for 30 minutes.

PER SERVING Calories: 436 | Fat: 17g | Sodium: 443mg | Fiber: 6g | Protein: 5g

Sweet Pineapple Cabbage Stir-Fry

Toss in a can of pineapple the last minute or 2 to just about any stir-fry recipe for a sweet treat, or try this recipe with a sweet and salty sauce.

INGREDIENTS | SERVES 6

1 15-ounce can diced pineapple
2 tablespoons red wine vinegar
1 tablespoon soy sauce
1 tablespoon brown sugar
2 teaspoons cornstarch
¼ teaspoon crushed red pepper flakes
2 cloves garlic, minced
1 onion, chopped
2 tablespoons olive oil
1 head broccoli, chopped
1 head Napa cabbage or ½ head green cabbage, chopped
1 batch Easy Fried Tofu (p. 242, optional)

1. Drain pineapple, reserving juice. Whisk together juice, vinegar, soy sauce, brown sugar, cornstarch, and red pepper flakes.

2. In a large skillet, heat garlic and onion in olive oil just until soft, about 3–4 minutes. Add broccoli, pineapple, and cabbage, stirring quickly to combine, and cook for another minute.

3. Reduce heat to medium, and add pineapple juice mixture. Bring to a slow simmer and heat just until mixture has thickened, stirring frequently.

4. Stir in fried tofu and serve over rice or whole grains.

PER SERVING Calories: 288 | Fat: 17g | Sodium: 357mg | Fiber: 5g | Protein: 13g

Cranberry Apple Stuffing

Why wait for Thanksgiving? Stuffing is a fabulous side dish anytime.
All the fresh herbs will flavor your kitchen with a home-cooked and nostalgic aroma.

INGREDIENTS | SERVES 6

3 tablespoons vegan margarine
1 yellow onion, diced
2 ribs celery, diced
⅔ cup sliced mushrooms
¾ teaspoon sage
¾ teaspoon thyme
½ teaspoon marjoram
12 slices dry bread, chopped into cubes
1 cup dried cranberries
1 apple, diced
½ cup apple juice
2 cups vegetable broth
Salt and pepper to taste

For an Extra Moist and Sweet Stuffing

Rehydrate your dried cranberries first in juice. Simply cover them with apple, orange, or even pineapple juice and allow them to sit until fat and plumped, about 15 minutes. If you want to get fancy, use a fruit liqueur instead of juice for a subtly gourmet flavor.

1. Preheat oven to 375°F.

2. In a pan melt margarine over low heat and add onion, celery, and mushrooms, heating and stirring just until mushrooms and onions are soft, about 4–5 minutes. Add sage, thyme, and marjoram and heat 1 more minute.

3. Combine onions-and-celery mixture with bread, cranberries, apple, apple juice, and vegetable broth, adding just enough vegetable broth to moisten well. You may need a little more or less than 2 cups. Season generously with salt and pepper.

4. Transfer to a large casserole or baking dish and bake for 20–25 minutes.

PER SERVING Calories: 281 | Fat: 8g | Sodium: 667mg | Fiber: 4g | Protein: 5g

Summer Squash Sauté

Green zucchini and yellow squash absorb flavors like magic, though little enhancement is needed with their fresh natural flavor. Toss these veggies with some cooked orzo or linguini to make it a main dish.

INGREDIENTS | SERVES 2

1 onion, chopped
2 cloves garlic, minced
2 tablespoons olive oil
2 zucchini, sliced into coins
2 yellow squash, sliced thin
1 large tomato, diced
2 teaspoons Italian seasoning
1 tablespoon nutritional yeast
2 teaspoons hot chili sauce (optional)

1. Sauté onions and garlic in olive oil for a minute or 2; then add zucchini, yellow squash, and tomato. Heat, stirring frequently, for 4–5 minutes until squash is soft.

2. Season with Italian seasoning and heat for 1 more minute.

3. Stir in nutritional yeast and hot sauce.

PER SERVING Calories: 205 | Fat: 14g | Sodium: 28mg | Fiber: 5g | Protein: 5g

Saucy Vaishnava Veggies

These simple, low-fat veggies will fill your kitchen with the smells and dreams of India as they simmer. Why not pick up a Bollywood movie to accompany your dinner?

INGREDIENTS | SERVES 4

1 28-ounce can diced tomatoes, undrained
2 potatoes, chopped small
½ teaspoon chili powder
2 teaspoons curry powder
1½ teaspoons cumin
½ teaspoon turmeric (optional)
1 head cauliflower, chopped
1 carrot, diced
¾ cup green peas
¾ teaspoon crushed red pepper flakes
¼ teaspoon salt, or to taste

1. Combine the tomatoes, potatoes, chili powder, curry powder, cumin, and turmeric in a large pot. Cover and cook for 10 minutes.

2. Add chopped cauliflower, carrot, green peas, and red pepper flakes and cook, covered, for 15 more minutes until potatoes and vegetables are soft, stirring occasionally. Season with salt, to taste.

Indian Vegan Options

In India, many vegetarians forswear eggs as well as onions and garlic for religious purposes, making Indian food an excellent choice for vegans. When eating at Indian restaurants, be sure to ask about ghee, Indian butter, which is a traditional ingredient, but easily and frequently substituted with oil.

PER SERVING Calories: 200 | Fat: 1g | Sodium: 494mg | Fiber: 12g | Protein: 9g

Garlic and Gingered Green Beans

Afraid of vampires? This garlicky recipe ought to scare them away.

INGREDIENTS | SERVES 4

1 pound fresh green beans, trimmed and chopped
2 tablespoons olive oil
4 cloves garlic, minced
1 teaspoon fresh minced ginger
½ teaspoon crushed red pepper flakes
Salt and pepper to taste

1. Boil green beans in water for just 3–4 minutes; do not overcook. Or steam for 4–5 minutes. Drain and rinse under cold water.

2. Heat olive oil in a skillet with garlic, ginger, green beans, and red pepper flakes. Cook, stirring frequently, for 3–4 minutes until garlic is soft.

3. Taste, and season lightly with salt and pepper.

PER SERVING Calories: 10 | Fat: 7g | Sodium: 8mg | Fiber: 4g | Protein: 2g

Sweetened Roast Squash

Naturally sweet squash is delicious in this simple quick side.
Serve as is, scooping it out of the skin, or remove the soft flesh and give it a quick mash.

INGREDIENTS | SERVES 4

1 butternut, acorn, or spaghetti squash
1 teaspoon sea salt
4 tablespoons orange juice
4 tablespoons maple syrup
Nutmeg or ginger to taste

Easy Roasted Squash Sides

Tossing squash in the oven couldn't be easier. A drizzle of olive oil and a dash of garlic powder, salt, nutritional yeast, and perhaps a touch of cayenne will also produce a satisfying roasted squash for a side dish you don't need to sweat over.

1. Preheat oven to 400°F.

2. Chop squash in fourths, and scrape out seeds. Place in a large casserole dish. Sprinkle each chunk of squash with a bit of sea salt, 1 tablespoon orange juice, and 1 tablespoon maple syrup, then a shake of nutmeg or ginger.

3. Cover with foil and bake for 40–45 minutes until squash is soft, basting with any extra sauce once or twice.

PER SERVING Calories: 91 | Fat: 0g | Sodium: 586mg | Fiber: 1g | Protein: 1g

Classic Green Bean Casserole

Shop for a vegan cream of mushroom soup to use in your traditional holiday recipe, or try this easy homemade vegan version. Delish!

INGREDIENTS | SERVES 4

1 12-ounce bag frozen green beans
¾ cup sliced mushrooms
2 tablespoons vegan margarine
2 tablespoons flour
1½ cups soy milk
1 tablespoon Dijon mustard
½ teaspoon garlic powder
½ teaspoon salt
¼ teaspoon sage
¼ teaspoon oregano
¼ teaspoon black pepper
1½ cups French-fried onions

Cut the Fat

For a slightly healthier version, top your green bean casserole with bread crumbs, crushed crackers, or a vegan cornflake cereal instead of the crispy fried onions.

1. Preheat oven to 375°F. Place green beans and mushrooms in a large casserole dish.

2. Melt vegan margarine over low heat. Stir in flour until pasty and combined. Add soy milk, mustard, garlic powder, salt, sage, oregano, and pepper, stirring continuously to combine until thickened.

3. Pour sauce over mushrooms and green beans and top with French-fried onions.

4. Bake for 16–18 minutes until onions are lightly browned and toasted.

PER SERVING Calories: 279 | Fat: 18g | Sodium: 642mg | Fiber: 3g | Protein: 5g

Baked Sweet Potato Fries

Brown sugar adds a sweet touch to these yummy sweet potato fries. If you like your fries with a kick, add some crushed red pepper flakes or a dash of cayenne pepper to the mix.

INGREDIENTS | SERVES 3

2 large sweet potatoes, sliced into fries
2 tablespoons olive oil
¼ teaspoon garlic powder
½ teaspoon paprika
½ teaspoon brown sugar
½ teaspoon chili powder
¼ teaspoon sea salt

1. Preheat oven to 400°F.

2. Spread sweet potatoes on a large baking sheet and drizzle with olive oil, tossing gently to coat.

3. In a small bowl, combine remaining ingredients. Sprinkle over potatoes, coating evenly and tossing as needed.

4. Bake in oven for 10 minutes, turning once. Taste, and sprinkle with a bit more sea salt if needed.

PER SERVING Calories: 203 | Fat: 9g | Sodium: 270mg | Fiber: 4g | Protein: 2g

Caramelized Baby Carrots

Baby carrots have a natural sweetness when cooked, and this recipe turns them into a treat even the pickiest veggie hater will gobble up.

INGREDIENTS | SERVES 4

4 cups baby carrots
1 teaspoon lemon juice
2 tablespoons vegan margarine
2 tablespoons brown sugar
¼ teaspoon sea salt

1. Simmer carrots in water until just soft, about 8–10 minutes; do not overcook. Drain and drizzle with lemon juice.

2. Heat together carrots, margarine, brown sugar, and sea salt, stirring frequently until glaze forms and carrots are well coated, about 5 minutes.

PER SERVING Calories: 119 | Fat: 6g | Sodium: 322mg | Fiber: 4g | Protein: 1g

Maple-Glazed Roasted Veggies

These easy roasted veggies make an excellent holiday side dish. The vegetables can be roasted in advance and reheated with the glaze to save on time if needed. If parsnips are too earthy for you, substitute one large potato.

INGREDIENTS | SERVES 4

3 carrots, chopped
2 small parsnips, chopped
2 sweet potatoes, chopped
2 tablespoons olive oil
Salt and pepper to taste
⅓ cup maple syrup
2 tablespoons Dijon mustard
1 tablespoon balsamic vinegar
½ teaspoon hot sauce

1. Preheat oven to 400°F.

2. On a large baking sheet, spread out chopped carrots, parsnips, and sweet potatoes. Drizzle with olive oil and season generously with salt and pepper. Roast for 40 minutes, tossing once.

3. In a small bowl, whisk together maple syrup, Dijon mustard, balsamic vinegar, and hot sauce.

4. Transfer the roasted vegetables to a large bowl and toss well with the maple mixture. Add more salt and pepper to taste.

PER SERVING Calories: 231 | Fat: 7g | Sodium: 158mg | Fiber: 5g | Protein: 5g

Root Love

This tangy and sweet glaze will lend itself well to a variety of roasted vegetables and combinations. Try it with roasted Brussels sprouts, beets, baby new potatoes, butternut or acorn squash, or even with roasted turnips or daikon radish.

Mango and Bell Pepper Stir-Fry

Add some marinated tofu to make it a main dish, or enjoy just the mango and veggies for a light lunch. Thaw frozen cubed mango if you can't find fresh.

INGREDIENTS | SERVES 4

2 tablespoons lime juice
2 tablespoons orange juice
1 tablespoon hot chili sauce
3 tablespoons soy sauce
2 cloves garlic, minced
2 tablespoons oil
1 red bell pepper, chopped
1 yellow or orange bell pepper, chopped
1 bunch broccoli, chopped
1 mango, cubed
3 scallions, chopped

1. Whisk together the lime juice, orange juice, hot sauce, and soy sauce.

2. Heat garlic in oil for just a minute or 2 then add bell peppers and broccoli and cook, stirring frequently, for another 2–3 minutes.

3. Add juice and soy sauce mixture, reduce heat, and cook for another 2–3 minutes until broccoli and bell peppers are almost soft.

4. Reduce heat to low, and add mango and scallions, gently stirring to combine. Heat for just another minute or 2 until mango is warmed.

PER SERVING Calories: 237 | Fat: 8g | Sodium: 783mg | Fiber: 10g | Protein: 11g

Roasted Garlic, Zucchini, and Onions

Roasting veggies brings out their natural flavors, so little additional seasoning is needed.

INGREDIENTS | SERVES 4

6 whole cloves garlic
4 zucchini, chopped
1 onion, chopped into rings
1 tablespoon balsamic vinegar
1 tablespoon olive oil
Salt and pepper, to taste
1 teaspoon fresh thyme
2 teaspoons nutritional yeast (optional)

1. Preheat oven to 400°F.

2. Arrange the garlic, zucchini, and onions on a baking sheet. Drizzle with vinegar and oil and season with salt and pepper, tossing to coat well.

3. Roast in oven for 20–25 minutes, then toss with fresh thyme, nutritional yeast, and additional salt and pepper to taste.

PER SERVING Calories: 83 | Fat: 4g | Sodium: 23mg | Fiber: 3g | Protein: 3g

Chapter 7

Rice Entrées and Sides

Italian White Beans and Rice

This is a quick, inexpensive, and hearty meal that will quickly become a favorite standby on busy nights. It's nutritious, filling, and can easily be doubled for a crowd.

INGREDIENTS | SERVES 4

½ onion, diced

2 ribs celery, diced

3 cloves garlic, minced

2 tablespoons olive oil

1 12-ounce can diced or crushed tomatoes

1 15-ounce can cannellini or great northern beans, drained

½ teaspoon parsley

½ teaspoon basil

1 cup rice, cooked

1 tablespoon balsamic vinegar

1. Sauté onion, celery, and garlic in olive oil for 3–5 minutes until onion and celery are soft.

2. Reduce heat to medium low and add tomatoes, beans, parsley, and basil. Cover and simmer for 10 minutes, stirring occasionally.

3. Stir in cooked rice and balsamic vinegar and cook, uncovered, for a few more minutes until liquid is absorbed.

PER SERVING Calories: 325 | Fat: 8g | Sodium: 135mg | Fiber: 8g | Protein: 12g

Spicy Southern Jambalaya

Make this spicy and smoky Southern rice dish a main meal by adding in some browned mock sausage or sautéed tofu.

INGREDIENTS | SERVES 6

1 onion, chopped

1 bell pepper, any color, chopped

1 rib celery, diced

2 tablespoons olive oil

1 14–ounce can diced tomatoes, undrained

3 cups water or vegetable broth

2 cups rice

1 bay leaf

1 teaspoon paprika

½ teaspoon thyme

½ teaspoon oregano

½ teaspoon garlic powder

1 cup corn or frozen mixed diced veggies (optional)

½ teaspoon cayenne or hot Tabasco sauce to taste

1. In a large skillet or stock pot, heat onion, bell pepper, and celery in olive oil until almost soft, about 3 minutes.

2. Reduce heat and add remaining ingredients, except frozen veggies and hot sauce. Cover, bring to a low simmer, and cook for 20 minutes until rice is done, stirring occasionally.

3. Add frozen veggies and cayenne or hot sauce and cook just until heated through, about 3 minutes. Adjust seasonings to taste. Remove bay leaf before serving.

PER SERVING Calories: 304 | Fat: 7g | Sodium: 100mg | Fiber: 4g | Protein: 7g

Got Leftovers?

Heat up some refried beans and wrap up your leftover jambalaya in tortillas with some salsa and shredded lettuce to make vegetable burritos!

Cuban Black Beans, Sweet Potatoes, and Rice

*Stir some plain steamed rice right into the pot, or serve it
alongside these well-seasoned beans.*

INGREDIENTS | SERVES 4

3 cloves garlic, minced
2 large sweet potatoes, chopped small
2 tablespoons olive oil
2 15-ounce cans black beans, drained
¾ cup vegetable broth
1 tablespoon chili powder
1 teaspoon paprika
1 teaspoon cumin
1 tablespoon lime juice
Hot sauce, to taste
2 cups rice, cooked

1. In a large skillet or pot, sauté garlic and sweet potatoes in olive oil for 2–3 minutes.

2. Reduce heat to medium low and add beans, vegetable broth, chili powder, paprika, and cumin. Bring to a simmer, cover, and allow to cook for 25–30 minutes until sweet potatoes are soft.

3. Stir in lime juice and hot sauce, to taste. Serve hot over rice.

PER SERVING Calories: 387 | Fat: 8g | Sodium: 491mg | Fiber: 13g | Protein: 13g

Spanish Artichoke and Zucchini Paella

Traditional Spanish paellas are always cooked with saffron, but this version with zucchini, artichokes, and bell peppers uses turmeric instead for the same golden hue.

INGREDIENTS | SERVES 4

3 cloves garlic, minced

1 yellow onion, diced

2 tablespoons olive oil

1 cup white rice, uncooked

1 15-ounce can diced or crushed tomatoes

1 green bell pepper, chopped

1 red or yellow bell pepper, chopped

½ cup artichoke hearts, chopped

2 zucchini, sliced

2 cups vegetable broth

1 tablespoon paprika

½ teaspoon turmeric

¾ teaspoon parsley

½ teaspoon salt

1. In the largest skillet you can find, heat garlic and onions in olive oil for 3–4 minutes until onions are almost soft. Add rice, stirring well to coat, and heat for another minute, stirring to prevent burning.

2. Add tomatoes, bell peppers, artichokes, and zucchini, stirring to combine. Add vegetable broth and remaining ingredients, cover, and simmer for 15–20 minutes, or until rice is done.

PER SERVING Calories: 260 | Fat: 1g | Sodium: 1,016mg | Fiber: 6g | Protein: 7g

Sun-Dried Tomato Risotto with Spinach and Pine Nuts

The tomatoes carry the flavor in this easy risotto—no butter, cheese, or wine is needed. But if you're a gourmand who keeps truffle, hazelnut, pine nut, or another gourmet oil on hand, now's the time to use it, instead of the margarine.

INGREDIENTS | SERVES 4

1 yellow onion, diced
4 cloves garlic, minced
2 tablespoons olive oil
1½ cups Arborio rice, uncooked
5–6 cups vegetable broth
⅔ cup rehydrated sun-dried tomatoes, sliced
½ cup fresh spinach
1 tablespoon chopped fresh basil (optional)
2 tablespoons vegan margarine (optional)
2 tablespoons nutritional yeast
Salt and pepper to taste
¼ cup pine nuts

Sun-Dried Tomatoes

If you're using dehydrated tomatoes, rehydrate them first by covering in water for at least 10 minutes, and add the soaking water to the broth. If you're using tomatoes packed in oil, add 2 tablespoons of the oil to risotto at the end of cooking, instead of the vegan margarine.

1. Heat onion and garlic in olive oil until just soft, about 2–3 minutes. Add rice and toast for 1 minute, stirring constantly.

2. Add ¾ cup vegetable broth and stir to combine. When most of the liquid has been absorbed, add another ½ cup, stirring constantly. Continue adding liquid ½ cup at a time until rice is cooked, about 20 minutes.

3. Add another ½ cup broth, tomatoes, spinach, and basil and reduce heat to low. Stir to combine well. Heat for 3–4 minutes until tomatoes are soft and spinach is wilted.

4. Stir in margarine and nutritional yeast. Taste, then season lightly with a bit of salt and pepper.

5. Allow to cool slightly, then top with pine nuts. Risotto will thicken a bit as it cools.

PER SERVING Calories: 441 | Fat: 13g | Sodium: 1,322mg | Fiber: 4g | Protein: 8g

Chinese Fried Rice with Tofu and Cashews

On busy weeknights, pick up some plain white rice from a Chinese take-out restaurant and turn it into a home-cooked meal in a jiffy. Garnish with fresh lime wedges and a sprinkle of sea salt and fresh black pepper on top.

INGREDIENTS | SERVES 3

2 cloves garlic, minced

1 12-ounce block silken tofu, mashed with a fork

3 tablespoons olive oil, divided

3 cups leftover rice, cooked

½ cup frozen mixed diced veggies

3 tablespoons soy sauce

1 tablespoon sesame oil

2 tablespoons lime juice

3 scallions (greens and whites), sliced

⅓ cup chopped cashews (optional)

Quick Healthy Meals

Like stir-fries and an easy pasta recipe, fried rice is a quick and easy meal you can turn to again and again. The formula is always the same: rice, oil, and seasonings, but the variations are endless. Besides tofu, try adding tempeh, seitan, or store-bought mock meats to fried rice. Add kimchi for a Korean spice, or season with a mixture of cumin, curry powder, ginger, and turmeric for an Indian-inspired dish.

1. In a large skillet or wok, sauté the garlic and tofu in 2 tablespoons olive oil over medium-high heat, stirring frequently, until tofu is lightly browned, about 6–8 minutes.

2. Add remaining 1 tablespoon olive oil, rice, and veggies, stirring well to combine.

3. Add soy sauce and sesame oil and combine well.

4. Allow to cook, stirring constantly, for 3–4 minutes.

5. Remove from heat and stir in remaining ingredients.

PER SERVING Calories: 477 | Fat: 22g | Sodium: 965mg | Fiber: 3g | Protein: 15g

Italian Rice Salad

Double this marinated rice salad recipe for a potluck or picnic.

INGREDIENTS | SERVES 4

⅓ cup red wine vinegar
1 tablespoon balsamic vinegar
2 teaspoons Dijon mustard
½ cup olive oil
4 cloves garlic, minced
1 teaspoon basil
⅓ cup chopped fresh parsley
2 cups rice, cooked
1 cup green peas
1 carrot, grated
½ cup roasted red peppers, chopped
½ cup green olives, sliced
Salt and pepper to taste

1. Whisk or shake together the red wine vinegar, balsamic vinegar, Dijon mustard, olive oil, garlic, basil, and parsley.

2. Combine rice with remaining ingredients in a large bowl. Toss with dressing mixture and coat well.

3. Taste, and season with just a bit of salt and pepper.

4. Chill for at least 30 minutes before serving to allow flavors to set, and gently toss again just before serving.

PER SERVING Calories: 439 | Fat: 32g | Sodium: 604mg | Fiber: 3g | Protein: 5g

Mexican Rice with Corn and Peppers

Although Mexican rice is usually just a filling for burritos or served as a side dish, this recipe loads up the veggies, making it hearty enough for a main dish. Use frozen or canned veggies if you need to save time.

INGREDIENTS | SERVES 4

2 cloves garlic, minced
1 cup rice, uncooked
2 tablespoons olive oil
3 cups vegetable broth
1 cup tomato paste (or 4 large tomatoes, puréed)
1 green bell pepper, chopped
1 red bell pepper, chopped
Kernels from 1 ear of corn
1 carrot, diced
1 teaspoon chili powder
½ teaspoon cumin
⅓ teaspoon oregano
⅓ teaspoon cayenne pepper (or to taste)
⅓ teaspoon salt

1. Add garlic, rice, and olive oil to a large skillet and heat on medium-high heat, stirring frequently. Toast the rice until just golden brown, about 2–3 minutes.

2. Reduce heat and add vegetable broth and remaining ingredients.

3. Bring to a simmer, cover, and allow to cook until liquid is absorbed and rice is cooked, about 20–25 minutes, stirring occasionally.

4. Adjust seasonings to taste.

PER SERVING Calories: 342 | Fat: 8g | Sodium: 1,442mg | Fiber: 6g | Protein: 8g

Vegan Burritos

Brown some vegetarian chorizo or mock sausage crumbles and wrap in tortillas, perhaps topped with some shredded vegan cheese, to make vegan burritos. Or, combine with TVP Taco "Meat" (p. 265) to turn this into a "meaty" Mexican main.

Mushroom and Rosemary Wild Rice

Top it off with some Lemon Basil Tofu slices (p. 238) for an herb-infused main dish.

INGREDIENTS | SERVES 4

1 tablespoon chopped fresh rosemary
1 yellow onion, diced
2 tablespoons olive oil
1 cup sliced mushrooms
1½ cups wild rice, uncooked
4½ cups vegetable broth
2 tablespoons vegan margarine
½ teaspoon lemon juice
¼ teaspoon ground sage
2 tablespoons nutritional yeast (optional)

1. In a large pan, heat rosemary and onion in olive oil until onions are just soft, about 3 minutes. Add mushrooms, and heat for another minute.

2. Add wild rice and vegetable broth and bring to a simmer. Cover and cook 40–45 minutes until rice is done and liquid is absorbed.

3. Remove from heat and stir in remaining ingredients.

PER SERVING Calories: 353 | Fat: 13g | Sodium: 1,144mg | Fiber: 4g | Protein: 10g

Coconut Rice

Serve coconut rice as a simple side dish or pair it with spicy Thai and Indian curries or stir-fries.

INGREDIENTS | SERVES 4

1 cup water
1 14-ounce can coconut milk
1½ cups white rice
⅓ cup coconut flakes
1 teaspoon lime juice
½ teaspoon salt

Toasted Coconut Flakes

Quickly toasting coconut flakes will help bring out their nutty bounty of flavor. Place the flakes directly onto a dry, ungreased skillet over low heat. Stirring constantly, heat the coconut just until you see the slightest bit of golden brown, then remove the pan from the heat. Use your toasted coconut to top vegan ice cream, cakes, or even a bowl of oatmeal or Chocolate Peanut Butter Breakfast Quinoa (p. 193).

1. In a large pot, combine the water, coconut milk, and rice and bring to a simmer. Cover and allow to cook 20 minutes, or until rice is done.

2. In a separate skillet, toast the coconut flakes over low heat until lightly golden, about 3 minutes. Gently stir constantly to avoid burning.

3. Combine coconut flakes with cooked rice and stir in lime juice and salt.

PER SERVING Calories: 480 | Fat: 25g | Sodium: 310mg | Fiber: 2g | Protein: 7g

Curried Rice and Lentils

This is a very simple one-pot side dish starter recipe.
Personalize it with some chopped greens, browned seitan, or a veggie mix.

INGREDIENTS | SERVES 4

1½ cups white or brown rice, uncooked
1 cup lentils
2 tomatoes, diced
3½ cups water or vegetable broth
1 bay leaf (optional)
1 tablespoon curry powder
½ teaspoon cumin
½ teaspoon turmeric
½ teaspoon garlic powder
Salt and pepper, to taste

1. Combine all ingredients except salt and pepper in a large soup or stock pot. Bring to a slow simmer, then cover and cook for 20 minutes, stirring occasionally, until rice is done and liquid is absorbed.

2. Taste, then add a bit of salt and pepper if needed. Remove bay leaf before serving.

PER SERVING Calories: 436 | Fat: 1g | Sodium: 13mg | Fiber: 17g | Protein: 18g

Stuff It!

Rice makes excellent stuffing for poblano or green bell peppers. Carefully remove the top of the bell peppers, or, for poblanos, slice down the middle. Fill with cooked Curried Rice and Lentils, Mexican Rice with Corn and Peppers (p. 129), or leftover Spanish Artichoke and Zucchini Paella rice (p. 125) and bake at 375°F for 25 minutes or 15 minutes for poblano peppers.

Greek Lemon Rice with Spinach

*Greek "spanakorizo" is seasoned with fresh lemon, herbs, and black pepper.
Serve with Lemon Basil Tofu (p. 238) for a citrusy meal.*

INGREDIENTS | SERVES 4

1 onion, chopped

4 cloves garlic, minced

2 tablespoons olive oil

¾ cup rice, uncooked

2½ cups water or vegetable broth

1 8-ounce can tomato paste

2 bunches fresh spinach, trimmed

2 tablespoons chopped fresh parsley

1 tablespoon chopped fresh mint or dill (optional)

2 tablespoons lemon juice

½ teaspoon salt

½ teaspoon fresh ground black pepper

1. Sauté onions and garlic in olive oil for just a minute or two; then add rice, stirring to lightly toast.

2. Add water or vegetable broth, cover, and heat for 10–12 minutes.

3. Add tomato paste, spinach, and parsley. Cover, and cook for another 5 minutes, or until spinach is wilted and rice is cooked.

4. Stir in fresh mint or dill, lemon juice, salt, and pepper.

PER SERVING Calories: 295 | Fat: 8g | Sodium: 488mg | Fiber: 7g | Protein: 10g

Indian Lemon Rice Pilaf

With an unexpected blend of flavors, lemon rice is a popular favorite to serve to the gods and their devotees in South Indian temples. Kick up the heat by adding a couple green chilies, or, if you can find them at an Indian grocer, heat some dried curry leaves with the mustard seeds.

INGREDIENTS | SERVES 4

1½ teaspoons black mustard seeds
2 tablespoons olive oil
½ teaspoon turmeric
1 cup rice, uncooked
1¾ cups vegetable broth or water
½ cup frozen peas
2 tablespoons lemon juice
¼ cup yellow raisins
2 tablespoons scallions, chopped
2 tablespoons chopped fresh cilantro (optional)

1. Heat mustard seeds in olive oil over medium heat for about 1 minute.

2. Add turmeric and rice and stir well to combine. Toast rice, stirring, for 1–2 minutes until lightly golden brown.

3. Add vegetable broth or water and bring to a slow simmer. Cover and allow to cook for about 15 minutes until rice is done.

4. Reduce heat to medium low and add peas and lemon juice, cooking for another minute or 2 until peas are heated through.

5. Remove from heat and stir in remaining ingredients.

PER SERVING Calories: 283 | Fat: 8g | Sodium: 434mg | Fiber: 2g | Protein: 5g

Squash and Sage Risotto

Risotto is easy to make, but it does take a bit of effort with all the stirring! This earthy recipe works well with just about any kind of squash. If you're in a hurry, use canned puréed pumpkin instead of fresh acorn squash or look for precooked butternut squash in your grocer's freezer section.

INGREDIENTS | SERVES 4

3 cloves garlic, minced
½ yellow onion, diced
2 tablespoons olive oil
1½ cups Arborio rice, uncooked
5 cups vegetable broth
2 whole cloves
1½ cups roasted puréed pumpkin, acorn, or butternut squash
1½ teaspoons sage
⅓ teaspoon salt
¼ teaspoon pepper

Quicker and Creamier

To save time, keep your vegetable broth simmering on the stove next to your risotto as it cooks. Adding hot liquid will help the rice cook faster and ensures an evenly cooked rice with a creamy sauce.

1. In a large skillet, sauté the garlic and onions in olive oil for 3 minutes over medium-high heat. Add uncooked rice and cook for 2 more minutes, stirring frequently to lightly toast the rice.

2. Add ¾ cup vegetable broth and cloves and stir well. When most of the liquid has been absorbed, add another ½ cup broth, stirring frequently. Continue adding vegetable broth ½ cup at a time until rice is just tender and sauce is creamy, about 20–25 minutes.

3. Reduce heat to medium low and stir in puréed squash and ¼ cup vegetable broth. Continue to stir well and allow to cook for 4–5 more minutes.

4. Stir in sage and season with salt and pepper.

5. Allow to cool, stirring occasionally, for at least 5 minutes. Risotto will thicken slightly as it cools. Remove cloves before serving.

PER SERVING Calories: 371 | Fat: 7g | Sodium: 1,370mg | Fiber: 4g | Protein: 6g

Hawaiian Pineapple and Mint Rice Salad

Pineapple and mint are a cooling combination, so this is perfect for a hot day.

INGREDIENTS | SERVES 6

4 cups white rice, cooked

2 ribs celery, diced

1 cup diced pineapple (fresh or canned)

⅓ cup chopped macadamia or cashew nuts

¼ cup dried papaya or raisins (optional)

⅓ cup pineapple juice

2 tablespoons olive or safflower oil

2 tablespoons red wine vinegar

¼ cup Toasted Coconut Flakes (p. 131)

2 tablespoons chopped fresh mint

1. Combine the cooked rice, celery, pineapple, macadamia, and dried papaya together in a large bowl.

2. In a separate small bowl, whisk together the pineapple juice, oil, and vinegar. Toss together with rice and coat well. Chill for at least 1 hour.

3. Gently toss with coconut flakes and mint just before serving.

PER SERVING Calories: 260 | Fat: 11g | Sodium: 14mg | Fiber: 2g | Protein: 4g

Macro-Inspired Veggie Bowl

Truly nourishing, this is a full meal in a bowl, inspired by macrobiotic cuisine.

INGREDIENTS | SERVES 6

2 cups brown rice, cooked

1 batch Sesame Baked Tofu (p. 242), chopped into cubes

1 head broccoli, steamed and chopped

1 red or yellow bell pepper, sliced thin

1 cup bean sprouts

1 cup You Are a Goddess Dressing (p. 69)

½ cup pumpkin seeds or sunflower seeds

2 teaspoons dulse or kelp seaweed flakes (optional)

1. Divide brown rice into six bowls.

2. Top each bowl with Sesame Baked Tofu, broccoli, bell pepper, and bean sprouts.

3. Drizzle with dressing, and sprinkle with seeds and seaweed flakes.

PER SERVING Calories: 547 | Fat: 37g | Sodium: 911 | Fiber: 11g | Protein: 28g

Live Long and Prosper

Although a macrobiotic diet includes seafood, it is an otherwise vegan diet originally from Japan. Macrobiotics combines a balance of nutrients with Japanese ingredients such as miso, plum vinegar, and seaweed; lots of organic grains; and veggies, while minimizing oils and fruits. A healthy diet, the philosophy goes, will lead to happiness and longevity.

"Cheesy" Broccoli and Rice Casserole

If you're substituting frozen broccoli, there's no need to cook it first, just thaw and use about 1¼ cups. Serve with ketchup for kids.

INGREDIENTS | SERVES 4

1 head broccoli, chopped small
1 onion, chopped
4 cloves garlic, minced
2 tablespoons olive oil
2 tablespoons flour
2 cups unsweetened soy milk
½ cup vegetable broth
2 tablespoons nutritional yeast
1 tablespoon vegan margarine
¼ teaspoon nutmeg
¼ teaspoon mustard powder
½ teaspoon salt
3½ cups rice, cooked
⅔ cup bread crumbs or crushed vegan crackers

1. Preheat oven to 325°F.

2. Steam or microwave broccoli until just barely soft; do not overcook.

3. Sauté onions and garlic in olive oil until soft, about 3–4 minutes. Reduce heat and add flour, stirring continuously to combine.

4. Add soy milk and vegetable broth and heat, stirring, until thickened. Remove from heat and stir in nutritional yeast, margarine, nutmeg, mustard powder, and salt.

5. Combine sauce, steamed broccoli, and cooked rice and transfer to a large casserole or baking dish. Sprinkle the top with bread crumbs or vegan crackers.

6. Cover and bake for 25 minutes. Uncover and cook for another 10 minutes.

PER SERVING Calories: 477 | Fat: 14g | Sodium: 401mg | Fiber: 7g | Protein: 16g

Indonesian Fried Rice (Nasi Goreng)

The kids might like some diced veggie dogs in this recipe, instead of or alongside the tempeh. Like any fried rice recipe, the vegetables you use are really up to you.

INGREDIENTS | SERVES 6

2 teaspoons molasses
2 tablespoons soy sauce
1 block tempeh, cubed
1 onion, diced
3 cloves garlic, minced
1 small chili, minced
3–4 tablespoons vegetable oil or peanut oil
3 cups rice, cooked
1 tablespoon sesame oil
2 tablespoons ketchup
2 tablespoons hot chili sauce
2 scallions, chopped
1 carrot, sliced thin
1 red or yellow bell pepper, diced
Dash Chinese five-spice powder (optional)

1. Whisk together the molasses and soy sauce, and set aside.

2. In a large skillet, sauté the tempeh, onion, garlic, and chili in oil for a few minutes until tempeh is lightly browned. Add rice and sesame oil, stirring to combine.

3. Add remaining ingredients, including molasses and soy sauce, and quickly stir to combine.

4. Cook for just a few minutes, stirring constantly, just until heated through.

PER SERVING Calories: 296 | Fat: 13g | Sodium: 433mg | Fiber: 2g | Protein: 10g

A Warung Favorite

In *warungs* (restaurants) across Indonesia, *nasi goreng* is guaranteed to be on the menu, as it's a favorite of visitors and locals alike. Top it off with some extra hot sauce to spice it up and some sliced cucumbers, to cool it back down. Browse an Asian grocery store for *kecap manis*, a sugary sauce you can use in place of the soy sauce and molasses mixture for a more authentic taste.

Caribbean Red Beans and Rice

Cook the beans from scratch and use the cooking liquid instead of the vegetable broth if you've got the time.

INGREDIENTS | SERVES 4

3 cloves garlic
1 small onion, chopped
3 ribs celery, chopped
2 tablespoons chopped fresh parsley
2 tablespoons olive oil
½ teaspoon rosemary
½ teaspoon thyme
¼ teaspoon cloves
1 15-ounce can kidney beans, drained
3 cups vegetable broth
2 bay leaves
1½ cups rice, uncooked
Dash salt and pepper to taste

1. Use a food processor to process the garlic, onion, celery, and parsley until finely grated or minced.

2. Heat onion mixture in olive oil, stirring frequently, for a few minutes until soft. Add rosemary, thyme, cloves, and beans, stirring to combine well. Cook for a few more minutes until fragrant.

3. Reduce heat and add vegetable broth, bay leaves, and rice. Bring to a slow simmer, cover, and cook for 30 minutes.

4. Reduce heat to low, uncover, and cook for 10 more minutes, or until most of the liquid is absorbed. Season with salt and pepper.

5. Remove bay leaves before serving.

PER SERVING Calories: 430 | Fat: 8g | Sodium: 1,046mg | Fiber: 8g | Protein: 11g

Cranberry Apple Wild Rice

To speed up the cooking time, soak the wild rice for 15–20 minutes before boiling.

INGREDIENTS | SERVES 4

1 rib celery, diced
1 red onion, diced
2 tablespoons olive oil
1 cup wild rice
3 cups water or vegetable broth
⅓ cup orange juice
½ cup dried cranberries or raisins
½ cup pine nuts or sliced almonds
2 scallions, chopped
1 apple, diced
Salt and pepper to taste

A High-Protein Rice?

Wild rice is not actually rice, but rather a seed. With almost 7 grams of protein per cup when cooked, wild rice can be an excellent source of protein. Add ¼ cup wild rice per cup of white rice to any recipe that calls for regular white rice for an extra protein boost.

1. In a large soup or stock pot, sauté celery and onion in olive oil for 3–4 minutes until soft.

2. Reduce heat and add wild rice and water or vegetable broth. Bring to a simmer, cover, and cook for 30 minutes. Add orange juice, and simmer for another 10–15 minutes, or until rice is cooked.

3. Remove from heat and add cranberries. Cover and let sit for 5 minutes.

4. Toss with remaining ingredients and serve hot or cold.

PER SERVING Calories: 427 | Fat: 19g | Sodium: 721mg | Fiber: 6g | Protein: 10g

Pineapple Lime Rice

Fresh cubed mango would also add a sweet flavor to this simple zesty side, instead of the pineapple.

INGREDIENTS | SERVES 4

2 tablespoons vegan margarine

2 cups rice, cooked

1½ tablespoons lime juice

⅓ cup chopped fresh cilantro

1 16-ounce can pineapple tidbits, drained

Dash sea salt

1. Stir vegan margarine into hot rice until melted and combined.

2. Add remaining ingredients, tossing gently to combine. Taste, and add a dash of salt, to taste.

PER SERVING Calories: 222 | Fat: 6g | Sodium: 83mg | Fiber: 2g | Protein: 3g

Baked Mexican Rice Casserole

A quick and easy side dish you can get into the oven in just a few minutes.

INGREDIENTS | SERVES 4

1 15-ounce can black beans
¾ cup salsa
2 teaspoons chili powder
1 teaspoon cumin
½ cup corn kernels
2 cups rice, cooked
½ cup grated vegan cheese (optional)
⅓ cup sliced black olives

Is Your Soy Cheese Vegan?

Many nondairy products do actually contain dairy, even if it says "nondairy" right there on the package! Nondairy creamer and soy cheeses are notorious for this. Look for casein or whey on the ingredients list, particularly if you suffer from dairy allergies, and, if you're allergic to soy, look for nut- or rice-based vegan cheeses.

1. Preheat oven to 350°F.

2. Combine the beans, salsa, chili powder, and cumin in a large pot over low heat, and partially mash beans with a large fork.

3. Remove from heat and stir in corn and rice. Transfer to a casserole dish.

4. Top with vegan cheese and sliced olives and bake for 20 minutes.

PER SERVING Calories: 289 | Fat: 2g | Sodium: 539mg | Fiber: 11g | Protein: 13g

Sesame Snow Pea Rice Pilaf

The leftovers from this rice pilaf can be enjoyed chilled the next day as a cold rice salad.

INGREDIENTS | SERVES 4

4 cups rice, cooked
2 tablespoons olive or safflower oil
1 tablespoon sesame oil
2 tablespoons soy sauce
3 tablespoons apple cider vinegar
1 teaspoon sugar
1 cup snow peas, chopped
¾ cup baby corn, chopped
3 scallions, chopped
2 tablespoons chopped fresh parsley
½ teaspoon sea salt

1. In a large pot over low heat, combine the rice, olive oil, sesame oil, soy sauce, vinegar, and sugar, stirring well to combine.

2. Add snow peas, baby corn, and scallions and heat until warmed through and vegetables are lightly cooked, stirring frequently, so the rice doesn't burn.

3. While still hot, stir in fresh parsley and season well with sea salt.

PER SERVING Calories: 345 | Fat: 11g | Sodium: 839mg | Fiber: 2g | Protein: 7g

Chapter 8

Classic Pastas

Artichoke and Spinach Pesto Pasta

Spinach, artichoke, and avocado combined with pesto is an impossibly delicious combination. Kermit would love this super-green dish!

INGREDIENTS | SERVES 4

1 cup basil
1 cup spinach leaves
3 cloves garlic
½ cup pine nuts or walnuts
1 tablespoon lemon juice
2 tablespoons nutritional yeast
½ teaspoon sea salt
¼ teaspoon pepper
2 tablespoons olive oil
1 cup chopped artichoke hearts
2 tablespoons vegan margarine
1 tablespoon flour
¾ cup soy milk
2 cups cooked pasta
1 avocado, diced (optional)

1. Process together the basil, spinach leaves, garlic, nuts, lemon juice, nutritional yeast, sea salt, and pepper until almost smooth. Add olive oil, then artichoke hearts, and process until artichokes are finely diced.

2. In a small saucepan, melt the vegan margarine and stir in the flour to form a paste. Add soy milk and heat until thickened.

3. Remove from heat and stir in basil and spinach pesto mixture.

4. Toss with prepared pasta and avocado.

PER SERVING Calories: 402 | Fat: 25g | Sodium: 612mg | Fiber: 5g | Protein: 11g

White Lasagna with Spinach

Feel free to dream of Italian opera houses or old Tuscany while savoring this chic cashew-butter lasagna by candlelight and listening to Pavarotti.

INGREDIENTS | SERVES 6

½ onion, diced
4 cloves garlic, minced
2 tablespoons olive oil
1 10-ounce box frozen spinach, thawed and pressed to remove moisture
½ teaspoon salt
1 block firm tofu, crumbled
¾ cup Tropical Cashew Nut Butter (p. 27)
2 cups soy milk
1 tablespoon miso
2 tablespoons soy sauce
2 tablespoons lemon juice
3 tablespoons nutritional yeast
2 teaspoons onion powder
1 12-ounce package lasagna noodles

Like the *Mona Lisa*

Although you might not be the next Michelangelo, lasagna—vegan or not— is a bit of an art form, with so many variants affecting the outcome: moisture, temperature, assembly, the thickness of the noodles. If you're worried about presenting a crumbly lasagna, prepare it in advance, and allow to cool completely. Then, reheat just before slicing and serving.

1. Sauté onion and garlic in olive oil until soft, about 4–5 minutes, and add spinach and salt, stirring to combine well and cooking just until spinach is heated through. Add crumbled tofu and mix well. Allow to cool completely.

2. In a small saucepan over low heat, combine the cashew butter, soy milk, miso, soy sauce, lemon juice, nutritional yeast, and onion powder until smooth and creamy.

3. Prepare lasagna noodles according to package instructions and preheat oven to 350°F.

4. In a lightly greased lasagna pan, place a thin layer of cashew sauce and then a layer of noodles. Next add spinach and more sauce, then a layer of noodles, continuing until all ingredients are used up. The top layer should be spinach and then sauce.

5. Bake for 40 minutes, or until done. Allow to cool for at least 10 minutes before serving, to allow lasagna to set.

PER SERVING Calories: 680 | Fat: 37g | Sodium: 675mg | Fiber: 6g | Protein: 24g

Zucchini and Fresh Basil Pomodoro

Pick out the finest fresh zucchini and tomatoes for this one, as pomodoro is a simple pasta dish with little added flavor.

INGREDIENTS | SERVES 4

2 zucchini, sliced

4 cloves garlic, minced

2 tablespoons olive oil

4 large tomatoes, diced

⅓ cup chopped fresh basil

2 cups prepared angel hair or spaghetti pasta

Salt and pepper to taste

Vegan Parmesan cheese or nutritional yeast (optional)

1. Heat zucchini and garlic over low heat in olive oil for just a minute or 2 until zucchini is just lightly softened. Add tomatoes and cook for another 4–5 minutes.

2. Toss zucchini and tomatoes with basil and pasta and season with salt and pepper, to taste. Serve topped with a sprinkle of vegan Parmesan cheese or nutritional yeast.

PER SERVING Calories: 224 | Fat: 8g | Sodium: 20mg | Fiber: 5g | Protein: 7g

Easy Pad Thai Noodles

Volumes could be written about Thailand's national dish. It's sweet, sour, spicy, and salty all at once, and filled with as much texture and flavor as the streets of Bangkok themselves.

INGREDIENTS | SERVES 4

1 pound thin rice noodles

¼ cup tahini

¼ cup ketchup

¼ cup soy sauce

2 tablespoons white, rice, or cider vinegar

3 tablespoons lime juice

2 tablespoons sugar

¾ teaspoon crushed red pepper flakes or cayenne

1 block firm or extra-firm tofu, diced small

3 cloves garlic

¼ cup vegetable or safflower oil

4 scallions, chopped

½ teaspoon salt

Optional toppings: bean sprouts, crushed toasted peanuts, extra scallions, sliced lime

1. Cover the noodles in hot water and set aside to soak until soft, about 5 minutes.

2. Whisk together the tahini, ketchup, soy sauce, vinegar, lime juice, sugar, and red pepper flakes.

3. In a large skillet, fry the tofu and garlic in oil until tofu is lightly golden brown. Add drained noodles, stirring to combine well, and fry for 2–3 minutes.

4. Reduce heat to medium and add tahini and ketchup sauce mixture, stirring well to combine. Allow to cook for 3–4 minutes until well combined and heated through. Add scallions and salt and heat 1 more minute, stirring well.

5. Serve with extra chopped scallions, bean sprouts, and crushed peanuts and a lime wedge or two.

PER SERVING Calories: 718 | Fat: 25g | Sodium: 1,401mg | Fiber: 3g | Protein: 11g

Truly Thai

Pad Thai is supposed to be a bit greasy—which is why the noodles are fried in the oil. If you're not worried about fat and have quick-cooking thin rice noodles, you can omit the presoaking in water and just toss the noodles in with the tofu and garlic and add extra oil. For an authentic pad Thai, however, you'll need tamarind juice or pulp, which you can often find at Mexican as well as Asian grocers.

Eggplant Puttanesca

Salty and garlicky puttanesca is a thick sauce traditionally served over pasta, but try it over a more wholesome grain, such as quinoa or even brown nice.

INGREDIENTS | SERVES 4

3 cloves garlic, minced
1 red bell pepper, chopped
1 eggplant, chopped
2 tablespoons olive oil
2 tablespoons capers, rinsed
⅓ cup sliced kalamata or black olives
½ teaspoon red pepper flakes
1 14-ounce can diced tomatoes
1 tablespoon balsamic vinegar
½ teaspoon parsley

1. In a large skillet or saucepan, sauté the garlic, bell pepper, and eggplant in olive oil for 4–5 minutes until eggplant is almost soft. Add capers, olives, and red pepper flakes, and stir to combine.

2. Reduce heat to low and add remaining ingredients. Cover and allow to simmer for 10–12 minutes until juice from tomatoes has reduced.

3. Serve over cooked pasta or rice.

PER SERVING Calories: 141 | Fat: 8g | Sodium: 378mg | Fiber: 7g | Protein: 3g

Classic Fettuccine Alfredo

Most vegan Alfredo recipes start with a roux of margarine and soy milk, but this one uses cashew cream instead for a sensually decadent white sauce. Go ahead and lick the spoons; nobody's watching.

INGREDIENTS | SERVES 6

½ cup raw cashews
1¼ cups water
1 tablespoon miso
2 tablespoons lemon juice
2 tablespoons tahini
¼ cup diced onion
1 teaspoon garlic
½ teaspoon salt
¼ cup nutritional yeast
2 tablespoons olive or safflower oil
1 12-ounce package fettuccine, cooked

Alfredo Sauce Lasagna

Make a double batch and use this cheesy sauce to create a layered White Lasagna with Spinach (p. 149). It's also great in macaroni and cheese for kids, or as a dip for veggies.

1. In a food processor or blender, blend together the cashews and water until completely smooth and creamy, about 90 seconds.

2. Add remaining ingredients, except oil and pasta, and purée until smooth. Slowly add oil until thick and oil is emulsified.

3. Heat in a saucepan over low heat for 4–5 minutes, stirring frequently. Serve over cooked fettuccine noodles.

PER SERVING Calories: 357 | Fat: 13g | Sodium: 281mg | Fiber: 4g | Protein: 12g

Gnocchi with Walnut Parsley Sauce

A simple and savory pasta sauce that pairs perfectly with earthy potato gnocchi.

INGREDIENTS | SERVES 4

1 cup chopped walnuts
2½ cups unsweetened soy milk
2 tablespoons vegan margarine
2 tablespoons all-purpose flour
¾ teaspoon parsley
2 teaspoons nutritional yeast (optional)
½ teaspoon salt
¼ teaspoon black pepper
Prepared Homemade Garlic and Herb Gnocchi (p. 155)

1. Heat walnuts and soy milk over low heat for 3–4 minutes, to soften the walnuts. Set aside.

2. In a small saucepan, heat vegan margarine over low heat until melted and whisk in flour, stirring continuously to prevent from burning.

3. Slowly stir in soy milk and walnuts, again stirring continuously. Heat until soy milk thickens into a sauce, about 4–5 minutes.

4. Remove from heat, stir in parsley, nutritional yeast, salt, and pepper, and pour over cooked gnocchi. Serve immediately.

PER SERVING Calories: 600 | Fat: 28g | Sodium: 889mg | Fiber: 6g | Protein: 6g

Homemade Garlic and Herb Gnocchi

Homemade gnocchi is well worth the effort if you have the time! Use a simple Walnut Parsley Sauce (p. 154) or minimal seasonings to make sure that the flavor from the gnocchi shines through.

INGREDIENTS | SERVES 4

2 large potatoes
¾ teaspoon garlic powder
½ teaspoon dried basil
½ teaspoon dried parsley
¾ teaspoon salt
1½ cups all-purpose flour
Water for boiling

Top It with . . .

When making the effort to create fresh gnocchi (pronounced *ny-OH-kee*), you want to taste the fresh doughy flavors, not a complex overpowering topping, so carefully choose your sauce. Melt a bit of vegan margarine with the gnocchi, or perhaps a flavored oil, and sprinkle with fresh herbs, salt, and pepper. Try a combination of garlic and nutritional yeast, or olive oil with a few crumbled sage or rosemary leaves.

1. Bake potatoes until done, about 50 minutes at 400°F. Allow to cool, then peel skins.

2. Using a fork, mash potatoes with garlic powder, basil, parsley, and salt until potatoes are completely smooth, with no lumps.

3. On a floured work surface, place half of the flour, and the potatoes on top. Use your hands to work the flour into the potatoes to form a dough. Continue to add only as much flour as is needed to form a dough. Knead smooth.

4. Working in batches, roll out a rope of dough about 1 inch thick. Slice into 1-inch-long pieces, and gently roll against a fork to make grooves in the dough. This helps the sauce stick to the dough.

5. Cook gnocchi in boiling water for 2–3 minutes until they rise to the surface. Serve immediately.

PER SERVING Calories: 281 | Fat: 1g | Sodium: 443mg | Fiber: 3g | Protein: 7g

Balsamic Dijon Orzo

Defying logic, this simple dish flavored with balsamic and Dijon is somehow exponentially greater than the sum of its parts. Add a dash of sugar or agave if you find the tangy Dijon overpowering.

INGREDIENTS | SERVES 4

3 tablespoons balsamic vinegar
1½ tablespoons Dijon mustard
1½ tablespoons olive oil
1 teaspoon basil
1 teaspoon parsley
½ teaspoon oregano
1½ cups orzo, cooked
2 medium tomatoes, chopped
½ cup sliced black olives
1 15-ounce can great northern or cannellini beans, drained
½ teaspoon salt
¼ teaspoon pepper

1. In a small bowl or container, whisk together the vinegar, mustard, olive oil, basil, parsley, and oregano until well mixed.

2. Over low heat, combine the orzo with the balsamic dressing and add tomatoes, olives, and beans. Cook for 3–4 minutes, stirring to combine.

3. Season with salt and pepper.

PER SERVING Calories: 356 | Fat: 8g | Sodium: 505mg | Fiber: 8g | Protein: 14g

Lazy and Hungry Garlic Pasta

It's not fancy, but that's the beauty of this recipe, which is, aptly, for those times when you're too hungry to cook and just want to fill your stomach.

INGREDIENTS | SERVES 6

2 cloves garlic, minced
2 tablespoons olive oil
3 cups pasta, cooked
2 tablespoons nutritional yeast
½ teaspoon parsley
Dash red pepper flakes (optional)
Salt and pepper to taste

1. Heat the garlic in olive oil for just a minute or 2 until almost browned.

2. Toss garlic and olive oil with remaining ingredients. Adjust seasonings to taste.

PER SERVING Calories: 157 | Fat: 5g | Sodium: 1mg | Fiber: 2g | Protein: 5g

Really Hungry? Really Lazy?
Garlic powder, nutritional yeast, and salt is a delicious seasoning combination, and will give you a bit of a B_{12} perk-up. Use it over toast, veggies, popcorn, bagels, baked potatoes, and, of course, cooked pasta if you're feeling, well, lazy and hungry!

California Picnic Pasta Salad

Lightly flavored with plenty of texture, this is a colorful salad that makes a meal on its own.

INGREDIENTS | SERVES 6

3 cups corkscrew or bow-tie pasta, cooked
2 large tomatoes, diced
½ cup jarred banana peppers, sliced thin
½ red onion, diced
½ cup sliced black olives
2 tablespoons olive oil
1 tablespoon lemon juice
2 teaspoons Dijon mustard
1 tablespoon red wine vinegar
½ teaspoon basil
½ teaspoon oregano
Salt and pepper to taste
2 avocados, diced

1. Combine the pasta, tomatoes, peppers, onion, and olives in a large bowl.

2. In a separate small bowl, whisk together the remaining ingredients, except avocado, until well mixed.

3. Pour the dressing over the pasta and toss to combine. Chill for at least 1 hour.

4. Add diced avocado and toss gently. Serve immediately.

PER SERVING Calories: 299 | Fat: 17g | Sodium: 324mg | Fiber: 7g | Protein: 6g

Artichoke and Olive Puttanesca

Use fresh basil and parsley if you have it on hand, but otherwise, dried is fine.

INGREDIENTS | SERVES 6

3 cloves garlic, minced
2 tablespoons olive oil
1 14-ounce can diced or crushed tomatoes
¼ cup sliced black olives
¼ cup sliced green olives
1 cup chopped artichoke hearts
2 tablespoons capers
½ teaspoon red pepper flakes
½ teaspoon basil
¾ teaspoon parsley
¼ teaspoon salt
1 12-ounce package pasta, cooked

1. Heat garlic in olive oil for 2–3 minutes. Reduce heat and add remaining ingredients, except pasta.

2. Cook over low heat, uncovered, for 10–12 minutes until most of the liquid from tomatoes is absorbed.

3. Toss with cooked pasta.

PER SERVING Calories: 297 | Fat: 7g | Sodium: 539mg | Fiber: 5g | Protein: 9g

Creamy Sun-Dried Tomato Pasta

Silken tofu makes a creamy low-fat sauce base. If using dried tomatoes, rather than oil-packed, be sure to rehydrate them well first.

INGREDIENTS | SERVES 6

1 block silken tofu, drained
¼ cup soy milk
2 tablespoons red wine vinegar
½ teaspoon garlic powder
½ teaspoon salt
1¼ cups sun-dried tomatoes, rehydrated
1 teaspoon parsley
1 12-ounce package pasta, cooked
2 tablespoons chopped fresh basil

Two in One

For another elegant twist on this dish, prepare this recipe with 1¼ cups chopped roasted red peppers instead of sun-dried tomatoes, or try a combination of the two.

1. Blend together the tofu, soy milk, vinegar, garlic powder, and salt in a blender or food processor until smooth and creamy. Add tomatoes and parsley and pulse until tomatoes are finely diced.

2. Transfer sauce to a small pot and heat over medium-low heat just until hot.

3. Pour sauce over pasta and sprinkle with fresh chopped basil.

PER SERVING Calories: 274 | Fat: 3g | Sodium: 441mg | Fiber: 3g | Protein: 12g

Basic Vegetable Marinara

No Parmesan is needed to top off this chunky vegetable marinara. Toss in a handful of TVP or browned store-bought mock meat crumbles for a "meaty" sauce.

INGREDIENTS | SERVES 4

4 cloves garlic, minced
1 carrot, sliced thin
2 ribs celery, chopped
2 tablespoons olive oil
1 28-ounce can diced or stewed tomatoes
1 6-ounce can tomato paste
1 teaspoon oregano
1 teaspoon parsley
2 tablespoons chopped fresh basil
2 bay leaves
½ cup corn (optional)
½ cup sliced black olives
1 tablespoon balsamic vinegar
½ teaspoon crushed red pepper flakes
½ teaspoon salt

In a Pinch

Don't have time to make marinara from scratch? Take 5 minutes to heat a store-bought variety on the stove and add in frozen veggies, Italian seasonings, and a bit of wine or balsamic vinegar for a fresh taste.

1. Heat garlic, carrot, and celery in olive oil over medium heat, stirring frequently, for 4–5 minutes.

2. Reduce heat to medium low, then add diced tomatoes, tomato paste, oregano, parsley, basil, and bay leaves, stirring well to combine.

3. Cover and heat for at least 30 minutes, stirring frequently.

4. Add corn, olives, balsamic vinegar, red pepper, and salt, and simmer for another 5 minutes, uncovered.

5. Remove bay leaves before serving, and adjust seasonings to taste.

PER SERVING Calories: 209 | Fat: 11g | Sodium: 864mg | Fiber: 7g | Protein: 6g

Pumpkin Cream Pasta Sauce

A simple recipe, but with such an unusual mix of flavors and ingredients, it's bound to impress. This sauce would also go well with Homemade Garlic and Herb Gnocchi (p. 155) or over stuffed Tofu "Ricotta" Manicotti (p. 241).

INGREDIENTS | SERVES 4

1 onion, chopped
2 cloves garlic, minced
2 tablespoons vegan margarine
1 15-ounce can puréed pumpkin
1½ cups soy cream
¼ cup nutritional yeast
½ teaspoon parsley
Salt and pepper, to taste

1. Heat onion and garlic in margarine until soft, about 3–4 minutes.

2. Reduce heat to medium low and add pumpkin and soy cream. Bring to a low simmer and cook for about 10 minutes, stirring frequently, until creamy.

3. Stir in nutritional yeast and parsley and season generously with salt and pepper, heating for just another minute or 2.

4. Serve over cooked pasta.

PER SERVING Calories: 199 | Fat: 12g | Sodium: 144mg | Fiber: 5g | Protein: 3g

Easy Creamy Pasta and Peas

*Great for the kids, but use artichoke hearts or broccoli to make it for adults,
or any frozen mixed veggies you like.*

INGREDIENTS | SERVES 6

1½ cups soy milk

1 teaspoon garlic powder

2 tablespoons vegan margarine

1 tablespoon flour

1½ cups green peas

⅓ cup nutritional yeast

1 12-ounce package pasta, cooked

Salt and pepper, to taste

1. In a medium pot, whisk together the soy milk, garlic powder, and margarine over low heat. Add flour and stir well to combine, heating just until thickened.

2. Add peas and nutritional yeast until heated and well mixed, then pour over pasta.

3. Season generously with salt and pepper, to taste.

PER SERVING Calories: 312 | Fat: 6g | Sodium: 124mg | Fiber: 4g | Protein: 13g

Basic Vegan White Sauce

Seeing a pattern? Melted vegan margarine, along with soy milk, is the base for many vegan cream sauces, roux, and cheese sauces. Flour is the simplest thickener, but cornstarch or arrowroot also work. Nutritional yeast is added for a cheesy flavor, and garlic powder, onion powder, and salt enhance the general flavor. Use an unsweetened soy milk for a more savory taste.

Lemon, Basil, and Artichoke Pasta

*The earthy rosemary, basil, and lemon flavor would complement gnocchi well;
otherwise, use a grooved pasta, such as corkscrews, to catch the sauce.*

INGREDIENTS | SERVES 6

12 ounces pasta, cooked

1 6-ounce jar artichoke hearts, drained and chopped

2 large tomatoes, chopped

½ cup fresh basil, chopped fine

½ cup sliced black olives

2 tablespoons olive oil

1 tablespoon lemon juice

½ teaspoon rosemary

2 tablespoons nutritional yeast

Salt and pepper, to taste

Over low heat, combine the cooked pasta with the remaining ingredients, combining well and heating just until well mixed and heated through, about 3–4 minutes.

PER SERVING Calories: 286 | Fat: 7g | Sodium: 196mg | Fiber: 4g | Protein: 9g

Sweet and Spicy Peanut Noodles

*Like the call of the siren, these noodles entice you with their sweet pineapple flavor,
then scorch your tongue with fiery chilies. Very sneaky, indeed.*

INGREDIENTS | SERVES 4

1 12-ounce package Asian-style noodles

⅓ cup peanut butter

2 tablespoons soy sauce

⅔ cup pineapple juice

2 cloves garlic, minced

1 teaspoon fresh ginger, grated

½ teaspoon salt

1 tablespoon olive oil

1 teaspoon sesame oil

2–3 small chilies, minced

¾ cup diced pineapple

1. Prepare noodles according to package instructions and set aside.

2. In a small saucepan, stir together the peanut butter, soy sauce, pineapple juice, garlic, ginger, and salt over low heat, just until well combined.

3. Place the olive oil and sesame oil in a large skillet and fry minced chilies and pineapple for 2–3 minutes, stirring frequently, until pineapple is lightly browned. Add noodles and fry for another minute, stirring well.

4. Reduce heat to low and add peanut butter sauce mixture, stirring to combine well. Heat for 1 more minute until heated through.

PER SERVING Calories: 329 | Fat: 16g | Sodium: 977mg | Fiber: 2g | Protein: 10g

Five-Minute Vegan Pasta Salad

Once you've got the pasta cooked and cooled, this takes just 5 minutes to assemble, as it's made with store-bought dressing. A balsamic vinaigrette or tomato dressing would also work well.

INGREDIENTS | SERVES 4

4 cups pasta, cooked
¾ cup vegan Italian salad dressing
3 scallions, chopped
½ cup sliced black olives
1 tomato, chopped
1 avocado, diced (optional)
Salt and pepper to taste

Toss together all ingredients. Allow to chill for at least 1½ hours before serving, if time allows, to allow flavors to combine.

PER SERVING Calories: 378 | Fat: 16g | Sodium: 877mg | Fiber: 4g | Protein: 9g

Instant Add-Ons

Open up a jar and instantly add color, flavor, and texture to a basic pasta salad. What's in your cupboard? Try capers, roasted red peppers, canned veggies, jarred pimentos or sun-dried tomatoes, or even mandarin oranges or sliced beets. Snip in any leftover fresh herbs you have on hand.

Orzo with White Wine and Mushrooms

Try using two different varieties of mushrooms for some extra color and depth of flavor.

INGREDIENTS | SERVES 4

1 cup sliced mushrooms
1 yellow onion, chopped
3 cloves garlic, minced
2 tablespoons olive oil
1½ cups vegetable broth
½ cup white wine
1½ cups orzo
2 tablespoons vegan margarine
2 tablespoons nutritional yeast or vegan Parmesan (optional)
2 tablespoons chopped fresh basil or parsley
Salt and pepper, to taste

1. Heat mushrooms, onions, and garlic in olive oil until just soft, about 3–4 minutes.

2. Reduce heat and add vegetable broth, white wine, and orzo. Cover and simmer for 8–10 minutes until orzo is cooked and liquid is absorbed.

3. While still hot, stir in margarine, nutritional yeast, and fresh basil or parsley, and season generously with salt and pepper, to taste.

PER SERVING Calories: 302 | Fat: 13g | Sodium: 439mg | Fiber: 2g | Protein: 6g

What Is Orzo?

Despite it's abundant use at gourmet eateries, there's really nothing fancy about orzo: its just a funny-sounding word for "small rice-shaped pasta." In other words, it's just pasta. Because of its small size, it can be used more like couscous and rice than other pastas, and it works well with lighter and thinner sauces and in pilaf-like salads.

Basic Tofu Lasagna

Seasoned tofu takes the place of ricotta cheese, and really does look and taste like the real thing. Fresh parsley adds flavor, and with store-bought sauce, it's quick to get in the oven.

INGREDIENTS | SERVES 6

1 block firm tofu
1 12-ounce block silken tofu
¼ cup nutritional yeast
1 tablespoon lemon juice
1 tablespoon soy sauce
1 teaspoon garlic powder
2 teaspoons basil
3 tablespoons chopped fresh parsley
1 teaspoon salt
4 cups spaghetti sauce
1 16-ounce package lasagna noodles, cooked

1. Preheat oven to 350°F.

2. In a large bowl, mash together the firm tofu, silken tofu, nutritional yeast, lemon juice, soy sauce, garlic powder, basil, parsley, and salt until combined and crumbly like ricotta cheese.

3. To assemble the lasagna, spread about ⅔ cup spaghetti sauce on the bottom of a lasagna pan, then add a layer of noodles.

4. Spread about ½ the tofu mixture on top of the noodles, followed by another layer of sauce. Place a second layer of noodles on top, followed by the remaining tofu and more sauce. Finish it off with a third layer of noodles and the rest of the sauce.

5. Cover and bake for 25 minutes.

PER SERVING Calories: 510 | Fat: 10g | Sodium: 1,256mg | Fiber: 8g | Protein: 21g

Stove Top Cheater's Mac 'n' Cheese

Yes, it's cheating just a little to make vegan macaroni and cheese starting with store-bought "cheese," but who cares? The secret to getting this recipe super-creamy and cheesy is using cream cheese as well as vegan Cheddar. It's not particularly healthy, but at least it's still cholesterol-free!

INGREDIENTS | SERVES 6

1 12-ounce package macaroni
1 cup soy milk
2 tablespoons vegan margarine
½ teaspoon onion powder
1 teaspoon garlic powder
½ cup vegan cream cheese
½ cup vegan Cheddar cheese
⅓ cup nutritional yeast
½ teaspoon salt
Black pepper, to taste

1. Prepare macaroni according to package instructions. Drain well and return to pot.

2. Over low heat, stir in soy milk and vegan margarine until melted.

3. Add remaining ingredients, stirring to combine over low heat until cheese is melted and ingredients are well mixed.

PER SERVING Calories: 411 | Fat: 13g | Sodium: 549mg | Fiber: 3g | Protein: 13g

Just Because It's Vegan . . .

Doesn't mean it's healthy! If health is your main concern for going vegan, you may do well to avoid recipes such as this one. Vegan cream cheese usually contains hydrogenated oils, which are admittedly nearly as bad for your system as red meat. Nonhydrogenated vegan cream cheese is available, but unfortunately, it just doesn't taste as good!

Lemon Thyme Orzo with Asparagus

The combination of lemon and thyme is understated and rustic; it smells and tastes good enough to bathe in. If asparagus isn't in season, use green peas or lightly steamed broccoli.

INGREDIENTS | SERVES 4

1½ cups orzo
1 bunch asparagus, chopped
2 tablespoons olive oil
Zest from 1 lemon
2 tablespoons lemon juice
½ teaspoon salt
¼ teaspoon pepper
2 teaspoons chopped fresh thyme

1. Cook orzo according to package instructions.

2. In a large skillet, heat asparagus in olive oil until just tender. Do not overcook.

3. Reduce heat to low and add orzo and remaining ingredients, stirring to combine well. Cook for just a minute or 2, until heated through, and adjust seasonings to taste.

PER SERVING Calories: 218 | Fat: 7g | Sodium: 294mg | Fiber: 2g | Protein: 6g

Peanut Butter Noodles for Kids

Drown your noodles in this mildly flavored peanut butter sauce recipe for kids. What kid doesn't love peanut butter?

INGREDIENTS | SERVES 4

1 pound Asian-style noodles (or use regular pasta)
⅓ cup peanut butter
⅓ cup water
3 tablespoons soy sauce
2 tablespoons lime juice
2 tablespoons rice vinegar
1 tablespoon sesame oil
½ teaspoon ginger powder
1 teaspoon sugar
½ teaspoon crushed red pepper flakes (optional)

1. Prepare noodles or pasta according to package instruction and set aside.

2. Whisk together remaining ingredients over low heat just until combined, about 3 minutes. Toss with noodles.

PER SERVING Calories: 584 | Fat: 16g | Sodium: 782mg | Fiber: 5g | Protein: 21g

Perfect Peanut Sauce

Experiment with the portions to get a ratio that works for you. Add fresh diced chilies for a perked-up version for adults, or, for a satay-style sauce, add a couple tablespoons of coconut milk. Use the sauce alone to dress steamed veggies or fried tofu—or to disguise anything the kids are reluctant to eat.

Asian Sesame Tahini Noodles

A creamy and nutty Chinese-inspired noodle dish.
If you don't have Asian-style noodles on hand, spaghetti will do.

INGREDIENTS | SERVES 4

1 pound Asian noodles
½ cup tahini
⅓ cup water
2 tablespoons soy sauce
1 clove garlic
2 teaspoons fresh ginger, minced
2 tablespoons rice vinegar
2 teaspoons sesame oil
1 red bell pepper, sliced thin
3 scallions, chopped
¾ cup snow peas, chopped
¼ teaspoon crushed red pepper flakes

1. Cook noodles according to package instructions; drain well.

2. Whisk or blend together the tahini, water, soy sauce, garlic, ginger, and rice vinegar.

3. In a large skillet, heat the sesame oil, bell pepper, scallions, and snow peas for 2–3 minutes. Add tahini sauce and noodles, stirring well to combine.

4. Cook over low heat just until heated, about 2–3 minutes.

5. Garnish with crushed red pepper flakes to taste.

PER SERVING Calories: 602 | Fat: 19g | Sodium: 1377mg | Fiber: 4g | Protein: 23g

Spaghetti with Italian "Meatballs"

These little TVP nuggets are so chewy and addicting, you just might want to make a double batch. If you can't find beef-flavored bouillon, just use what you've got. Don't be tempted to add extra water to the TVP, as it needs to be a little dry for this recipe.

INGREDIENTS | SERVES 6

⅔ cup hot water
½ vegetarian beef-flavored bouillon cube (optional)
⅔ cup TVP
Egg replacer for 2 eggs
½ onion, minced
2 tablespoons ketchup or barbecue sauce
½ teaspoon garlic powder
1 teaspoon basil
1 teaspoon parsley
½ teaspoon sage
½ teaspoon salt
½ cup bread crumbs
⅔–¾ cup flour
Oil for pan-frying
3 cups prepared spaghetti sauce
1 12-ounce package spaghetti noodles, cooked

TVP Veggie Burgers

This recipe makes excellently chewy veggie burger patties. Cut down on the basil, sage, and parsley, and add some "beefier" seasonings: paprika, chili powder, seasoning salt, or pepper. Shape into patties, instead of balls, and pan fry in oil on both sides. Delish!

1. Dissolve bouillon cube in hot water, and pour over TVP to reconstitute. Allow to sit for 6–7 minutes. Gently press to remove any excess moisture.

2. In a large bowl, combine the TVP, egg replacer, onion, ketchup or barbecue sauce, and seasonings until well mixed.

3. Add bread crumbs and combine well, then add flour, a few tablespoons at a time, mixing well to combine until mixture is sticky and thick. You may need a little more or less than ⅔ cup.

4. Using lightly floured hands, shape into balls 1½–2 inches thick.

5. Pan fry "meatballs" in a bit of oil over medium heat, rolling them around in the pan to maintain the shape, until golden brown on all sides.

6. Reduce heat to medium low and add spaghetti sauce, heating thoroughly. Serve over cooked spaghetti noodles.

PER SERVING Calories: 495 | Fat: 9g | Sodium: 850mg | Fiber: 8g | Protein: 18g

Baked Macaroni and Cheese

Vegan chefs all take pride in seeing who can create the best dairy-free macaroni and cheese ever. Join in the friendly rivalry with this recipe. Don't tell anyone that the silken tofu is the secret ingredient for super creaminess.

INGREDIENTS | SERVES 6

1 12-ounce package macaroni
1 block silken tofu
1 cup soy milk
2 tablespoons tahini
2 tablespoons lemon juice
1 tablespoon miso
1 teaspoon garlic powder
1 teaspoon onion powder
¼ cup nutritional yeast
2 tablespoons vegan margarine
1 cup bread crumbs
⅓ teaspoon nutmeg (optional)
½ teaspoon salt
½ teaspoon pepper

1. Prepare macaroni according to package instructions. Drain well and place in a large casserole or baking dish.

2. In a blender or food processor, purée together the tofu, soy milk, tahini, lemon juice, miso, garlic and onion powders, and nutritional yeast until smooth and creamy, scraping the sides to blend well.

3. Heat oven to 350°F.

4. Combine tofu mixture with macaroni in the casserole dish.

5. In a small skillet, melt the vegan margarine and add bread crumbs, stirring to coat. Spread bread crumbs on top of macaroni and sprinkle with nutmeg, salt, and pepper.

6. Bake for 20–25 minutes, or until slightly crispy.

PER SERVING Calories: 409 | Fat: 16g | Sodium: 486mg | Fiber: 4g | Protein: 16g

Chapter 9

Whole Grains

Lemon Quinoa Veggie Salad

If you prefer to use fresh veggies, any kind will do.
Steamed broccoli or fresh tomatoes would work well.

INGREDIENTS | SERVES 4

4 cups vegetable broth
1½ cups quinoa
1 cup frozen mixed veggies, thawed
¼ cup lemon juice
¼ cup olive oil
1 teaspoon garlic powder
½ teaspoon sea salt
¼ teaspoon black pepper
2 tablespoons chopped fresh cilantro or parsley (optional)

1. In a large pot, bring vegetable broth to a boil. Add quinoa, cover, and simmer for 15–20 minutes, stirring occasionally, until liquid is absorbed and quinoa is cooked. Add mixed veggies and stir to combine.

2. Remove from heat and combine with remaining ingredients. Serve hot or cold.

PER SERVING Calories: 408 | Fat: 18g | Sodium: 1,261mg | Fiber: 7g | Protein: 11g

Maple Cinnamon Breakfast Quinoa

Quinoa is a filling and healthy breakfast and has more protein than regular oatmeal.
This is a deliciously sweet and energizing way to kick off your day.

INGREDIENTS | SERVES 2

1 cup quinoa
2–2½ cups water
1 teaspoon vegan margarine
⅔ cup soy milk
½ teaspoon cinnamon
2 tablespoons maple syrup
2 tablespoons raisins (optional)
2 bananas, sliced (optional)

1. Heat the quinoa and water in a small saucepan and bring to a boil. Reduce to a simmer and allow to cook, covered, for 15 minutes, until liquid is absorbed.

2. Remove from heat and fluff the quinoa with a fork. Cover, and allow to sit for 5 minutes.

3. Stir in the margarine and soy milk, then remaining ingredients.

PER SERVING Calories: 416 | Fat: 8g | Sodium: 77mg | Fiber: 7g | Protein: 14g

Bulgur Wheat Tabbouleh Salad with Tomatoes

Though you'll need to adjust the cooking time, of course, you can try this tabbouleh recipe with just about any whole grain. Bulgur wheat is traditional, but quinoa, millet, or amaranth would also work.

INGREDIENTS | SERVES 4

1¼ cups boiling water or vegetable broth
1 cup bulgur wheat
3 tablespoons olive oil
¼ cup lemon juice
1 teaspoon garlic powder
½ teaspoon sea salt
½ teaspoon pepper
3 scallions, chopped
½ cup chopped fresh mint
½ cup chopped fresh parsley
1 15-ounce can chickpeas, drained (optional)
3 large tomatoes, diced

1. Pour boiling water over bulgur wheat. Cover, and allow to sit for 30 minutes, or until bulgur wheat is soft.

2. Toss bulgur wheat with olive oil, lemon juice, garlic powder, and salt, stirring well to coat. Combine with remaining ingredients, adding in tomatoes last.

3. Allow to chill for at least 1 hour before serving.

PER SERVING Calories: 252 | Fat: 11g | Sodium: 315mg | Fiber: 10g | Protein: 7g

Leftover Tabbouleh Sandwiches

Spread a slice of bread or a tortilla with some hummus, then layer leftover tabbouleh, sweet pickle relish, thinly sliced cucumbers, and some lettuce and make a quick sandwich or wrap for lunch.

Barley and Mushroom Pilaf

*An earthy-flavored pilaf with mushrooms and nutty toasted barley.
This one will really stick to your ribs!*

INGREDIENTS | SERVES 4

1 cup sliced porcini mushrooms

1 cup sliced shiitake mushrooms

2 ribs celery, diced

½ onion, chopped

3 tablespoons vegan margarine or olive oil, divided

1¼ cups barley

3¾ cups vegetable broth

1 bay leaf

¼ teaspoon sage

½ teaspoon parsley

½ teaspoon thyme

1. In a large skillet or stock pot, sauté mushrooms, celery, and onion in 2 tablespoons margarine or olive oil until almost soft, about 2–3 minutes. Add barley and remaining 1 tablespoon of margarine and allow to toast for a minute or 2, stirring frequently.

2. When barley starts to turn brown, add vegetable broth and seasonings. Bring to a simmer, cover, and allow to cook for 20–25 minutes, stirring occasionally, until liquid is absorbed and barley is cooked. Remove bay leaf before serving.

PER SERVING Calories: 323 | Fat: 9g | Sodium: 1,025mg | Fiber: 11g | Protein: 8g

Cooking Barley

Be sure you pick up either pearl or quick-cooking barley, and not the hulled variety, which takes ages to cook. Pearl barley is done in 20–25 minutes, and quick-cooking barley is done in about 10, so adjust the cooking times as needed. Barley can also be cooked in your rice steamer with about 2½ cups liquid for each cup of barley.

Easy Garlic Quinoa

A simple way to spruce up plain quinoa to serve as a side dish,
or top with cooked veggies, a stir-fry, or some baked tofu.

INGREDIENTS | SERVES 4

1 yellow onion, diced
4 cloves garlic, minced
2 tablespoons olive oil or vegan margarine
3 cups vegetable broth
1½ cups quinoa
½ teaspoon salt
3 tablespoons nutritional yeast

1. In a large skillet, heat onion and garlic in oil or margarine for 3–4 minutes until onions are soft.

2. Add vegetable broth and quinoa, cover, and bring to a simmer. Allow to cook for 15 minutes until liquid is absorbed.

3. Fluff quinoa with a fork and stir in salt and nutritional yeast.

PER SERVING Calories: 342 | Fat: 11g | Sodium: 1,002mg | Fiber: 6g | Protein: 12g

Mediterranean Quinoa Pilaf

Inspired by the flavors of the Mediterranean, bring this vibrant whole-grain entrée
to a vegan potluck and watch it magically disappear.

INGREDIENTS | SERVES 4

1½ cups quinoa
3 cups vegetable broth
3 tablespoons balsamic vinegar
2 tablespoons olive oil
1 tablespoon lemon juice
⅓ teaspoon salt
½ cup sun-dried tomatoes, chopped
½ cup artichoke hearts, chopped
½ cup black or kalamata olives, sliced

1. In a large skillet or saucepan, bring the quinoa and vegetable broth to a boil then reduce to a simmer. Cover, and allow quinoa to cook until liquid is absorbed, about 15 minutes. Remove from heat, fluff quinoa with a fork, and allow to stand another 5 minutes.

2. Stir in the balsamic vinegar, olive oil, lemon juice, and salt, then add remaining ingredients, gently tossing to combine. Serve hot.

PER SERVING Calories: 522 | Fat: 31g | Sodium: 1,168mg | Fiber: 6g | Protein: 11g

Quinoa and Fresh Herb Stuffing

Substitute dried herbs if you have to, but fresh is best in this untraditional stuffing recipe.

INGREDIENTS | SERVES 6

1 yellow onion, chopped
2 ribs celery, diced
¼ cup vegan margarine
1 teaspoon chopped fresh rosemary
2 teaspoons chopped fresh marjoram
1½ tablespoons chopped fresh thyme
1 tablespoon chopped fresh sage
6 slices dried bread, cubed
1¼ cups vegetable broth
2 cups cooked quinoa
¾ teaspoon salt
½ teaspoon pepper

1. Preheat oven to 400°F.

2. Heat onion and celery in vegan margarine and cook until soft, about 6–8 minutes. Add fresh herbs and heat for another minute, just until fragrant.

3. Remove from heat and add bread, combining well. Add vegetable broth to moisten bread; you may need a bit more or less than 1¼ cups.

4. Add cooked quinoa, salt, and pepper, and combine well.

5. Cover and bake for 30 minutes.

PER SERVING Calories: 220 | Fat: 10g | Sodium: 739mg | Fiber: 3g | Protein: 5g

Stuffed-Up Stuffing

Stuffing works best with dried bread to better absorb all that flavor and moisture. Leave your bread out for a couple days, or lightly toast in a 275°F oven for 20 minutes on each side. For a more textured stuffing, add in ¾ cup chopped dried apricots, ¾ cup chopped nuts (walnuts, cashews, or pecans), or sauté some mushrooms or a grated carrot along the with onions and celery.

Orange and Raisin Curried Couscous

Another whole-grain salad or pilaf that can be served either hot or cold.
Cranberries, currants, or dates may be used instead of raisins.

INGREDIENTS | SERVES 4

2 cups water or vegetable broth

1½ cups couscous

½ cup orange juice

1 onion, chopped

2 tablespoons olive oil

½ teaspoon coriander powder

1 teaspoon curry powder

2 scallions, chopped

¾ cup golden raisins

¾ cup sliced almonds or pine nuts

What Is Couscous?

Couscous isn't technically a whole grain but rather whole-wheat semolina pasta. But its small size and grainy texture gives it more in common with whole grains than pasta.

1. Bring water or vegetable broth to a boil. Add couscous and remove from heat. Stir in orange juice, cover, and allow to sit for 15 minutes until most of the liquid is absorbed and couscous is soft.

2. Heat onion in olive oil for a minute or 2, then add spices and heat for 1 more minute until fragrant.

3. Combine couscous with spices, and add scallions, raisins, and nuts.

PER SERVING Calories: 520 | Fat: 16g | Sodium: 483mg | Fiber: 7g | Protein: 14g

Black Bean and Barley Taco Salad

Adding barley to a taco salad gives a bit of a whole-grain and fiber boost to this low-fat recipe.

INGREDIENTS | SERVES 2

1 15-ounce can black beans, drained

½ teaspoon cumin

½ teaspoon oregano

2 tablespoons lime juice

1 teaspoon hot chili sauce (optional)

1 cup cooked barley

1 head iceberg lettuce, shredded

¾ cup salsa

Handful tortilla chips, crumbled

2 tablespoons vegan Italian dressing (optional)

1. Mash together the beans, cumin, oregano, lime juice, and hot sauce until beans are mostly mashed, then combine with barley.

2. Layer lettuce with beans and barley and top with salsa and tortilla chips. Drizzle with Italian dressing.

PER SERVING Calories: 516 | Fat: 5g | Sodium: 929mg | Fiber: 26g | Protein: 25g

Quinoa "Mac 'n' Cheese" Casserole

Craving mac and cheese but don't want the carbs, or the cheese, for that matter?
Try this filling whole-grain substitute.

INGREDIENTS | SERVES 4

1½ cups quinoa
3 cups vegetable broth
1 onion, chopped
3 cloves garlic, minced
2 tablespoons olive oil
1 bunch broccoli, diced small
1 large tomato, diced
1 tablespoon flour
¾ cup soy milk
½ teaspoon sea salt
1 cup shredded vegan cheese
½ teaspoon dried parsley
1 cup seasoned bread crumbs (optional)
¼ teaspoon nutmeg (optional)

What Is Quinoa?

Pronounced "keen-wa," this is actually a seed disguised as a whole grain. Quinoa has been a staple food in South America since ancient times, as it's one of the few crops that thrives in the high altitudes of the Andes. Look for these tiny round seeds in the bulk food bin or baking aisle of natural-foods stores, or in the natural-foods section of a well-stocked supermarket.

1. Preheat oven to 350°F.

2. Simmer quinoa in vegetable broth, covered, until liquid is absorbed, about 15 minutes.

3. In a medium skillet or saucepan, heat onion and garlic in olive oil and add broccoli and tomato. Heat, stirring frequently, for 3–4 minutes.

4. Add flour, stirring to coat well, then add soy milk and sea salt, stirring until thick, about 3 minutes.

5. Combine quinoa with broccoli and soy milk mixture and half of the vegan cheese in a large casserole dish. Sprinkle the other half of the cheese on top, along with parsley and optional bread crumbs and nutmeg.

6. Bake for 10–12 minutes, or until cheese is melted.

PER SERVING Calories: 473 | Fat: 16g | Sodium: 1,269mg | Fiber: 10g | Protein: 19g

Spiced Couscous Salad with Bell Pepper and Zucchini

A full meal for lunch or dinner, or a side salad, depending on how hungry you are!

INGREDIENTS | SERVES 4

2 cups vegetable broth
2 cups couscous
1 teaspoon cumin
½ teaspoon turmeric
½ teaspoon paprika
¼ teaspoon cayenne pepper
1 tablespoon lemon juice
2 zucchini, sliced
1 red bell pepper, chopped
1 yellow bell pepper, chopped
3 cloves garlic, minced
2 tablespoons olive oil
2 tablespoons chopped fresh parsley
Salt and pepper to taste

1. Combine vegetable broth and couscous and bring to a boil. Add cumin, turmeric, paprika, and cayenne pepper, and stir to combine.

2. Turn off heat, cover, and allow to sit for at least 15 minutes, until couscous is soft and liquid is absorbed. Fluff couscous with a fork and add lemon juice.

3. Sauté zucchini, bell pepper, and garlic in olive oil just until soft; combine with couscous.

4. Add parsley, taste, and season lightly with salt and pepper.

PER SERVING Calories: 441 | Fat: 8g | Sodium: 495mg | Fiber: 7g | Protein: 14g

Baked Millet Patties

Serve these nutty whole-grain patties topped with Mushroom Gravy (p. 26),
You Are a Goddess Dressing (p. 69), or another dressing or sauce.

INGREDIENTS | YIELDS 8 PATTIES

1½ cups cooked millet
½ cup tahini
1 cup bread crumbs
1 teaspoon parsley
¾ teaspoon garlic powder
½ teaspoon onion powder (optional)
⅓ teaspoon salt

For the Birds?

In the United States, millet is most frequently spotted being used as a bird-friendly rice alternative at weddings and as a filler in bird feeders. But it's also a healthy whole grain used in one form or another across much of Africa. With a longer cooking time and harder texture than other grains, it tends to be less popular than other whole-grain options, but this recipe uses it well.

1. Preheat oven to 350°F.

2. Combine all ingredients together in a bowl, mashing to mix well.

3. Use your hands to press firmly into patties, about 1 inch thick, and place on a baking sheet.

4. Bake for 10–12 minutes on each side.

PER 1 PATTY Calories: 285 | Fat: 10g | Sodium: 214mg | Fiber: 5g | Protein: 9g

Lemon Cilantro Couscous

*This flavorful couscous is a light and easy side dish, or top it off with
a vegetable stew or some stir-fried or roasted veggies.*

INGREDIENTS | SERVES 4

2 cups vegetable broth
1 cup couscous
⅓ cup lemon juice
½ cup chopped fresh cilantro
¼ teaspoon sea salt, or to taste

1. Bring vegetable broth to a simmer and add couscous. Cover and let stand for 10 minutes, until soft, then fluff with a fork.

2. Stir in lemon juice and cilantro, and season generously with sea salt.

PER SERVING Calories: 174 | Fat: 0g | Sodium: 621mg | Fiber: 2g | Protein: 6g

Tropical Breakfast Couscous

This recipe is like having a piña colada for breakfast. What could be better?
Stick a flower behind your ear, and enjoy this breakfast barefoot in the sun.

INGREDIENTS | SERVES 2

1 cup coconut milk
1 cup pineapple juice or orange juice
1 cup couscous
½ teaspoon vanilla
2 tablespoons maple syrup or agave nectar
Sliced fresh fruit (optional)

1. In a small saucepan, heat coconut milk and juice until just about to simmer. Do not boil.

2. Add couscous and heat for 1 minute. Stir in vanilla, cover, and turn off heat. Allow to sit, covered, for 5 minutes, until couscous is cooked.

3. Fluff couscous with a fork and stir in maple syrup. Garnish with fresh fruit.

PER SERVING Calories: 665 | Fat: 25g | Sodium: 28mg | Fiber: 5g | Protein: 14g

Couscous for Breakfast

Couscous is an excellent choice for breakfast, as it is much quicker to cook than other grains and doesn't need to be watched. Boil some water, add your couscous, turn off the stove, and cover the couscous; then go brush your teeth and tie your shoes. By the time you finish, breakfast is ready!

Confetti "Rice" with TVP

If the kids like Mexican rice, try this whole-grain version with barley and TVP.

INGREDIENTS | SERVES 6

1 onion, chopped
2 cloves garlic, minced
2 tablespoons olive oil
1 cup barley
1 15-ounce can diced tomatoes
2 cups vegetable broth
1 teaspoon chili powder
½ teaspoon cumin
¾ cup TVP
1 cup hot water or vegetable broth
1 tablespoon soy sauce
1 cup frozen veggie mix (peas, corn, and carrots)
1 teaspoon parsley
½ teaspoon salt

1. In a large skillet, heat the onion and garlic in olive oil for a minute or 2, then add barley. Toast for 1 minute, stirring constantly.

2. Add canned tomatoes including liquid, vegetable broth, and chili powder and cumin. Cook until barley is almost soft, about 15 minutes.

3. While barley is cooking, combine TVP with hot water or vegetable broth and soy sauce and allow to sit for 8–10 minutes until TVP is rehydrated. Drain any excess liquid.

4. When barley is almost done cooking, add rehydrated TVP, veggies, parsley, and salt. Heat for another 5 minutes, or until done.

PER SERVING Calories: 258 | Fat: 5g | Sodium: 628mg | Fiber: 11g | Protein: 12g

Turn It into Tacos

Use this "meaty" Mexican "rice" as a base for burritos or crunchy tacos instead of meat, along with some shredded lettuce, vegan cheese, and nondairy sour cream, or, serve alongside some cooked beans for a healthy Mexican meal.

Summer Squash and Barley Risotto

A smooth and saucy risotto with barley instead of rice. Fresh asparagus instead of squash would also be lovely in this untraditional risotto. Top it off with some vegan Parmesan cheese, if you happen to have some on hand.

INGREDIENTS | SERVES 4

4 cloves garlic, minced
½ onion, diced
1 zucchini, chopped
1 yellow squash, chopped
2 tablespoons olive oil
1 cup pearled barley
3–4 cups vegetable broth
2 tablespoons chopped fresh basil
2 tablespoons nutritional yeast
2 tablespoons vegan margarine
Salt and pepper, to taste

1. Sauté garlic, onions, zucchini, and yellow squash in olive oil until soft, about 3–4 minutes. Add barley and heat for 1 minute, stirring to coat well with oil and to prevent burning.

2. Add 1 cup vegetable broth and bring to a simmer. Cover and allow to cook for a few minutes until almost absorbed.

3. Add another cup of vegetable broth and continue cooking until barley is soft, about 20–25 minutes, adding more vegetable broth as needed.

4. When barley is done, add an additional ¼ cup vegetable broth and basil, stirring well to combine just until heated through.

5. Stir in nutritional yeast and vegan margarine and season generously with salt and pepper, to taste.

PER SERVING Calories: 323 | Fat: 13g | Sodium: 797mg | Fiber: 9g | Protein: 7g

Barley Baked Beans

If you've got a slow cooker, you can dump all the ingredients in and cook it on a medium setting for about 6 hours.

INGREDIENTS | SERVES 8

2 cups cooked barley

2 15-ounce cans pinto or navy beans, drained

1 onion, diced

1 28-ounce can crushed or diced tomatoes

½ cup water

¼ cup brown sugar

⅓ cup barbecue sauce

2 tablespoons molasses

2 teaspoons mustard powder

1 teaspoon garlic powder

1 teaspoon salt

1. Preheat oven to 300°F.

2. Combine all ingredients in a large casserole or baking dish. Cover, and bake for 2 hours, stirring occasionally.

3. Uncover and bake for 15 more minutes or until thick and saucy.

PER SERVING Calories: 224 | Fat: 1g | Sodium: 849mg | Fiber: 9g | Protein: 8g

Millet and Butternut Squash Casserole

Slightly sweet, slightly savory, top this millet medley with some Easy Fried Tofu (p. 242) to make it a main meal.

INGREDIENTS | SERVES 4

1 cup millet
2 cups vegetable broth
1 small butternut squash, peeled, seeded, and chopped
½ cup water
1 teaspoon curry powder
½ cup orange juice
2 tablespoons nutritional yeast
½ teaspoon sea salt

1. In a small pot, cook millet in vegetable broth until done, about 20–30 minutes.

2. In a separate pan, heat butternut squash in water. Cover and allow to cook for 10–15 minutes until squash is almost soft. Remove lid and drain extra water.

3. Combine millet with squash over low heat and add curry powder and orange juice, stirring to combine well. Heat for 3–4 more minutes, add nutritional yeast, and season with sea salt.

PER SERVING Calories: 242 | Fat: 2g | Sodium: 767mg | Fiber: 6g | Protein: 7g

Vegetarian "Beef" and Barley Stew

*Classic and comforting, you can't go wrong with this warming
"beef" and barley stew on a cold night.*

INGREDIENTS | SERVES 6

1 onion, chopped

2 ribs celery, chopped

1 carrot, chopped

1 green bell pepper, chopped

2 tablespoons olive oil

1 cup water

2½ cups tomato or mixed vegetable
juice

⅓ cup barley

1½ teaspoons chili powder

1½ teaspoons parsley or Italian
seasoning

2 bay leaves

4 veggie burgers, crumbled

Salt and pepper, to taste

1. Heat the onion, celery, carrot, and bell pepper in olive oil in a large soup or stock pot, just until veggies are almost soft, about 4–5 minutes.

2. Add water, tomato juice, and barley, stirring well to combine, then add chili powder, parsley or Italian seasoning, and bay leaves.

3. Cover and cook over medium-low heat for 20 minutes. Add veggie burgers, and cook for another 5 minutes, uncovered, or until barley is soft.

4. Season with salt and pepper to taste; remove bay leaves before serving.

PER SERVING Calories: 187 | Fat: 7g | Sodium: 480mg | Fiber: 5g | Protein: 13g

Bean and Barley Stew

TVP or a store-bought meat substitute could work in this stew, but the chewiness of the veggie burgers provides a nice complement to the equally chewy barley. If you don't have any of these on hand, add some beans instead for a thick and hearty meal.

Quinoa and Hummus Sandwich Wrap

Lunch is the perfect time to fill up on whole grains. If you've got leftover tabbouleh (p. 175), use that in place of the cooked quinoa.

INGREDIENTS | SERVES 1

1 tortilla or flavored wrap, warmed

3 tablespoons hummus

⅓ cup cooked quinoa

½ teaspoon lemon juice

2 teaspoons Italian or vinaigrette salad dressing

1 roasted red pepper, sliced into strips

¼ cup sprouts

1. Spread a warmed tortilla or wrap with a layer of hummus, then quinoa, and drizzle with lemon juice and salad dressing.

2. Layer red pepper and sprouts on top, and wrap.

PER SERVING Calories: 332 | Fat: 12g | Sodium: 627mg | Fiber: 6g | Protein: 11g

Barley Pilaf with Edamame and Roasted Red Peppers

Don't forget! Freshly ground sea salt and hand-cracked pepper will give the best flavor to all your recipes, including this one. Serve chilled like a salad, or heat the edamame lightly first for a warmed and high-protein pilaf.

INGREDIENTS | SERVES 6

2 cups frozen shelled edamame, thawed and drained

2 cups cooked barley

½ cup chopped roasted red peppers

⅔ cup green peas

⅔ cup corn (fresh, canned, or frozen)

1½ tablespoons Dijon mustard

2 tablespoons lemon or lime juice

¾ teaspoon garlic powder

2 tablespoons olive oil

Salt and pepper, to taste

¼ cup chopped fresh cilantro

1 avocado, diced (optional)

1. Combine the edamame, barley, peppers, peas, and corn in a large bowl.

2. In a separate small bowl, whisk together the mustard, lemon or lime juice, garlic powder, and olive oil, then drizzle over barley mixture, tossing gently to coat well.

3. Season generously with salt and pepper and toss lightly with cilantro and avocado.

PER SERVING Calories: 190 | Fat: 4g | Sodium: 100mg | Fiber: 9g | Protein: 9g

Whole-Grain Bean Salads

If you like bean salads, try adding in a portion of cooked barley or quinoa to your favorite recipe. Stretch leftover bean salads by tossing in some extra dressing and cooked whole grains.

Quinoa "Tapioca" Pudding

Instead of tapioca pudding or baked rice pudding, try this whole-grain version made with quinoa. Healthy enough to eat for breakfast, but sweet enough for dessert, too.

INGREDIENTS | SERVES 4

1 cup quinoa
2 cups water
2 cups soy milk or soy cream
2 tablespoons maple syrup or brown rice syrup
1 teaspoon cornstarch
2 bananas, sliced thin
½ teaspoon vanilla
⅓ cup raisins
Dash cinnamon or nutmeg (optional)

1. In a medium saucepan, simmer quinoa in water over medium heat, covered, stirring frequently, for 10–15 minutes, until done and water is absorbed.

2. Reduce heat to medium low and stir in soy milk, maple syrup or brown rice syrup, cornstarch, and bananas, combining well. Heat, stirring constantly, for 6–8 minutes, until bananas are soft and pudding has thickened.

3. Stir in vanilla and raisins while still hot and sprinkle with a dash of cinnamon or nutmeg, to taste.

PER SERVING Calories: 325 | Fat: 5g | Sodium: 67mg | Fiber: 5g | Protein: 11g

Chocolate Peanut Butter Breakfast Quinoa

Chocolate and peanut butter is a flavor combination from heaven. Even with a bit of cocoa and sweetener, this breakfast cereal is still much more nutritious than the sugar-packed, processed, and refined cardboard-box brands in the supermarket.

INGREDIENTS | SERVES 1

½ cup quinoa
1½ cups soy milk
2 tablespoons peanut butter
1½ tablespoons cocoa
1½ tablespoons maple syrup or brown rice syrup (optional)

1. Combine the quinoa and soy milk over medium-low heat. Cover and cook for 15 minutes or until quinoa is done, stirring frequently.

2. While still hot, stir in peanut butter, cocoa, and sweetener.

PER SERVING Calories: 668 | Fat: 28g | Sodium: 337mg | Fiber: 12g | Protein: 31g

Try Quinoa Flakes

If you discover you like eating quinoa for breakfast, try quinoa flakes instead of whole quinoa. The flakes are quicker to cook, like oatmeal, but provide the same protein and amino acids that make quinoa such a great choice for vegans.

Couscous and Bean Pilaf

A quick side or lunch that can be served hot or cold.
With a few veggies tossed in, this could also be a full meal.

INGREDIENTS | SERVES 4

2 cups water or vegetable broth

2 cups couscous

2 tablespoons olive oil

2 tablespoons red wine vinegar

½ teaspoon crushed red pepper flakes

1 15-ounce can great northern or cannellini beans, drained

2 tablespoons minced pimiento peppers

2 tablespoons chopped fresh parsley

Salt and pepper to taste

1. Bring the water or vegetable broth to a simmer and add couscous. Cover, turn off heat, and allow to sit for at least 15 minutes to cook couscous. Fluff with a fork.

2. Whisk together the olive oil, red wine vinegar, and red pepper flakes and toss with cooked couscous.

3. Combine beans, pimiento peppers, and parsley with couscous, tossing gently to combine. Season generously with salt and pepper.

PER SERVING Calories: 509 | Fat: 8g | Sodium: 32mg | Fiber: 10g | Protein: 19g

Barley and Bell Pepper Chili

*With all the flavors and ingredients of traditional vegetarian chili,
this recipe just adds a bit of whole-grain goodness to the mix.*

INGREDIENTS | SERVES 6

3 cloves garlic, minced
1 onion, chopped
1 green bell pepper, chopped
1 red bell pepper, chopped
2 tablespoons olive oil
½ cup barley
2½ cups water or vegetable broth
1 15-ounce can diced tomatoes
1 15-ounce can black beans or kidney beans
2 tablespoons chili powder
1 teaspoon cumin
½ teaspoon oregano
2 tablespoons chopped fresh cilantro (optional)

1. In a large stock pot, heat the garlic, onion, and bell peppers in olive oil for 2–3 minutes. Add barley and toast, stirring frequently, for just 1 minute.

2. Reduce heat to medium low and add water or vegetable broth, tomatoes, beans, chili powder, cumin, and oregano. Bring to a slow simmer, cover, and heat for at least 35 minutes, stirring occasionally.

3. Uncover and adjust seasonings to taste, then top with fresh chopped cilantro.

PER SERVING Calories: 241 | Fat: 6g | Sodium: 290mg | Fiber: 12g | Protein: 10g

Whole-Grain Chili

Tossing in some cooked whole grains is a great way to stretch out your leftover chili, or just to add some healthy fiber and a touch of homemade goodness to canned chili or even canned baked beans. Although barley has a great texture for pairing with beans, leftover quinoa or millet would also work.

Fruited Fall Quinoa

Cranberries and apricots make a sweet combo; add some sage and thyme to give it some more warming flavors and it would make an excellent Thanksgiving entrée.

INGREDIENTS | SERVES 4

1 cup quinoa
2 cups apple juice
1 cup water
½ onion, diced
2 ribs celery, diced
2 tablespoons vegan margarine
½ teaspoon nutmeg
½ teaspoon cinnamon
¼ teaspoon cloves
½ cup dried cranberries
½ cup dried apricots, chopped
1 teaspoon parsley
¼ teaspoon salt

1. In a large pot, combine quinoa, apple juice, and water. Cover and simmer for 15 minutes or until done.

2. In a large skillet, heat onion and celery in margarine, stirring frequently, until soft.

3. Over low heat, combine onions and celery with quinoa and add remaining ingredients, tossing gently to combine. Heat for 3–4 more minutes.

PER SERVING Calories: 360 | Fat: 9g | Sodium: 252mg | Fiber: 6g | Protein: 7g

Bell Peppers Stuffed with Couscous

Baked stuffed peppers are always a hit with those who appreciate presentation, and this recipe takes very little effort.

INGREDIENTS | SERVES 4

4 cups water or vegetable broth
3 cups couscous
2 tablespoons olive oil
2 tablespoons lemon or lime juice
1 cup frozen peas or corn, thawed
2 green onions, sliced
½ teaspoon cumin
½ teaspoon chili powder
4 green bell peppers

1. Preheat oven to 350°F.

2. Bring water or vegetable broth to a boil and add couscous. Cover, turn off heat, and let sit for 10–15 minutes until couscous is cooked. Fluff with a fork.

3. Combine couscous with olive oil, lemon or lime juice, peas or corn, green onions, cumin, and chili powder.

4. Cut the tops off the bell peppers and remove seeds.

5. Stuff couscous into bell peppers and place the tops back on, using a toothpick to secure if needed.

6. Transfer to a baking dish and bake for 15 minutes.

PER SERVING Calories: 602 | Fat: 8g | Sodium: 62mg | Fiber: 10g | Protein: 20g

Chapter 10

Miscellaneous Mains

Black Bean and Butternut Squash Chili

Squash is an excellent addition to vegetarian chili in this Southwestern-style dish.

INGREDIENTS | SERVES 4

1 onion, chopped

3 cloves garlic, minced

2 tablespoons oil

1 medium butternut squash, chopped into chunks

2 15-ounce cans black beans, drained

1 28-ounce can stewed or diced tomatoes, undrained

¾ cup water or vegetable broth

1 tablespoon chili powder

1 teaspoon cumin

¼ teaspoon cayenne pepper, or to taste

½ teaspoon salt

2 tablespoons chopped fresh cilantro (optional)

1. In a large stock pot, sauté onion and garlic in oil until soft, about 4 minutes.

2. Reduce heat and add remaining ingredients, except cilantro.

3. Cover and simmer for 25 minutes. Uncover and simmer another 5 minutes. Top with fresh cilantro just before serving.

PER SERVING Calories: 455 | Fat: 9g | Sodium: 1,247mg | Fiber: 25g | Protein: 23g

Caramelized Onion and Barbecue Sauce Pizza

Sweet onions and barbecue sauce are the perfect pair in this tofu-topped pizza.

INGREDIENTS | SERVES 4

⅔ cup barbecue sauce
1 vegan pizza crust
2 red onions, chopped
3 tablespoons olive oil
1 block tofu, diced small
½ cup diced pineapple
⅓ teaspoon garlic powder
Salt and pepper, to taste

Vegan Pizza

More and more pizzerias are offering vegan cheese, but cheeseless pizza is more delicious than you might think. When ordering out, fill your pizza with tons of extra toppings, and sprinkle it with nutritional yeast if you want that cheesy flavor, or make some Dairy-Free Ranch Dressing (p. 61) to dip it in.

1. Preheat oven to 450°F. Spread barbecue sauce on pizza crust.

2. Heat onions in olive oil for 2–3 minutes, stirring occasionally. Add tofu, and sauté until tofu is lightly crisped and onions are soft and caramelized.

3. Top pizza with tofu, onions, and pineapple. Sprinkle with garlic powder and a generous amount of salt and pepper.

4. Bake for 12–14 minutes, or according to instructions on pizza dough.

PER SERVING Calories: 461 | Fat: 17g | Sodium: 1,009mg | Fiber: 3g | Protein: 14g

Breaded Eggplant "Parmesan"

*Slowly baking these breaded eggplant cutlets brings out the best flavor,
but they can also be pan fried in a bit of oil.*

INGREDIENTS | SERVES 4

1 medium eggplant
½ teaspoon salt
¾ cup flour
1 teaspoon garlic powder
⅔ cup soy milk
Egg replacer for 2 eggs
1½ cups bread crumbs
2 tablespoons Italian seasoning
¼ cup nutritional yeast
1½ cups marinara sauce

1. Slice eggplant into ¾-inch-thick slices and sprinkle with salt. Allow to sit for 10 minutes. Gently pat dry to remove extra moisture.

2. In a shallow bowl or pie tin, combine flour and garlic powder. In a separate bowl, whisk together the soy milk and egg replacer. In a third bowl, combine the bread crumbs, Italian seasoning, and nutritional yeast.

3. Coat each eggplant slice with flour, then carefully dip in the soy milk mixture, then coat with the bread crumb mixture and place in a lightly greased casserole dish.

4. Bake for 20–25 minutes, then top with marinara sauce, and return to oven until sauce is hot, about 5 minutes.

PER SERVING Calories: 409 | Fat: 6g | Sodium: 1,009mg | Fiber: 11g | Protein: 14g

Basic Creamy Polenta

Whether for breakfast, lunch, or dinner, entrée or side, polenta is versatile, simple, and great for families on a budget. This is a basic recipe, so add spices, if you prefer, or a bit of soy milk for a creamier texture.

INGREDIENTS | SERVES 4

6½ cups water
2 cups cornmeal
3 tablespoons vegan margarine
1½ teaspoons garlic powder
¼ cup nutritional yeast
½ teaspoon salt

Properties of Polenta

Homemade polenta can be eaten as it is, all soft and creamy, or, transfer it to a loaf pan, smoothing the top with the back of a spoon. Chill it in the refrigerator, and it will firm up into a loaf in about an hour or two. You can then slice it and pan fry it in a bit of oil, or just reheat the loaf in your oven. The stuff you buy in a tube at the store is already cooked, so all you need to do is fry it up or heat it in the oven.

1. Bring the water to a boil, then slowly add cornmeal, stirring to combine.

2. Reduce heat to low, and cook for 20 minutes, stirring frequently and scraping the bottom of the pot to prevent sticking and burning. Polenta is done when it is thick and sticky.

3. Stir in margarine, garlic powder, nutritional yeast, and salt.

PER SERVING Calories: 463 | Fat: 18g | Sodium: 545mg | Fiber: 4g | Protein: 8g

Italian Veggie and Pasta Casserole

Veggies and pasta are baked into an Italian-spiced casserole with a crumbly topping.
Add in a handful of TVP crumbles or some kidney beans if you want a protein boost.

INGREDIENTS | SERVES 6

1 16-ounce package pasta (use a medium pasta like bow ties, corkscrews, or small shells)
1 onion, chopped
3 zucchini, sliced
1 red bell pepper, chopped
4 cloves garlic, minced
2 tablespoons olive oil
1 28-ounce can diced tomatoes
¾ cup corn kernels
1 teaspoon parsley
1 teaspoon basil
½ teaspoon oregano
½ teaspoon crushed red pepper flakes
¼ teaspoon black pepper
1 cup bread crumbs
½ cup grated vegan cheese

1. Cook pasta according to package instructions, drain well, and layer in a baking dish.

2. Preheat oven to 425°F.

3. Sauté onion, zucchini, bell pepper, and garlic in olive oil just until soft, about 3–4 minutes. Add tomatoes, corn, parsley, basil, oregano, and crushed red pepper. Simmer for 8–10 minutes and season with black pepper.

4. Cover pasta with zucchini and tomato mixture. Sprinkle with bread crumbs and vegan cheese.

5. Bake for 10–12 minutes.

PER SERVING Calories: 500 | Fat: 8g | Sodium: 386mg | Fiber: 8g | Protein: 18g

Tofu and Portobello Enchiladas

Turn up the heat by adding some fresh minced or canned chilies. If you're addicted to vegan cheese, add a handful of grated cheese to the filling as well as on top.

INGREDIENTS | SERVES 4

1 block firm tofu, diced small
5 portobello mushrooms, chopped
1 onion, diced
3 cloves garlic, minced
2 tablespoons oil
2 teaspoons chili powder
½ cup sliced black olives
1 15-ounce can enchilada sauce
8–10 flour tortillas
½ cup vegan cheese (optional)

Vegetable Enchiladas

Omit the mushrooms and grate a couple carrots and zucchini to use in the filling instead. They'll bake quickly when grated, so no need to precook.

1. Preheat oven to 350°F.

2. In a large skillet, heat the tofu, mushrooms, onion, and garlic in oil until tofu is just lightly sautéed, about 4–5 minutes. Add chili powder and heat for 1 more minute, stirring to coat well.

3. Remove from heat and add black olives and ⅓ cup enchilada sauce, and combine well.

4. Spread a thin layer of enchilada sauce in the bottom of a baking pan or casserole dish.

5. Place about ¼ cup of the tofu and mushrooms in each flour tortilla and roll, placing snugly in the baking dish. Top with remaining enchilada sauce, coating the tops of each tortilla well.

6. Sprinkle with vegan cheese if desired, and bake for 25–30 minutes.

PER SERVING Calories: 516 | Fat: 18g | Sodium: 1,582mg | Fiber: 6g | Protein: 21g

Pumpkin and Lentil Curry

Red lentils complement the pumpkin and coconut best in this salty sweet curry, but any kind you have on hand will do. Look for frozen chopped squash to cut the preparation time.

INGREDIENTS | SERVES 3

1 yellow onion, chopped

2 cups chopped pumpkin or butternut squash

2 tablespoons olive oil

1 tablespoon curry powder

1 teaspoon cumin

2 small red chilies, minced, or ½ teaspoon red pepper flakes

2 whole cloves

3 cups water or vegetable broth

1 cup lentils

2 tomatoes, chopped

8–10 fresh green beans, trimmed and chopped

¾ cup coconut milk

1. Sauté onion and pumpkin in olive oil until onions are soft, about 4 minutes. Add curry powder, cumin, chilies, and cloves, and toast for 1 minute, stirring frequently.

2. Reduce heat slightly and add water or vegetable broth and lentils. Cover and cook for about 10–12 minutes, stirring occasionally.

3. Uncover and add tomatoes, green beans, and coconut milk, stirring well to combine. Heat uncovered for 4–5 more minutes, just until tomatoes and beans are cooked.

4. Serve over rice or whole grains.

PER SERVING Calories: 430 | Fat: 16g | Sodium: 26mg | Fiber: 23g | Protein: 20g

Black and Green Veggie Burritos

Black bean burritos filled with zucchini or yellow summer squash. Just add in the fixings—salsa, avocado slices, some nondairy sour cream—the works!

INGREDIENTS | SERVES 4

1 onion, chopped
2 zucchini or yellow squash, cut into thin strips
1 bell pepper, any color, chopped
2 tablespoons olive oil
½ teaspoon oregano
½ teaspoon cumin
1 15-ounce can black beans, drained
1 4-ounce can green chilies
1 cup cooked rice
4 large flour tortillas, warmed

Gluten-Free Bean Burritos

If you're gluten-free or just want an extra protein and nutrition boost, use a cooked grain other than rice in these burritos and shop for a gluten-free flatbread to wrap it up in. Quinoa in particular works well in burritos, as it is lighter than other grains.

1. Heat onion, zucchini, and bell pepper in olive oil until vegetables are soft, about 4–5 minutes.

2. Reduce heat to low and add oregano, cumin, black beans, and chilies, combining well. Cook, stirring, until well combined and heated through.

3. Place ¼ cup rice in the center of each flour tortilla and top with the bean mixture. Fold the bottom of the tortilla up, then snugly wrap one side, then the other.

4. Serve as is, or bake in a 350°F oven for 15 minutes for a crispy burrito.

PER SERVING Calories: 377 | Fat: 10g | Sodium: 554mg | Fiber: 13g | Protein: 15g

Polenta and Chili Casserole

Using canned chili and thawed frozen veggies, you can get this quick one-pot casserole meal in the oven in just about 10 minutes.

INGREDIENTS | SERVES 4

3 cans vegetarian chili (or about 6 cups, homemade)
2 cups diced veggie mixture, any kind
1 cup cornmeal
2½ cups water
2 tablespoons vegan margarine
1 tablespoon chili powder

1. Combine vegetarian chili and vegetables and spread in the bottom of a lightly greased casserole dish.

2. Preheat oven to 375°F.

3. Over low heat, combine cornmeal and water in a saucepan. Simmer, stirring frequently, for 10 minutes. Stir in vegan margarine.

4. Spread cornmeal mixture over chili and sprinkle the top with chili powder.

5. Bake uncovered for 20–25 minutes.

PER SERVING Calories: 546 | Fat: 8g | Sodium: 1,298mg | Fiber: 19g | Protein: 23g

The Easiest Black Bean Burger Recipe in the World

Veggie burgers are notorious for falling apart. If you're sick of crumbly burgers, try this simple method for making black bean patties. It's 100 percent guaranteed to stick together.

INGREDIENTS | YIELDS 6 PATTIES

1 15-ounce can black beans, drained
3 tablespoons minced onions
1 teaspoon salt
1½ teaspoons garlic powder
2 teaspoons parsley
1 teaspoon chili powder
⅔ cup flour
Oil for pan frying

Veggie Burger Tips

Although this recipe is foolproof, if you have trouble with your veggie burgers crumbling, try adding egg replacer to bind the ingredients, and chill the mixture before forming into patties. Veggie burger patties can be grilled, baked, or pan fried, but they do tend to dry out a bit in the oven. Not a problem, just smother with extra ketchup!

1. Process the black beans in a blender or food processor until halfway mashed, or mash with a fork.

2. Add minced onions, salt, garlic powder, parsley, and chili powder and mash to combine.

3. Add flour, a bit at a time, again mashing together to combine. You may need a little bit more or less than ⅔ cup. Beans should stick together completely.

4. Form into patties and pan fry in a bit of oil for 2–3 minutes on each side. Patties will appear to be done on the outside while still a bit mushy on the inside, so fry them a few minutes longer than you think they need.

PER 1 PATTY Calories: 210 | Fat: 8g | Sodium: 559mg | Fiber: 7g | Protein: 8g

Cilantro Potato and Pea Curry

A simple curried potato recipe with peas. Turn up the heat by adding in some fresh chilies or cayenne pepper, or sweeten it for kids by adding some pineapple.

INGREDIENTS | SERVES 4

3 cloves garlic
¼ cup water
¼ cup tomato paste
1 teaspoon fresh ginger, minced
2 tablespoons curry powder
1 teaspoon sugar (optional)
2 tablespoons soy sauce
½ onion, chopped
1 tablespoon sesame oil
4 medium potatoes, chopped
2 tablespoons olive oil
1½ cups frozen green peas, thawed
1 14-ounce can coconut milk
3 tablespoons chopped fresh cilantro

1. Combine garlic, water, tomato paste, ginger, curry powder, sugar, soy sauce, onion, and sesame oil in a blender or food processor and process until smooth.

2. In a large skillet, sauté potatoes in olive oil for 3–4 minutes, then add spice mix and peas and simmer, covered, for 10–12 minutes, stirring occasionally.

3. Add coconut milk and simmer for another 5–6 minutes, stirring well to combine.

4. Remove from heat and add fresh cilantro.

PER SERVING Calories: 505 | Fat: 32g | Sodium: 550mg | Fiber: 9g | Protein: 10g

Sweet Stuffed Butternut Squash

For a Thanksgiving side dish or even an entrée that everyone will "ooh" and "ahh" over, try this stuffed squash. It has a beautiful presentation, but is super easy to prepare. Use raisins if you don't like cranberries.

INGREDIENTS | SERVES 4

2 small butternut squash
½ cup apple juice or orange juice (optional)
2 apples, diced
½ cup chopped pecans or walnuts
⅓ cup frozen or rehydrated dried cranberries
¼ cup maple syrup
2 tablespoons vegan margarine, melted
½ teaspoon cinnamon
¼ teaspoon nutmeg

How to Chop Squash

Even the finest chef armed with the sharpest knife may have a bit of trouble chopping squash. To make the task easier, pierce the squash several times with a fork and microwave for 3–4 minutes, just to soften it up a bit. Your knife will run through much easier afterward.

1. Preheat oven to 350°F. Chop the squash in half lengthwise and scrape out any stringy bits and seeds.

2. Pour apple or orange juice into a rimmed baking sheet, and place squash cut-side down. Roast in the oven for 20 minutes. Alternatively, you can microwave squash for 10 minutes. Remove from oven.

3. In a large bowl, combine the apples, nuts, and cranberries. Stir in maple syrup, melted vegan margarine, cinnamon, and nutmeg, tossing to coat well.

4. Stuff each half of squash with apple filling, piling any extra filling on top, and roast another 20–25 minutes.

PER SERVING Calories: 312 | Fat: 16g | Sodium: 89mg | Fiber: 7g | Protein: 3g

Black Bean Polenta Cakes with Salsa

All the flavors of the Southwest combine in this colorful confetti polenta loaf.
Pan fry individual slices, if you like, or just enjoy it as it is.

INGREDIENTS | SERVES 4

1 15-ounce can black beans, drained
6 cups water
2 cups cornmeal
½ red or yellow bell pepper, diced small
¾ teaspoon cumin
1 teaspoon chili powder
1 teaspoon garlic powder
¾ teaspoon oregano
½ teaspoon salt
½ teaspoon black pepper
2 tablespoons vegan margarine
Salsa

1. Place black beans in a bowl and mash with a fork until halfway mashed. Set aside.

2. Bring the water to a boil, then slowly add cornmeal, stirring to combine.

3. Reduce heat to low, and cook for 10 minutes, stirring frequently and scraping the bottom of the pot to prevent sticking and burning.

4. Add bell pepper, cumin, chili powder, garlic powder, oregano, salt, and pepper and stir well to combine. Continue to heat, stirring frequently for 8–10 more minutes.

5. Add vegan margarine and stir well to combine, then add black beans, combining well.

6. Gently press into a lightly greased loaf pan, smoothing the top with the back of a spoon. Chill until firm, at least 1 hour. Reheat, slice, and serve topped with prepared salsa.

PER SERVING Calories: 494 | Fat: 8g | Sodium: 633mg | Fiber: 13g | Protein: 16g

Portobello and Pepper Fajitas

Chopped seitan could take the place of the portobellos if you prefer,
or look for vegetarian "steak" or "chicken" strips.

INGREDIENTS | SERVES 4

2 tablespoons olive oil

2 large portobello mushrooms, cut into strips

1 green bell pepper, cut into strips

1 red bell pepper, cut into strips

1 onion, cut into strips

¾ teaspoon chili powder

¼ teaspoon cumin

Dash hot sauce (optional)

1 tablespoon chopped fresh cilantro (optional)

4 flour tortillas, warmed

Toppings: salsa, avocado, vegan sour cream, etc.

1. Heat olive oil in a large skillet and add mushrooms, bell peppers, and onions. Allow to cook for 3–5 minutes until vegetables are almost done.

2. Add chili powder, cumin, and hot sauce and stir to combine. Cook for 2–3 more minutes until mushrooms and peppers are soft. Remove from heat and stir in fresh cilantro.

3. Layer the mushrooms and peppers in flour tortillas and top with vegan sour cream, salsa, or fresh sliced avocados.

PER SERVING Calories: 243 | Fat: 11g | Sodium: 299mg | Fiber: 4g | Protein: 6g

Time-Saving Tips

Fresh is always best, but you can usually find frozen bell pepper strips ready to go in your grocery freezer, and a taco seasoning blend can take the place of the individual spices.

Savory Stuffed Acorn Squash

All the flavors of fall baked into one nutritious dish. Use fresh herbs if you have them, and breathe deep to savor the impossibly magical aromas coming from your kitchen.

INGREDIENTS | SERVES 4

2 acorn squash
1 teaspoon garlic powder
½ teaspoon salt
2 ribs celery, chopped
1 onion, diced
½ cup sliced mushrooms
2 tablespoons vegan margarine or oil
¼ cup chopped walnuts
1 tablespoon soy sauce
1 teaspoon parsley
½ teaspoon thyme
½ teaspoon sage
Salt and pepper, to taste
½ cup grated vegan cheese (optional)

1. Preheat oven to 350°F. Chop the squash in half lengthwise and scrape out any stringy bits and seeds.

2. Drizzle squash with garlic powder and salt, then place cut-side down on a baking sheet and bake for 30 minutes or until almost soft; remove from oven.

3. In a large skillet, heat celery, onion, and mushrooms in vegan margarine until soft, about 4–5 minutes.

4. Add walnuts, soy sauce, parsley, thyme, and sage, stirring to combine well, and season generously with salt and pepper. Heat for another minute or 2 until fragrant.

5. Fill squash with mushroom mixture and sprinkle with vegan cheese. Bake another 5–10 minutes until squash is soft.

PER SERVING Calories: 151 | Fat: 10g | Sodium: 616mg | Fiber: 3g | Protein: 3g

Easy Vegan Pizza Bagels

Need a quick lunch or after-school snack for the kids? Pizza bagels to the rescue!
For a real treat, shop for vegetarian "pepperoni" slices to top it off!

INGREDIENTS | SERVES 4

⅓ cup pizza sauce or tomato sauce
½ teaspoon garlic powder
¼ teaspoon salt
½ teaspoon basil
½ teaspoon oregano
4 bagels, sliced in half
8 slices vegan cheese, or 1 cup grated vegan cheese
¼ cup sliced mushrooms (optional)
¼ cup sliced black olives

1. Preheat oven to 325°F.

2. Combine pizza sauce, garlic powder, salt, basil, and oregano.

3. Spread sauce over each bagel half, and top with cheese, mushrooms, olives, or any other toppings.

4. Heat in oven for 8–10 minutes or until cheese is melted.

PER SERVING Calories: 308 | Fat: 9g | Sodium: 900mg | Fiber: 2g | Protein: 13g

Individual Pizzas

Flour tortillas (use two stacked together) and pita bread also make an easy base for individual pizza servings.

Chickpea Soft Tacos

For an easy and healthy taco filling wrapped up in flour tortillas, try using chickpeas! Short on time? Pick up taco seasoning packets to use instead of the spice blend—but watch out for added MSG.

INGREDIENTS | SERVES 6

2 15-ounce cans chickpeas, drained
½ cup water
1 6-ounce can tomato paste
1 tablespoon chili powder
1 teaspoon garlic powder
½ teaspoon onion powder
½ teaspoon cumin
¼ cup chopped fresh cilantro (optional)
4 flour tortillas
Optional taco fillings: shredded lettuce, black olives, vegan cheese, nondairy sour cream

1. Combine chickpeas, water, tomato paste, chili, garlic and onion powder, and cumin in a large skillet. Cover and simmer for 10 minutes, stirring occasionally. Uncover and simmer another minute or 2 until most of the liquid is absorbed.

2. Uncover and use a fork or potato masher to mash the chickpeas until half mashed. Stir in fresh cilantro.

3. Spoon mixture into flour tortillas, add toppings, and wrap.

PER SERVING Calories: 285 | Fat: 4g | Sodium: 641mg | Fiber: 8g | Protein: 11g

Caramelized Onion and Mushroom Cheeseless Quesadillas

*Sure, you can easily make vegan quesadillas using vegan cheese,
but try this more nutritious version filled with a cheesy bean spread.*

INGREDIENTS | SERVES 6

½ onion, chopped

1 cup sliced mushrooms

2 cloves garlic

2 tablespoons olive oil

Dash salt and pepper

1 15-ounce can white beans, any kind, drained

1 medium tomato

3 tablespoons nutritional yeast

3 tablespoons lemon juice

½ teaspoon cumin

6 flour tortillas

Oil for frying

"Chicken" Quesadillas

Pick up some store-bought "chicken" strips and make cheesy "chicken" quesadillas, omitting the onions and mushrooms. A great lunch for kids, or add some canned jalapeño slices for an easy game-day snack for adults!

1. Sauté onion, mushrooms, and garlic in olive oil in a large skillet and add a dash of salt and pepper. Cook, stirring occasionally, until onions and mushrooms are browned and caramelized, about 8 minutes.

2. In a food processor or blender, purée together the white beans, tomato, nutritional yeast, lemon juice, and cumin until smooth.

3. Spread ⅓ of the bean mixture on each of three tortillas, then top with a portion of the mushrooms and onions. Top with additional tortillas.

4. Lightly fry in oil for 2–3 minutes on each side, just until tortillas are lightly crispy.

PER SERVING Calories: 333 | Fat: 13g | Sodium: 316mg | Fiber: 6g | Protein: 11g

Cheesy Macaroni and "Hamburger" Casserole

Reminiscent of the boxed version, this is guilt-free vegan comfort food at its finest.

INGREDIENTS | SERVES 6

1 12-ounce bag macaroni noodles

4 veggie burgers, thawed and crumbled, or 1 12-ounce package vegetarian beef crumbles

1 tomato, diced

1 tablespoon olive oil

1 teaspoon chili powder

1 cup soy milk

2 tablespoons vegan margarine

2 tablespoons flour

1 teaspoon garlic powder

1 teaspoon onion powder

¼ cup nutritional yeast

Salt and pepper, to taste

1. Prepare macaroni noodles according to package instructions.

2. Sauté the veggie burgers and tomatoes in oil until burgers are lightly browned and season with chili powder.

3. In a separate small skillet, melt together the soy milk and margarine over low heat until well mixed. Stir in flour and heat until thickened, then stir in garlic and onion powder and nutritional yeast and remove from heat.

4. Combine macaroni, veggie burgers, tomatoes, and sauce, gently tossing to coat.

5. Season generously with salt and pepper and allow to cool slightly before serving to allow ingredients to combine.

PER SERVING Calories: 395 | Fat: 12g | Sodium: 259mg | Fiber: 5g | Protein: 21g

Lentil and Rice Loaf

Made from two of the cheapest ingredients on the planet, this one is a great filler for families on a budget. Serve with mashed potatoes and Mushroom Gravy (p. 26) for an all-American meal. Use poultry seasoning in place of the individual herbs, if you prefer.

INGREDIENTS | SERVES 6

3 cloves garlic
1 large onion, diced
2 tablespoons oil
3½ cups cooked lentils
2¼ cups rice, cooked
⅓ + 3 tablespoons cup ketchup
2 tablespoons flour
Egg replacer for 1 egg
½ teaspoon parsley
½ teaspoon thyme
½ teaspoon oregano
¼ teaspoon sage
¾ teaspoon salt
½ teaspoon black pepper

Perfect Loaf Tips

Cook the rice and lentils in vegetable broth and add a bay leaf for maximum flavor. Overcook the lentils a bit, so they'll be soft and mash easily, but let them cool before mashing. To avoid a mushy loaf, allow both the rice and lentils to cool completely before making your loaf, as they'll be drier that way. Finally, smother the top with loads of ketchup—that's the best part!

1. Preheat oven to 350°F.

2. Sauté garlic and onions in oil until onions are soft and clear, about 3–4 minutes.

3. In a large bowl, use a fork or a potato masher to mash the lentils until about ⅔ mashed.

4. Add garlic and onions, rice, ⅓ cup ketchup, and flour and combine well, then add egg replacer and remaining seasonings, mashing to combine.

5. Gently press the mixture into a lightly greased loaf pan. Drizzle the remaining 3 tablespoons ketchup on top.

6. Bake for 60 minutes. Allow to cool at least 10 minutes before serving, as loaf will firm slightly as it cools.

PER SERVING Calories: 295 | Fat: 5g | Sodium: 528mg | Fiber: 10g | Protein: 13g

Easy Falafel Patties

Health food stores sell a vegan instant falafel mix, but it's not very much work at all to make your own from scratch.

INGREDIENTS | SERVES 4

1 15-ounce can chickpeas, well drained
½ onion, minced
1 tablespoon flour
1 teaspoon cumin
¾ teaspoon garlic powder
¾ teaspoon salt
Egg substitute for 1 egg
¼ cup chopped fresh parsley
2 tablespoons chopped fresh cilantro (optional)

Falafel Sandwiches

Stuff falafel into a pita bread with some sliced tomatoes and lettuce and top it off with a bit of Homemade Tahini (p. 21), Vegan Tzatziki (p. 29), or hummus for a middle Eastern sandwich.

1. Preheat oven to 375°F.

2. Place chickpeas in a large bowl and mash with a fork until coarsely mashed. Or pulse in a food processor until chopped.

3. Combine chickpeas with onion, flour, cumin, garlic powder, salt, and egg substitute, mashing together to combine. Add parsley and cilantro.

4. Shape mixture into 2-inch balls or 1-inch-thick patties and bake in oven for 15 minutes, or until crisp. Falafel can also be fried in oil for about 5–6 minutes on each side.

PER SERVING Calories: 141 | Fat: 1g | Sodium: 752mg | Fiber: 5g | Protein: 6g

Green Olive and Artichoke Focaccia Pizza

A gourmet vegan pizza with plenty of Italian seasonings; no cheese needed.

INGREDIENTS | SERVES 3

1 loaf vegan focaccia bread
1 tablespoon olive oil
½ teaspoon salt
½ teaspoon rosemary
½ teaspoon basil
⅓ cup tomato paste
½ cup sliced green olives
¾ cup chopped artichoke hearts
½ cup sliced mushrooms
3 cloves garlic, minced
½ teaspoon parsley
¼ teaspoon oregano
½ teaspoon red pepper flakes (optional)

1. Preheat oven to 400°F.

2. Drizzle focaccia with olive oil and sprinkle with salt, rosemary, and basil.

3. Spread a thin layer of tomato paste on the focaccia, then top with olives, artichoke hearts, mushrooms, and garlic.

4. Sprinkle with parsley, oregano, and red pepper flakes, then bake for 20 minutes, or until done.

PER SERVING Calories: 441 | Fat: 14g | Sodium: 1,923mg | Fiber: 7g | Protein: 13g

Focaccia Pizza

Sure, you could use this recipe with a regular pizza crust, but vegan food is all about maximum flavor, and focaccia has much more than a regular crust. If you do prefer a store-bought pizza crust, drizzle it with olive oil and herbs, as in this recipe, on both sides.

Maple Baked Beans

Tailor these saucy Boston-style baked beans to your liking by adding extra molasses, a bit of cayenne, or some TVP crumbles for a meaty texture.

INGREDIENTS | SERVES 6

3 cups navy or pinto beans
9 cups water
1 onion, chopped
⅔ cup maple syrup
¼ cup barbecue sauce
2 tablespoons molasses
1 tablespoon Dijon mustard
1 tablespoon chili powder
1 teaspoon paprika
1½ teaspoons salt
¾ teaspoon pepper

1. Cover beans in water and allow to soak at least 8 hours or overnight. Drain.

2. Preheat oven to 350°F.

3. In a large Dutch oven or sturdy pot, combine beans and remaining ingredients. Bring to a rolling boil on the stove.

4. Cover and bake beans for 1½ hours, stirring once or twice. Uncover and cook 1 more hour.

5. Alternatively, beans can be simmered over low heat for 1½–2 hours on the stovetop.

PER SERVING Calories: 487 | Fat: 2g | Sodium: 740mg | Fiber: 26g | Protein: 24g

Potato and Veggie Fritters

These easy potato fritters are similar to an Indian snack, called bajji, *or* pakoras. *To get the idea, add a few shakes of some Indian spices: cumin, curry powder, turmeric, or garam masala and cayenne.*

INGREDIENTS | SERVES 3

3 medium potatoes
¼ cup soy milk
¼–⅓ cup flour
½ teaspoon garlic powder
½ teaspoon onion powder
½ teaspoon chili powder (optional)
½ cup frozen peas, corn, and diced carrot mix
Salt and pepper, to taste
Oil for frying

Leftover Baked Potatoes

This recipe is a great way to use leftover baked potatoes. Looking for more ideas for leftover potatoes? Make Potato and Leek Soup (p. 90) or No Shepherd, No Sheep Pie (p. 270).

1. Boil potatoes in water until cooked, about 20 minutes. Drain and allow to cool.

2. Mash potatoes together with soy milk, flour, garlic powder, onion powder, chili powder, veggies, and salt and pepper until mixture is thick and potatoes are well mashed, adding a little less soy milk and more flour as needed. Mixture should be dry but sticky.

3. Form into patties and pan fry in oil over medium heat for 3–4 minutes on each side or until browned and crispy.

PER SERVING Calories: 330 | Fat: 14g | Sodium: 47mg | Fiber: 6g | Protein: 6g

Baked Polenta with Italian Herbs

If you don't feel like stirring your polenta over the stove, it can also be baked; here's how. Use fresh herbs, if you have them on hand.

INGREDIENTS | SERVES 2

1 cup cornmeal
4 cups vegetable broth
1 teaspoon parsley
¼ teaspoon sage
¼ teaspoon oregano
½ teaspoon salt
¼ teaspoon black pepper
1 tablespoon chopped fresh basil
3 tablespoons vegan margarine, melted
2 tablespoons nutritional yeast (optional)

1. Preheat oven to 450°F.

2. Combine cornmeal and vegetable broth in a casserole dish. Add parsley, sage, oregano, salt, and pepper.

3. Cover and bake for 25 minutes. Uncover and bake another 5–10 minutes until liquid is mostly absorbed.

4. Stir in fresh basil, vegan margarine, and optional nutritional yeast.

5. Serve as is, or transfer to a loaf pan, chill until firm, then slice and pan fry in a bit of oil.

PER SERVING Calories: 392 | Fat: 10g | Sodium: 2,587mg | Fiber: 3g | Protein: 6g

Southwest Sweet Potato Enchiladas

Enchiladas freeze well, so make a double batch and thaw and reheat when you're hungry!

INGREDIENTS | SERVES 4

2 medium sweet potatoes, baked and diced

½ onion, minced

3 cloves garlic, minced

1 15-ounce can black beans, drained

2 teaspoons lime juice

2 tablespoons sliced green chilies (optional)

2 teaspoons chili powder

1 teaspoon cumin

1 15-ounce can green chili enchilada sauce

½ cup water

10–12 corn tortillas, warmed

Sweet Potato Burritos

Sweet potatoes and black beans make lovely vegan burritos as well as enchiladas. Omit the enchilada sauce and wrap the mixture in flour tortillas along with the usual taco fixings.

1. Preheat oven to 350°F.

2. In a large bowl, combine the sweet potatoes, onion, garlic, beans, lime juice, chilies, chili powder, and cumin until well mixed.

3. In a separate bowl, combine the enchilada sauce and water. Add ¼ cup of this mixture to the beans and sweet potatoes and combine well.

4. Spread about ⅓ cup sauce in the bottom of a casserole or baking dish.

5. Place about ⅓ cup bean and potato mixture in each tortilla and wrap, then place in the casserole dish. Repeat until filling is used.

6. Spread a generous layer of the remaining enchilada sauce over the top of the rolled tortillas, being sure to coat all the edges and corners well. You may have a little sauce left over.

7. Bake for 25–30 minutes. If enchiladas dry out while baking, top with more sauce.

PER SERVING Calories: 374 | Fat: 2g | Sodium: 1,208mg | Fiber: 17g | Protein: 16g

Easy Three-Bean Casserole

If you like baked beans, you'll like this easy bean casserole.
It's an easy entrée you can get in the oven in just a few minutes.

INGREDIENTS | SERVES 8

1 15-ounce can vegetarian baked beans
1 15-ounce can black beans, drained
1 15-ounce can kidney beans, drained
1 onion, chopped
⅓ cup ketchup
3 tablespoons apple cider vinegar
⅓ cup brown sugar
2 teaspoons mustard powder
2 teaspoons garlic powder
4 vegan hot dogs, cooked and chopped
(optional)

1. Preheat oven to 350°F.

2. Combine all ingredients except vegan hot dogs in a large casserole dish.

3. Bake for 55 minutes, uncovered. Add precooked vegan hot dogs just before serving.

PER SERVING Calories: 202 | Fat: 1g | Sodium: 553mg | Fiber: 10g | Protein: 10g

Chapter 11

Tofu

Cajun-Spiced Cornmeal-Breaded Tofu

Reminiscent of oven-fried breaded catfish, this is a Southern-inspired breaded tofu that can be baked or fried.

INGREDIENTS | SERVES 3

⅔ cup soy milk
2 tablespoons lime juice
¼ cup flour
⅓ cup cornmeal
1 tablespoon Cajun seasoning
1 teaspoon onion powder
½ teaspoon cayenne pepper, or to taste
½ teaspoon salt
½ teaspoon black pepper
1 block firm or extra-firm tofu, well pressed

1. Preheat oven to 375°F and lightly grease a baking pan.

2. Combine soy milk and lime juice in a wide shallow bowl. In a separate bowl, combine flour, cornmeal, Cajun seasoning, onion powder, cayenne, and salt and pepper.

3. Slice tofu into triangles or rectangular strips and dip in soy milk and lime juice mixture. Next, coat well with cornmeal and flour mixture

4. Transfer to baking pan and bake for 8–10 minutes on each side. Serve with hot sauce or barbecue sauce.

5. Alternatively, you can pan fry in a bit of oil for 2–3 minutes on each side.

PER SERVING Calories: 203 | Fat: 6g | Sodium: 428mg | Fiber: 2g | Protein: 13g

Mexican Spice–Crusted Tofu

These little bites are packed with spices, so no dipping sauce is needed. Use them to top off Mexican Rice with Corn and Peppers (p. 129) or Confetti "Rice" with TVP (p. 185), or just eat plain.

INGREDIENTS | SERVES 3

3 tablespoons soy sauce

3 tablespoons hot chili sauce

1 teaspoon sugar

1 block firm or extra-firm tofu, sliced into strips

1 teaspoon garlic powder

1 teaspoon onion powder

1 tablespoon chili powder

¾ teaspoon cumin

¾ teaspoon oregano

2 tablespoons flour

1. Whisk together the soy sauce, chili sauce, and sugar in a shallow pan and add tofu. Marinate tofu for at least 1 hour.

2. In a separate dish, combine the garlic powder, onion powder, chili powder, cumin, oregano, and flour to form a spice rub. Carefully dip each piece of tofu in the spices on each side, then transfer to a lightly greased baking sheet.

3. Bake at 350°F for 7–9 minutes, turning once.

PER SERVING Calories: 126 | Fat: 5g | Sodium: 1,144mg | Fiber: 2g | Protein: 11g

Pressing and Freezing Tofu

Tofu doesn't taste like much on its own, but soaks up spices and marinades wonderfully. It's like a sponge: the drier it is, the more flavor it absorbs. Wrap firm tofu in a couple layers of paper towels and place a can of beans or another light weight on top. After 10 minutes, flip the tofu over and let it sit weighted down for another 10 minutes. "Pressing" firm and extra-firm tofu will substantially enhance just about every recipe.

Pineapple-Glazed Tofu

If you like orange chicken or sweet-and-sour dishes, try this saucy, sweet, Pineapple-Glazed Tofu, excellent for kids. Toss with some noodles, or add some diced veggies to make it an entrée.

INGREDIENTS | SERVES 3

½ cup pineapple preserves
2 tablespoons balsamic vinegar
2 tablespoons soy sauce
⅔ cup pineapple juice
1 block firm or extra-firm tofu, cubed
3 tablespoons flour
2 tablespoons oil
1 teaspoon cornstarch

1. Whisk together the pineapple preserves, vinegar, soy sauce, and pineapple juice.

2. Coat tofu in flour, then sauté in oil for a few minutes, just until lightly golden. Reduce heat to medium low and add pineapple sauce, stirring well to combine and coat tofu.

3. Heat for 3–4 minutes, stirring frequently, then add cornstarch, whisking to combine and avoid lumps. Heat for a few more minutes, stirring, until sauce has thickened.

PER SERVING Calories: 360 | Fat: 14g | Sodium: 639mg | Fiber: 2g | Protein: 11g

Tofu "Fish" Sticks

Adding seaweed and lemon juice to baked and breaded tofu gives it a "fishy" taste. Crumbled nori sushi sheets would work well too if you can't find kelp or dulse flakes. You could also pan fry these fish sticks in a bit of oil instead of baking, if you prefer.

INGREDIENTS | SERVES 3

½ cup flour
⅓ cup soy milk
2 tablespoons lemon juice
1½ cups fine ground bread crumbs
2 tablespoons kelp or dulse seaweed flakes
1 tablespoon Old Bay seasoning blend
1 teaspoon onion powder
1 block extra-firm tofu, well pressed

Tartar Sauce

To make a simple vegan tartar sauce, combine Vegan Mayonnaise (p. 23) with sweet pickle relish and a generous squeeze of lemon juice. Or dip your fishy tofu sticks in ketchup or barbecue sauce.

1. Preheat oven to 350°F.

2. Place flour in a shallow bowl or pie tin and set aside. Combine the soy milk and lemon juice in a separate shallow bowl or pie tin. In a third bowl or pie tin, combine the bread crumbs, kelp, Old Bay, and onion powder.

3. Slice tofu into twelve ½-inch-thick strips. Place each strip into the flour mixture to coat well, then dip into the soy milk. Next, place each strip into the bread crumbs, gently patting to coat well.

4. Bake for 15–20 minutes, turn once, then bake for another 10–15 minutes or until crispy.

5. Serve with ketchup or a vegan tartar sauce.

PER SERVING Calories: 344 | Fat: 8g | Sodium: 1,070mg | Fiber: 4g | Protein: 18g

Eggless Egg Salad

Vegan egg salad looks just like the real thing and is much quicker to make. Use this recipe to make egg salad sandwiches, or serve it on a bed of lettuce with tomato slices and enjoy it just as it is.

INGREDIENTS | SERVES 4

1 block firm tofu
1 block silken tofu
½ cup vegan mayonnaise
⅓ cup sweet pickle relish
¾ teaspoon apple cider vinegar
½ stalk celery, diced
2 tablespoons minced onion
1½ tablespoons Dijon mustard
2 tablespoons chopped chives (optional)
2 tablespoons vegetarian bacon bits (optional)
1 teaspoon paprika

1. In a medium-size bowl, use a fork to mash the tofu together with the rest of the ingredients, except the bacon bits and paprika.

2. Chill for at least 15 minutes before serving to allow flavors to mingle.

3. Garnish with vegetarian bacon bits and paprika just before serving.

PER SERVING Calories: 318 | Fat: 24 g | Sodium: 428mg | Fiber: 2g | Protein: 11g

Indian Tofu Palak

*Palak paneer is a popular Indian dish of creamed spinach and soft cheese.
This version uses tofu for a similar dish.*

INGREDIENTS | SERVES 4

3 cloves garlic, minced

1 block firm or extra-firm tofu, cut into small cubes

2 tablespoons olive oil

2 tablespoons nutritional yeast

½ teaspoon onion powder

4 bunches fresh spinach

3 tablespoons water

1 tablespoon curry powder

2 teaspoons cumin

½ teaspoon salt

½ cup plain soy yogurt

1. Heat garlic and tofu in olive oil over low heat and add nutritional yeast and onion powder, stirring to coat tofu. Heat for 2–3 minutes until tofu is lightly browned.

2. Add spinach, water, curry powder, cumin, and salt, stirring well to combine. Once spinach starts to wilt, add soy yogurt and heat just until spinach is fully wilted and soft.

PER SERVING Calories: 234 | Fat: 13g | Sodium: 576mg | Fiber: 10g | Protein: 19g

Types of Tofu

Made from cooked, coagulated soybeans and little else, tofu is a minimally processed, low-fat source of calcium and protein. Plain tofu comes in either firm, extra-firm, or silken (also called silk or soft tofu), and many grocers stock a variety of prebaked or flavored tofu. Firm or extra-firm tofu is used in stir-fries and baked dishes when you want the tofu to hold shape. For creamy sauces, use silken tofu.

Tofu "Chicken" Nuggets

If the kids like chicken nuggets, try this tofu version with poultry seasoning instead.

INGREDIENTS | SERVES 4

¼ cup soy milk
2 tablespoons mustard
3 tablespoons nutritional yeast
½ cup bread crumbs
½ cup flour
1 teaspoon poultry seasoning
1 teaspoon garlic powder
1 teaspoon onion powder
½ teaspoon salt
¼ teaspoon pepper
1 block firm or extra-firm tofu, sliced into thin strips
Oil for frying (optional)

1. In a large shallow pan, whisk together the soy milk, mustard, and nutritional yeast. In a separate bowl, combine the bread crumbs with the flour, poultry seasoning, garlic and onion powder, salt, and pepper.

2. Coat each piece of tofu with the soy milk mixture, then coat well in bread crumbs and flour mixture.

3. Fry in hot oil until lightly golden brown, about 3–4 minutes on each side, or bake in 375°F oven for 20 minutes, turning over once.

PER SERVING Calories: 131 | Fat: 5g | Sodium: 492mg | Fiber: 2g | Protein: 10g

Italian Balsamic Baked Tofu

A sweet and crunchy Italian-inspired baked tofu delicious on its own or in salads or pastas. The extra marinade makes a great salad dressing!

INGREDIENTS | SERVES 3

1 tablespoon soy sauce
½ teaspoon sugar
¼ cup balsamic vinegar
½ teaspoon garlic powder
2 tablespoons olive oil
½ teaspoon parsley
½ teaspoon basil
¼ teaspoon thyme or oregano
¼ teaspoon salt
¼ teaspoon black pepper
2 blocks firm or extra-firm tofu, well pressed

Press, Marinate, Bake!

Now that you know how to make baked tofu, try creating your own marinades with your favorite spices and flavors. For quick and easy baked tofu dishes, try a store-bought salad dressing, teriyaki sauce, barbecue sauce, or steak marinade. Thicker dressings may need to be thinned with a bit of water first, and to get the best glazing action make sure there's a bit of sugar added.

1. Whisk together all ingredients except tofu and transfer to a wide, shallow pan or ziplock bag.

2. Slice the tofu into ½-inch-thick strips or triangles.

3. Place the tofu in the marinade and coat well. Allow to marinate for at least 1 hour or overnight, being sure tofu is well coated in marinade.

4. Preheat oven to 400°F. Coat a baking sheet well with nonstick spray or olive oil, or line with foil. Place tofu on sheet.

5. Bake for 15–20 minutes, turn over, then bake for another 5–10 minutes or until done.

PER SERVING Calories: 255 | Fat: 18g | Sodium: 250mg | Fiber: 2g | Protein: 18g

Lemon Basil Tofu

Moist and chewy, this zesty baked tofu is reminiscent of lemon chicken.
Serve over steamed rice with extra marinade.

INGREDIENTS | SERVES 6

3 tablespoons lemon juice
1 tablespoon soy sauce
2 teaspoons apple cider vinegar
1 tablespoon Dijon mustard
¾ teaspoon sugar
3 tablespoons olive oil
2 tablespoons chopped basil, plus extra for garnish
2 blocks firm or extra-firm tofu, well pressed

1. Whisk together all ingredients, except tofu, and transfer to a baking dish or casserole pan.

2. Slice the tofu into ½-inch-thick strips or triangles.

3. Place the tofu in the marinade and coat well. Allow to marinate for at least 1 hour or overnight, being sure tofu is well coated in marinade.

4. Preheat oven to 350°F.

5. Bake for 15 minutes, turn over, then bake for another 10–12 minutes or until done. Garnish with a few extra bits of chopped fresh basil.

PER SERVING Calories: 143 | Fat: 11g | Sodium: 192mg | Fiber: 1g | Protein: 9g

Tofu BBQ Sauce "Steaks"

These chewy tofu "steaks" have a hearty texture and a meaty flavor. Delicious as is, or add it to a sandwich. If you've never cooked tofu before, this is a super-easy foolproof recipe to start with.

INGREDIENTS | SERVES 3

⅓ cup barbecue sauce

¼ cup water

2 teaspoons balsamic vinegar

2 tablespoons soy sauce

1–2 tablespoons hot sauce, or to taste

2 teaspoons sugar

2 blocks firm or extra-firm tofu, well pressed

½ onion, chopped

2 tablespoons olive oil

Tofu vs. Seitan

This recipe, like many pan-fried or stir-fried tofu recipes, will also work well with seitan, though seitan needs a bit longer to cook all the way through; otherwise, it ends up tough and chewy.

1. In a small bowl, whisk together the barbecue sauce, water, vinegar, soy sauce, hot sauce, and sugar until well combined. Set aside.

2. Slice pressed tofu into ¼-inch-thick strips.

3. Sauté onions in oil, and carefully add tofu. Fry tofu on both sides until lightly golden brown, about 2 minutes on each side.

4. Reduce heat and add barbecue sauce mixture, stirring to coat tofu well. Cook over medium-low heat until sauce absorbs and thickens, about 5–6 minutes.

PER SERVING Calories: 294 | Fat: 18g | Sodium: 1,056mg | Fiber: 3g | Protein: 19g

Braised Tofu and Veggie Cacciatore

If you'd like a more "grown up" Italian dish, use ½ cup white cooking wine in place of ½ cup broth. Serve over pasta or try it with rice, whole grains, or even baked potatoes or polenta.

INGREDIENTS | SERVES 4

½ yellow onion, chopped

½ cup mushrooms, sliced

1 carrot, chopped

3 cloves garlic, minced

2 blocks firm or extra-firm tofu, chopped into cubes

2 tablespoons olive oil

1½ cups vegetable broth

1 14-ounce can diced tomatoes or 3 large fresh tomatoes, diced

1 6-ounce can tomato paste

1 bay leaf (optional)

½ teaspoon salt

1 teaspoon parsley

1 teaspoon basil

1 teaspoon oregano

1. Sauté the onion, mushrooms, carrot, garlic, and tofu in olive oil for 4–5 minutes, stirring frequently.

2. Reduce heat to medium low, and add vegetable broth, diced tomatoes, tomato paste, bay leaf, salt, and herbs.

3. Cover and allow to simmer for 20 minutes, stirring occasionally. Remove bay leaf before serving.

PER SERVING Calories: 256 | Fat: 14g | Sodium: 845mg | Fiber: 6g | Protein: 17g

Tofu "Ricotta" Manicotti

Check the label on your manicotti package, as some need to be precooked and some can be placed straight into the oven.

INGREDIENTS | SERVES 4

12 large manicotti
2 blocks firm tofu, crumbled
2 tablespoons lemon juice
2 tablespoons olive oil
2 tablespoons soy milk
¼ cup nutritional yeast
½ teaspoon garlic powder
½ teaspoon onion powder
¼ teaspoon salt
1 teaspoon basil
2 tablespoons fresh chopped parsley
3 cups prepared marinara sauce
⅓ cup grated vegan cheese (optional)

Mani—Canne—What?

If you can't find manicotti noodles (sometimes called *cannelloni*), use a large shell pasta. Or cook some lasagna noodles al dente, then place the filling on top of a noodle and roll it up. Place seam-side down in your casserole dish, and stuff them in tight to get them to stick together.

1. Precook the manicotti shells according to package instructions, if needed. Preheat oven to 350°F.

2. In a large bowl, mash together the tofu, lemon juice, olive oil, soy milk, nutritional yeast, garlic powder, onion powder, salt, basil, and parsley until well mixed, crumbly, and almost smooth.

3. Stuff each manicotti noodle with the tofu mixture.

4. Spread half of the marinara sauce in the bottom of a casserole or baking dish, then place the manicotti on top. Sprinkle with grated vegan cheese if desired, and cover with the remaining sauce.

5. Cover and bake for 30 minutes.

PER SERVING Calories: 570 | Fat: 20g | Sodium: 964mg | Fiber: 9g | Protein: 26g

Easy Fried Tofu

*A simple fried tofu that you can serve with just about any dipping sauce
for a snack, or add to salads or stir-fries instead of plain tofu.*

INGREDIENTS | SERVES 3

1 block firm or extra-firm tofu, cubed
¼ cup soy sauce (optional)
2 tablespoons flour
2 tablespoons nutritional yeast
1 teaspoon garlic powder
¼ teaspoon salt
Dash pepper
Oil for frying

1. Marinate sliced tofu in soy sauce for at least 1 hour. This step is optional.

2. In a small bowl, combine flour, nutritional yeast, garlic powder, salt, and pepper.

3. Coat tofu well with flour mixture on all sides, then fry in hot oil until crispy and lightly golden brown on all sides, about 4–5 minutes.

PER SERVING Calories: 232 | Fat: 19g | Sodium: 208mg | Fiber: 2g | Protein: 11g

Sesame Baked Tofu

*This is a quick and basic marinade to try if you're new to baking tofu, which makes it
meaty and chewy. Serve these marinated tofu strips as an entrée or
use as a salad topper or as a meat substitute in a sandwich.*

INGREDIENTS | SERVES 6

¼ cup soy sauce
2 tablespoons sesame oil
¾ teaspoon garlic powder
½ teaspoon ginger powder
2 blocks firm or extra-firm tofu, well pressed

Marinating Tofu

For marinated baked tofu dishes, a ziplock bag can be helpful in getting the tofu well covered with marinade. Place the tofu in the bag, pour the marinade in, seal, and set in the fridge, turning and lightly shaking occasionally to coat all sides of the tofu.

1. Whisk together the soy sauce, sesame oil, and garlic and ginger powder and transfer to a wide, shallow pan.

2. Slice the tofu into ½-inch-thick strips or triangles.

3. Place the tofu in the marinade and coat well. Allow to marinate for at least 1 hour or overnight.

4. Preheat oven to 400°F. Coat a baking sheet well with nonstick spray or olive oil, or line with foil. Place tofu on sheet.

5. Bake for 20–25 minutes, turn over, then bake for another 10–15 minutes or until done.

PER SERVING Calories: 99 | Fat: 7g | Sodium: 314mg | Fiber: 1g | Protein: 9g

Saucy Kung Pao Tofu

Try adding in a few more Asian ingredients to stretch this recipe: bok choy, water chestnuts, or bamboo shoots, perhaps, and spoon on top of cooked noodles or plain rice.

INGREDIENTS | SERVES 6

3 tablespoons soy sauce

2 tablespoons rice vinegar or cooking sherry

1 tablespoon sesame oil

2 blocks firm or extra-firm tofu, chopped into 1-inch cubes

1 red bell pepper, chopped

1 green bell pepper, chopped

⅔ cup sliced mushrooms

3 cloves garlic

3 small red or green chili peppers, diced small

1 teaspoon red pepper flakes

2 tablespoons oil

1 teaspoon ginger powder

½ cup water or vegetable broth

½ teaspoon sugar

1½ teaspoons cornstarch

2 green onions, chopped

½ cup peanuts

1. Whisk together the soy sauce, rice vinegar, and sesame oil in a shallow pan or ziplock bag. Add tofu and marinate for at least 1 hour; the longer, the better. Drain tofu, reserving marinade.

2. Sauté bell peppers, mushrooms, garlic, chili peppers, and red pepper flakes in oil for 2–3 minutes, then add tofu and heat for another minute or 2 until veggies are almost soft.

3. Reduce heat to medium low and add marinade, ginger powder, water or vegetable broth, sugar, and cornstarch, whisking in the cornstarch to avoid lumps.

4. Heat a few more minutes, stirring constantly, until sauce has almost thickened.

5. Add green onions and peanuts and heat for 1 more minute.

PER SERVING Calories: 535 | Fat: 51g | Sodium: 520mg | Fiber: 3g | Protein: 13g

Sticky Teriyaki Tofu Cubes

Cut tofu into wide slabs or triangular cutlets for a main dish or smaller cubes to add to a salad, or just for an appetizer or snack.

INGREDIENTS | SERVES 3

⅓ cup soy sauce

3 tablespoons barbecue sauce

2 teaspoons hot chili sauce

¼ cup maple syrup

¾ teaspoon garlic powder

1 block firm or extra-firm tofu, cut into thin chunks

1. Preheat oven to 375°F.

2. In a casserole or baking dish, whisk together the soy sauce, barbecue sauce, chili sauce, maple syrup, and garlic powder.

3. Add tofu and cover with sauce.

4. Bake for 35–40 minutes, tossing once.

PER SERVING Calories: 191 | Fat: 5g | Sodium: 1,846mg | Fiber: 2g | Protein: 11g

Storing and Freezing Tofu

Freezing firm or extra-firm tofu creates an even meatier and chewier texture, which some people prefer, and makes it even more absorbent. After pressing your tofu, stick it in the freezer until solid and thaw just before using. If you don't use the whole block, cover any leftover bits of uncooked tofu with water in a sealed container and stick it in the fridge.

Simmered Coconut Curried Tofu

Serve on top of Coconut Rice (p. 131) or Pineapple Lime Rice (p. 143).

INGREDIENTS | SERVES 3

1 block firm or extra-firm tofu, cubed
1 tablespoon olive oil
2 teaspoons sesame oil
3 tablespoons peanut butter
2 tablespoons soy sauce
2 tablespoons water
1 teaspoon curry powder
¼ cup coconut flakes
2 tablespoons fresh cilantro, minced

1. Sauté tofu in olive oil for just a few minutes until lightly golden brown.

2. Reduce heat to medium low and add sesame oil, peanut butter, soy sauce, water, and curry powder, stirring well to combine. Heat, gently stirring, for 4–5 minutes.

3. Add coconut flakes and cilantro and heat just until well combined, about 1 more minute.

PER SERVING Calories: 277 | Fat: 23g | Sodium: 693mg | Fiber: 3g | Protein: 13g

Agave Mustard–Glazed Tofu

Miss honey mustard–glazed ham? Try this vegan version with agave and tofu.

INGREDIENTS | SERVES 3

2 tablespoons lemon juice
2 tablespoons water
1 teaspoon soy sauce
¼ cup agave nectar
2 tablespoons prepared mustard
½ teaspoon garlic powder
½ teaspoon sugar
¾ teaspoon curry powder (optional)
1 block firm or extra-firm tofu, chopped into 1-inch cubes

1. Whisk together all sauce ingredients in a shallow pan and add tofu. Allow to marinate for at least 1 hour, flipping tofu and basting with sauce.

2. Preheat oven to 400°F.

3. Transfer tofu to a baking sheet or casserole dish, basting with extra sauce. Bake tofu for 20–25 minutes, turning over once and spooning extra marinade over the top.

PER SERVING Calories: 168 | Fat: 5g | Sodium: 225mg | Fiber: 1g | Protein: 9g

Honey: To Bee or Not to Bee?

Many vegans assume honey is cruelty-free and gently collected from bees that are producing it naturally. This is simply not true. According to the manifesto set forth by the British Vegan Society in 1944, honey is an animal by-product and therefore not vegan.

Mexico City Protein Bowl

A quick meal-for-one in a bowl, reminiscent of Mexico City street food stalls, but healthier and with less pollution.

INGREDIENTS | SERVES 1

½ block firm tofu, diced small
1 scallion, chopped
1 tablespoon olive oil
½ cup peas
½ cup corn kernels
½ teaspoon chili powder
1 can black beans, drained
2 corn tortillas
Hot sauce, to taste

1. Heat tofu and scallion in olive oil for 2–3 minutes, then add peas, corn, and chili powder. Cook another minute or 2, stirring frequently.

2. Reduce heat to medium low, and add black beans. Heat for 4–5 minutes until well combined and heated through.

3. Place 2 corn tortillas in the bottom of a bowl, and spoon beans and tofu over the top. Season with hot sauce to taste.

PER SERVING Calories: 1,198 | Fat: 26g | Sodium: 1,120mg | Fiber: 50g | Protein: 66g

Spicy Chili Basil Tofu

This saucy stir-fry is a favorite in Thailand when made with chicken and fish sauce, but many restaurants offer a vegetarian version with soy sauce and tofu instead. Serve with rice or rice noodles to sop up all the sauce.

INGREDIENTS | SERVES 3

4 cloves garlic, minced
5 small red or green chilies, diced
3 shallots, diced
2 tablespoons oil
1 block firm tofu, diced
¼ cup soy sauce
1 tablespoon vegetarian oyster mushroom sauce
1 teaspoon sugar
1 bunch Thai or holy basil leaves, whole

1. In a large skillet, sauté garlic, chilies, and shallots in oil until fragrant and browned, about 3–4 minutes.

2. Add tofu and heat for another 2–3 minutes until tofu is just lightly golden brown.

3. Reduce heat to medium low and add soy sauce, mushroom sauce, and sugar, whisking to combine and dissolve sugar. Heat 2–3 more minutes, stirring frequently, then add basil and heat, stirring 1 more minute, just until basil is wilted.

PER SERVING Calories: 202 | Fat: 14g | Sodium: 1,380mg | Fiber: 2g | Protein: 12g

Make It Last

If tofu and chilies aren't enough for you, add in some onions, mushrooms, or green bell peppers to fill it out. Or, for a bit of variety, try it with half basil and half fresh mint leaves.

Chili and Curry Baked Tofu

If you like tofu and Indian- or Thai-style curries, you'll love this spicy baked tofu, which tastes like a slowly simmered curry in each bite. Use the extra marinade to dress a bowl of plain steamed rice.

INGREDIENTS | SERVES 3

⅓ cup coconut milk
½ teaspoon garlic powder
1 teaspoon cumin
1 teaspoon curry powder
½ teaspoon turmeric
2–3 small chilies, minced
2 tablespoons maple syrup
1 block firm or extra-firm tofu, sliced into thin strips

1. Whisk together coconut milk, garlic powder, cumin, curry powder, turmeric, chilies, and maple syrup in a shallow bowl. Add tofu and marinate for at least 1 hour, flipping once or twice to coat well.

2. Preheat oven to 425°F.

3. Transfer tofu to a casserole dish in a single layer, reserving marinade.

4. Bake for 8–10 minutes. Turn tofu over, and spoon 1–2 tablespoons of marinade over the tofu. Bake 10–12 more minutes.

PER SERVING Calories: 165 | Fat: 10g | Sodium: 19mg | Fiber: 1g | Protein: 10g

Beer-Battered Tofu Fillet

Who needs eggs for a tangy and light batter, when beer works just as well?
Add some fries for a British pub–style "fish 'n chips" meal.

INGREDIENTS | SERVES 8

2 teaspoons garlic powder

2 teaspoons onion powder

2 teaspoons paprika

1 teaspoon salt

½ teaspoon black pepper

3 blocks extra-firm tofu, chopped into chunks

1 12-ounce bottle of beer

1⅓ cups flour

Oil for frying

1. Combine the garlic powder, onion powder, paprika, salt, and pepper. Sprinkle the mixture over the tofu, gently pressing to stick.

2. Pour the beer into a large bowl and add flour, stirring to combine.

3. Dip the tofu in the beer batter, then fry in plenty of oil on both sides until crispy.

PER SERVING Calories: 224 | Fat: 10g | Sodium: 308mg | Fiber: 2g | Protein: 12g

Bourbon Street Treats

Venture south to New Orleans and into the heart of the city and you might be lucky enough to find an old jazz restaurant humbly serving battered fried pickles, a New Orleans cult favorite. Sound odd? Try this recipe using dill pickle slices instead of tofu (or okra if you're less adventurous but still want a taste of the Big Easy) and taste for yourself.

Nutty Pesto-Crusted Tofu

Make sure your basil leaves are completely dry before trying these nutty, crispy, herbed tofu cutlets.

INGREDIENTS | SERVES 3

½ cup roasted cashews
½ cup basil, packed
3 cloves garlic
½ cup nutritional yeast
⅔ cup bread crumbs
½ teaspoon salt
¼ teaspoon pepper
⅔ cup flour
⅔ cup soy milk
2 blocks firm or extra-firm tofu, pressed
Oil for pan frying (optional)

Why Do Vegans Love Tofu So Much?

Aside from the low cost and ease of preparation, tofu is beloved by vegans as an excellent source of protein, calcium, and iron. Plain sautéed tofu with a dash of salt is a quick addition to just about any meal, and many grocery stores offer premarinated and even prebaked tofu that is ready to go out of the package. What's not to love?

1. In a blender or food processor, process the nuts until coarse and fine but not powdery. Separately, process the basil and garlic until finely minced.

2. Combine the cashews, basil, garlic, nutritional yeast, bread crumbs, salt, and pepper in a bowl. Place the flour in a separate shallow bowl and the soy milk in a third bowl.

3. Slice each block of tofu into triangular cutlets, about ¾ inch thick. Using tongs, dip in flour and coat well, then dip in soy milk. Next, coat well with the basil and bread crumb mixture and transfer to a lightly greased baking sheet.

4. Pan fry in oil over medium heat a few minutes on each side until lightly crispy. Alternatively, tofu can be baked for 10–12 minutes at 350°F, or until lightly crispy.

PER SERVING Calories: 540 | Fat: 22g | Sodium: 684mg | Fiber: 7g | Protein: 34g

Easy Lemon Thyme Marinated Tofu

The leftover marinade can be whisked with some extra olive oil for a lemony salad dressing.

INGREDIENTS | SERVES 3

3 tablespoons lemon juice
3 tablespoons soy sauce
1 tablespoon olive oil
3 tablespoons water
1 tablespoon chopped fresh or 2 teaspoons dried thyme
1 block firm or extra-firm tofu, pressed
Dash salt and pepper

1. In a shallow pan, whisk together the lemon juice, soy sauce, olive oil, water, and thyme.

2. Slice pressed tofu into desired shape, about ½ inch thick, and cover with marinade. Allow to marinate for at least 1 hour, preferably longer.

3. Heat oven to 400°F and transfer tofu to a lightly greased baking sheet or casserole dish. Sprinkle with a bit of salt and pepper.

4. Bake tofu for 10–12 minutes or until lightly crispy.

PER SERVING Calories: 142 | Fat: 11g | Sodium: 464mg | Fiber: 1g | Protein: 9g

Five-Spice Glazed Tofu

Chinese five-spice powder is a blend of spices with an exotic and unique taste. Everyone will be asking you what it is!

INGREDIENTS | SERVES 3

1 block firm tofu, well pressed
½ cup water
2 tablespoons soy sauce
1 tablespoon sesame oil
1 tablespoon brown sugar
2 cloves garlic, minced
¾ teaspoon Chinese five-spice powder

1. Slice tofu into ½-inch-thick slabs or triangles.

2. Whisk together the water, soy sauce, sesame oil, brown sugar, garlic, and five-spice in a shallow pan, and add tofu, covering well. Allow to marinate for at least 30 minutes.

3. Transfer tofu and marinade to a baking sheet or casserole dish and bake at 350°F for 10–15 minutes on each side.

PER SERVING Calories: 135 | Fat: 9g | Sodium: 616mg | Fiber: 1g | Protein: 10g

Orange-Glazed "Chicken" Tofu

If you're missing Chinese restaurant–style orange-glazed chicken, try this easy tofu version. It's slightly sweet, slightly salty, and, if you add some crushed red pepper, it'll have a bit of spice as well! Double the sauce and add some veggies for a full meal over rice.

INGREDIENTS | SERVES 3

⅔ cup orange juice
2 tablespoons soy sauce
2 tablespoons rice vinegar
1 tablespoon maple syrup
½ teaspoon red pepper flakes (optional)
2 tablespoons olive oil
1 block firm or extra-firm tofu, well pressed and chopped into 1-inch cubes
3 cloves garlic, minced
1½ teaspoons cornstarch
2 tablespoons water

1. Whisk together the orange juice, soy sauce, vinegar, maple syrup, and red pepper flakes and set aside.

2. In a large skillet, heat the oil and add tofu and garlic. Lightly fry just a few minutes over medium heat.

3. Reduce heat to medium low and add in orange juice mixture. Bring to a very low simmer and allow to cook for 7–8 minutes over low heat.

4. Whisk together the cornstarch and water in a small bowl until cornstarch is dissolved. Add to tofu mixture, stirring well to combine.

5. Bring to a simmer and heat for 3–4 minutes until sauce thickens. Serve over rice or another whole grain if desired.

PER SERVING Calories: 219 | Fat: 14g | Sodium: 616mg | Fiber: 1g | Protein: 10g

Chapter 12

Seitan, TVP, and Tempeh

Super-Meaty TVP Meatloaf

With a pinkish hue and chewy texture, this meatloaf impersonates the real thing well. Top with gravy for a Thanksgiving entrée.

INGREDIENTS | SERVES 6

2 cups TVP
1¾ cups hot vegetable broth
1 onion, chopped
1 tablespoon oil
¼ cup ketchup
⅓ cup + 3 tablespoons barbecue sauce
1 cup vital wheat gluten flour
1 cup bread crumbs
1 teaspoon parsley
½ teaspoon sage
½ teaspoon salt
¼ teaspoon pepper

1. Combine TVP with hot vegetable broth and allow to sit for 6–7 minutes until rehydrated. Gently squeeze out any excess moisture.

2. Heat onion in oil until translucent, about 3–4 minutes.

3. Preheat oven to 400°F.

4. In a large bowl, combine TVP, onions, ketchup, and ⅓ cup barbecue sauce. Add vital wheat gluten flour, bread crumbs, and seasonings and combine well.

5. Gently press mixture into a lightly greased loaf pan. Drizzle 3 tablespoons of barbecue sauce on top and bake for 45–50 minutes until lightly browned. Allow to cool for at least 10 minutes before serving, as loaf will set as it cools.

PER SERVING Calories: 321 | Fat: 4g | Sodium: 967mg | Fiber: 7g | Protein: 33g

Southern Fried Seitan

Deep-fried seitan is one the best things about eating vegan. Feel free to gloat when eating this amazing dish—those omnivores don't know what they're missing!

INGREDIENTS | SERVES 4

2 tablespoons soy sauce
¼ cup soy milk
3 tablespoons mustard
⅔ cup flour
¼ cup nutritional yeast
1 tablespoon baking powder
1 teaspoon garlic powder
1 teaspoon onion powder
½ teaspoon paprika
½ teaspoon salt
½ teaspoon black pepper
1 16-ounce package prepared seitan
Oil for frying

1. In a small bowl, combine the soy sauce, soy milk, and mustard. In a separate medium bowl, combine the flour, nutritional yeast, and remaining ingredients, except for oil and seitan.

2. Coat the seitan pieces well with the soy milk and mustard mixture, then coat well with the flour and nutritional yeast mixture.

3. Fry in oil, turning as needed, for 4–5 minutes, or until golden brown, and drain on paper towels.

PER SERVING Calories: 383 | Fat: 23g | Sodium: 1,407mg | Fiber: 3g | Protein: 27g

Any Way You Slice It . . .

For an appetizer or snack, chop your seitan into 2-inch chunks and dip in ketchup or barbecue sauce. Or flatten your seitan into patties for Southern fried "chicken steak" and top with Mushroom Gravy (p. 26) and a side of Roasted-Garlic Mashed Potatoes (p. 99).

Massaman Curried Seitan

With its Indian influences and popularity among Muslim communities in southern Thailand, massaman curry is a truly global dish. This version is simplified but still has a distinct kick. Diced tomatoes, baby corn, or green peas would go well in this recipe if you want to add veggies.

INGREDIENTS | SERVES 4

1 tablespoon Chinese five-spice powder
½ teaspoon fresh ginger, grated
½ teaspoon turmeric
¼ teaspoon cayenne pepper, or to taste
1 tablespoon oil
1½ cups coconut milk
1 cup vegetable broth
2 potatoes, chopped
1½ cups seitan, chopped small
2 whole cloves
1 teaspoon salt
1 tablespoon peanut butter
¼ teaspoon cinnamon
2 teaspoons brown sugar
⅓ cup peanuts or cashews (optional)

1. In a large skillet or stock pot, heat five-spice powder, ginger, turmeric, and cayenne in oil for just 1 minute, stirring constantly, until fragrant.

2. Reduce heat to medium low and add coconut milk and vegetable broth, stirring to combine. Add potatoes, seitan, cloves, and salt; cover and cook for 15–20 minutes, stirring occasionally.

3. If you prefer a thicker curry, dissolve 1 tablespoon cornstarch in 3 tablespoons water and add to curry, simmering for 2–3 minutes, until thick.

4. Uncover, add peanut butter, cinnamon, sugar, and peanuts or cashews, and heat for 1 more minute. Serve over rice.

PER SERVING Calories: 386 | Fat: 24g | Sodium: 1,210mg | Fiber: 4g | Protein: 21g

Basic Homemade Seitan

*Homemade seitan may seem like a lot of work at first, but it's quite simple
once you get the hang of it, and it's just a fraction of the cost of store-bought.*

INGREDIENTS | SERVES 8

1 cup vital wheat gluten

1 teaspoon onion powder

1 teaspoon garlic powder

2 tablespoons soy sauce

6¾ cups strong vegetable broth, divided

Seitan Tips

Shop for vital wheat gluten, also called
wheat gluten flour, at your natural foods
store in the bulk section or baking aisle.
Note that this recipe is for a basic, raw
seitan. It won't be too tasty if you eat it
plain, as it still needs to be cooked, even
after all that boiling! Make a batch, then
use it in any of the recipes in this book
calling for seitan. Seitan expands when it
cooks, so use more broth and a larger pot
than you think you might need, and add
an extra bouillon cube for maximum flavor,
if you like.

1. Combine the vital wheat gluten with the onion powder
   and garlic powder. In a separate bowl, combine the soy
   sauce and ¾ cup vegetable broth.

2. Slowly add the soy sauce mixture to the wheat gluten
   mixture, mixing with your hands until all of the flour is
   combined. You'll have one big rubbery ball of dough,
   and you may need a bit more or less than ¾ cup broth.

3. Knead the dough a few times to get an even texture.
   Let dough rest for a few minutes, then knead again for
   a minute or 2.

4. Divide dough into 3 (or more) pieces and stretch and
   press to about 1 inch thickness.

5. Slowly simmer in 6 cups vegetable broth for
   45 minutes–1 hour over low heat.

PER SERVING WITHOUT COOKING LIQUID Calories: 28 |
Fat: 0g | Sodium: 119mg | Fiber: 0g | Protein: 6g

Homemade Baked Seitan

Homemade seitan can be baked instead of boiled, for a similar result. This version is deliciously chewy straight out of the oven, and makes an excellent deli-style lunch "meat" when sliced thin.

INGREDIENTS | SERVES 8

1 12-ounce block silken tofu
⅔ cup water
⅓ cup olive oil
⅓ cup barbecue sauce
2 teaspoons hot chili sauce (optional)
1 teaspoon onion powder
1 teaspoon garlic powder
1 teaspoon seasoning salt
2¼ cups vital wheat gluten

1. Preheat oven to 350°F and grease a loaf pan well.

2. Purée the tofu, water, and olive oil until smooth and creamy, at least 1 minute. Stir in barbecue sauce, hot chili sauce, onion and garlic powders, and seasoning salt.

3. Combine vital wheat gluten and mix in with your hands to form a dough. Knead the dough a few times to get an even texture. Let dough rest for a few minutes, then knead again for a minute or 2.

4. Firmly press into a small loaf pan, forming a compacted loaf.

5. Bake for 35–40 minutes or until just starting to brown. Cool completely before using.

PER SERVING Calories: 234 | Fat: 11g | Sodium: 127mg | Fiber: 0g | Protein: 26g

Chickeny Seitan

Use a vegetarian chicken-flavored broth instead of regular vegetable broth,
or add vegetarian chicken-flavored bouillon to the broth, if you can find it.

INGREDIENTS | SERVES 8

1 cup vital wheat gluten flour
1 tablespoon nutritional yeast
½ teaspoon sage
¼ teaspoon thyme
½ teaspoon garlic powder
½ teaspoon onion powder
6¾ cups vegetable broth, divided

Seitan Stylings

When making homemade seitan, experiment with different seasonings to determine what you like best; no two batches ever seem to turn out the same anyway. Try adding lemon juice and minced seaweed for a fishy taste, and try out different vegetable broths and bouillon flavorings.

1. Combine the vital wheat gluten with the nutritional yeast, sage, thyme, and garlic and onion powder.

2. Slowly add ¾ cup vegetable broth to the wheat gluten, mixing with your hands until all of the flour is combined. You'll have one big rubbery ball of dough, and you may need a bit more or less than ¾ cup broth.

3. Knead the dough a few times to get an even texture. Let dough rest for a few minutes, then knead again for a minute or 2.

4. Divide dough into 3 (or more) pieces and stretch and press to about 1-inch thickness.

5. Slowly simmer in 6 cups vegetable broth for 45 minutes–1 hour over low heat.

PER SERVING WITHOUT COOKING LIQUID Calories: 55 | Fat: 0g | Sodium: 92mg | Fiber: 0g | Protein: 11g

Rosemary Tempeh Hash

Diner-style breakfast hash with tempeh for protein and a little less grease on your spoon.
Use a tablespoon of fresh rosemary, if you have some in your herb garden, instead of dried.

INGREDIENTS | SERVES 4

2 potatoes, diced
1 8-ounce package tempeh, cubed
2 tablespoons olive oil
2 green onions, chopped
1 teaspoon chili powder
1 teaspoon rosemary
Salt and pepper to taste

1. Cover the potatoes with water in a large pot and bring to a boil. Cook just until potatoes are almost soft, about 15 minutes. Drain.

2. In a large pan, sauté the potatoes and tempeh in olive oil for 3–4 minutes, lightly browning tempeh on all sides.

3. Add green onions, chili powder, and rosemary, stirring to combine, and heat for 3–4 more minutes. Season well with salt and pepper.

PER SERVING Calories: 207 | Fat: 13g | Sodium: 10mg | Fiber: 1g | Protein: 11g

Seitan Buffalo Wings

To tame these spicy wings, dip in cooling Dairy-Free Ranch Dressing (p. 61),
or serve with chilled cucumber slices.

INGREDIENTS | SERVES 4

⅓ cup vegan margarine

⅓ cup Louisiana hot sauce

1 cup flour

1 teaspoon garlic powder

1 teaspoon onion powder

¼ teaspoon pepper

½ cup soy milk

Oil for frying

1 16-ounce package seitan or mock chicken, chopped

Baked, Not Fried

This is, admittedly, not the healthiest of vegan recipes, but you can cut some of the fat out by skipping the breading and deep-frying. Instead, lightly brown the seitan in a bit of oil, then coat with the sauce. Alternatively, bake the seitan with the sauce for 25 minutes at 325°F.

1. Over low heat, combine the margarine and hot sauce, just until margarine is melted. Set aside.

2. In a small bowl, combine the flour, garlic powder, onion powder, and pepper. Place soy milk in a separate bowl and heat oil.

3. Dip each piece of seitan in the soy milk, then dredge in flour mixture. Carefully place in hot oil and deep-fry until lightly golden browned on all sides, about 4–5 minutes.

4. Coat fried seitan with margarine and hot sauce mixture.

PER SERVING Calories: 525 | Fat: 37g | Sodium: 1,198mg | Fiber: 2g | Protein: 26g

TVP Taco "Meat"

Whip up this meaty and economical taco filling in just a few minutes using prepared salsa, and have diners fill their own tacos according to their taste. Nondairy sour cream, fresh tomatoes, shredded lettuce, and extra hot sauce are a must, as well as sliced avocados or vegan cheese if you have room.

INGREDIENTS | SERVES 6

2 cups TVP flakes
2 cups hot water
1 yellow onion, diced
½ red or yellow bell pepper, diced
½ green bell pepper, diced
2 tablespoons olive oil
2 teaspoons chili powder
1 teaspoon cumin
½ cup salsa
½ teaspoon hot sauce, or to taste
5–6 flour tortillas or taco shells

TVP: Cheap, Chewy, and Meaty

TVP is inexpensive and has such a meaty texture that many budget-conscious nonvegetarian cooks use it to stretch their dollar, adding it to homemade burgers and meatloaf. For the best deal, buy it in bulk. TVP is usually found in small crumbles, but some specialty shops also sell it in strips or chunks.

1. Combine TVP with hot water and allow to sit for 5–10 minutes to reconstitute. Drain.

2. In a large skillet, heat onion and bell peppers in olive oil. Add TVP, chili powder, and cumin. Cook, stirring frequently, for 4–5 minutes or until peppers and onions are soft.

3. Add salsa and hot sauce, stirring to combine. Remove from heat.

4. Wrap TVP mixture in flour tortillas or spoon into taco shells and serve with taco fillings.

PER SERVING (WITH FLOUR TORTILLA) Calories: 311 | Fat: 8g | Sodium: 378mg | Fiber: 8g | Protein: 21g

Tandoori Seitan

*You can enjoy the flavors of traditional Indian tandoori without firing up
your grill by simmering the seitan on the stove top.*

INGREDIENTS | SERVES 6

⅔ cup soy yogurt

2 tablespoons lemon juice

1½ tablespoons tandoori spice blend

½ teaspoon cumin

½ teaspoon garlic powder

¼ teaspoon salt

1 16-ounce package prepared seitan, chopped

1 bell pepper, chopped

1 onion, chopped

1 tomato, chopped

2 tablespoons oil

1. Whisk together the yogurt, lemon juice, and all the spices in a shallow bowl or pan and add seitan. Allow to marinate for at least 1 hour. Reserve marinade.

2. Sauté pepper, onion, and tomato in oil until just barely soft. Reduce heat to low and add seitan. Cook, tossing seitan occasionally, for 8–10 minutes.

3. Serve topped with extra marinade.

PER SERVING Calories: 148 | Fat: 6g | Sodium: 419mg | Fiber: 2g | Protein: 16g

Sweet and Sour Tempeh

With maple syrup instead of white sugar, this is a sweet and sour that's slightly less sweet than other versions. There's plenty of sauce, so plan on serving with some plain white rice or another grain to mop it all up. A handful of broccoli or baby corn could go in along with the bell peppers, if you have some on hand.

INGREDIENTS | SERVES 4

1 cup vegetable broth
2 tablespoons soy sauce
1 8-ounce package tempeh, diced into cubes
2 tablespoons barbecue sauce
½ teaspoon ground ginger
2 tablespoons maple syrup
⅓ cup rice vinegar or apple cider vinegar
1 tablespoon cornstarch
1 15-ounce can pineapple chunks, drained, reserving juice
2 tablespoons olive oil
1 green bell pepper, chopped
1 red bell pepper, chopped
1 yellow onion, chopped

Like Sweet and Sour?

This sauce would go equally well with some sautéed tofu, lightly browned seitan, or any vegetables that you like.

1. Whisk together the vegetable broth and soy sauce, and bring to a simmer in a large skillet. Simmer the tempeh for 10 minutes. Remove tempeh from the pan, and reserve ½ cup vegetable broth mix.

2. In a small bowl, whisk together the barbecue sauce, ginger, maple syrup, vinegar, cornstarch, and juice from pineapples until cornstarch is dissolved. Set aside.

3. Heat olive oil in skillet, and add tempeh, bell peppers, and onions. Sauté for just a minute or 2, then add sauce mixture and bring to a simmer.

4. Allow to cook until sauce thickens, about 6–8 minutes. Reduce heat and stir in pineapples. Serve over rice or another whole grain.

PER SERVING Calories: 325 | Fat: 13g | Sodium: 795mg | Fiber: 2g | Protein: 13g

"Sloppy Jolindas" with TVP

TVP "Sloppy Jolindas" are reminiscent of those goopy sloppy Joes served up in school cafeterias, with all of the nostalgic comfort and none of the gristle or mystery meat. The TVP is only partially rehydrated, the better to absorb all the flavors.

INGREDIENTS | SERVES 8

1¾ cups TVP
1 cup hot water or vegetable broth
1 onion, chopped
1 green bell pepper, chopped small
2 tablespoons oil
1 16-ounce can tomato sauce
¼ cup barbecue sauce
2 tablespoons chili powder
1 tablespoon mustard powder
1 tablespoon soy sauce
2 tablespoons molasses
2 tablespoons apple cider vinegar
1 teaspoon hot sauce, or to taste
1 teaspoon garlic powder
½ teaspoon salt

1. Combine the TVP with water or vegetable broth and allow to sit at least 5 minutes.

2. In a large soup or stock pot, sauté onion and bell pepper in oil until soft.

3. Reduce heat to medium low and add TVP and remaining ingredients. Simmer, covered, for at least 15 minutes, stirring occasionally.

4. For thicker and less sloppy "Sloppy Jolindas," simmer a bit longer, uncovered, to reduce the liquid.

PER SERVING Calories: 158 | Fat: 4g | Sodium: 795mg | Fiber: 6g | Protein: 12g

Baked Mexican Tempeh Cakes

Like tofu, tempeh can be baked in a flavorful sauce,
but it does need to be simmered first, just to soften it up a bit.

INGREDIENTS | SERVES 4

2 8-ounce packages tempeh
1 cup water or vegetable broth
⅓ cup tomato paste
3 cloves garlic, minced
2 tablespoons soy sauce
2 tablespoons apple cider vinegar
3 tablespoons water
1½ teaspoons chili powder
½ teaspoon oregano
¼ teaspoon cayenne, or to taste
Tomato salsa or hot sauce

1. If your tempeh is thicker than ¾ inch, slice it in half through the middle to create two thinner halves. Then, slice each block of tempeh in fourths. Simmer in water or vegetable broth for 10 minutes, and drain well.

2. Whisk together the tomato paste, garlic, soy sauce, vinegar, water, chili powder, oregano, and cayenne. Add tempeh, and allow to marinate for at least 1 hour or overnight.

3. Preheat oven to 375°F.

4. Transfer tempeh to a lightly greased baking sheet or casserole dish and baste with a bit of the marinade.

5. Bake for 15–17 minutes. Turn tempeh pieces over and baste with a bit more marinade. Bake another 15–17 minutes. Serve topped with tomato salsa or hot sauce.

PER SERVING Calories: 246 | Fat: 12g | Sodium: 494mg | Fiber: 1g | Protein: 22g

No Shepherd, No Sheep Pie

Sheep- and shepherd-less pie is a hearty vegan entrée for big appetites!

INGREDIENTS | SERVES 6

1½ cups TVP
1½ cups hot water or vegetable broth
½ onion, chopped
2 cloves garlic, minced
1 large carrot, sliced thin
2 tablespoons olive oil
¾ cup sliced mushrooms
½ cup green peas
½ cup vegetable broth
½ cup + 3 tablespoons soy milk
1 tablespoon flour
5 medium potatoes, cooked
2 tablespoons vegan margarine
¼ teaspoon rosemary
¼ teaspoon sage
½ teaspoon paprika (optional)
½ teaspoon salt
¼ teaspoon black pepper

1. Preheat oven to 350°F.

2. Combine TVP with hot water or vegetable broth and allow to sit for 6–7 minutes. Gently drain any excess moisture.

3. In a large skillet, sauté onions, garlic, and carrots in oil until onions are soft, about 5 minutes. Add mushrooms, green peas, vegetable broth, and ½ cup soy milk. Whisk in flour just until sauce thickens, then transfer to a casserole dish.

4. Mash together the potatoes, margarine, and 3 tablespoons soy milk with the rosemary, sage, paprika, and salt and pepper, and spread over the vegetables.

5. Bake for 30–35 minutes, or until lightly browned on top.

PER SERVING Calories: 273 | Fat: 4g | Sodium: 373mg | Fiber: 9g | Protein: 17g

Pineapple TVP Baked Beans

*Add a kick to these saucy homemade vegetarian baked beans
with a bit of cayenne pepper if you'd like.*

INGREDIENTS | SERVES 4

2 15-ounce cans pinto or navy beans,
partially drained
1 onion, diced
⅔ cup barbecue sauce
2 tablespoons prepared mustard
2 tablespoons brown sugar
1 cup TVP
1 cup hot water
1 8-ounce can diced pineapple, drained
¾ teaspoon salt
½ teaspoon pepper

Canadian Baked Beans

Why not omit the brown sugar and
use pure maple syrup for sweetened
Canadian-style baked beans, eh?

1. In a large stock pot, combine beans and about half
   their liquid, onion, barbecue sauce, mustard, and brown
   sugar and bring to a slow simmer. Cover and allow to
   cook for at least 10 minutes, stirring occasionally.

2. Combine TVP with hot water and allow to sit for 6–8
   minutes to rehydrate TVP. Drain.

3. Add TVP, pineapple, salt, and pepper to beans; cover
   and slowly simmer another 10–12 minutes.

PER SERVING Calories: 389 | Fat: 2g | Sodium: 1,461mg |
Fiber: 15g | Protein: 23g

Spicy Seitan Taco "Meat"

Finely dice the seitan, or pulse it in the food processor until diced small for maximum surface area and spice in this recipe, and pile up the taco fixings!

INGREDIENTS | SERVES 6

½ onion, diced

½ green or red bell pepper, chopped small

1 large tomato, chopped

1 package prepared seitan, chopped small (about 2½ cups)

2 tablespoons oil

1 tablespoon soy sauce

1 teaspoon hot sauce, or to taste

2 teaspoons chili powder

½ teaspoon cumin

1. In a large skillet, sauté onion, bell pepper, tomato, and seitan in oil, stirring frequently, until seitan is browned and tomatoes and pepper are soft.

2. Reduce heat and add soy sauce, hot sauce, chili powder, and cumin, coating well. Heat for 1 more minute.

PER SERVING Calories: 130 | Fat: 6g | Sodium: 497mg | Fiber: 2g | Protein: 16g

Seitan Barbecue "Meat"

Sooner or later, all vegans discover the magically delicious combination of seitan and barbecue sauce in some variation of this classic favorite.

INGREDIENTS | SERVES 6

1 package prepared seitan, chopped into thin strips (about 2 cups)

1 large onion, chopped

3 cloves garlic, minced

2 tablespoons oil

1 cup barbecue sauce

2 tablespoons water

1. Heat seitan, onions, and garlic in oil, stirring frequently, until onions are just soft and seitan is lightly browned.

2. Reduce heat to medium low and stir in barbecue sauce and water. Allow to simmer, stirring to coat seitan, until most of the liquid has been absorbed, about 10 minutes.

PER SERVING Calories: 190 | Fat: 5g | Sodium: 784mg | Fiber: 2g | Protein: 15g

Seitan Sandwiches

Piled on top of sourdough along with some vegan mayonnaise, lettuce, and tomato, this makes a perfect sandwich. Melt some vegan cheese for a simple Philly "cheesesteak"–style sandwich, or pile on the vegan Thousand Island and sauerkraut for a seitan Reuben.

Greek Seitan Gyros

Wander the streets of Manhattan or Cairo and you'll find that these messy sandwiches have a huge cult following among street-food lovers. If raw onion isn't your thing, just leave it out.

INGREDIENTS | SERVES 6

1 16-ounce package seitan, thinly sliced
2 tablespoons oil
¾ teaspoon paprika
½ teaspoon parsley
¼ teaspoon garlic powder
¼ teaspoon oregano
Salt and pepper, to taste
6 pitas
2 tomatoes, sliced thin
1 onion, chopped (optional)
½ head iceberg lettuce, shredded
1 cup Vegan Tzatziki (p. 29) or nondairy sour cream

1. Sauté seitan in oil and coat well with seasonings. Heat until seitan is lightly browned and spices are fragrant, about 5–7 minutes.

2. Top each pita with a portion of seitan, tomatoes, onion, lettuce, and about 2 tablespoons Vegan Tzatziki or nondairy sour cream, and fold in half to eat.

PER SERVING Calories: 341 | Fat: 8g | Sodium: 651mg | Fiber: 4g | Protein: 23g

Crispy Tempeh Fries

Frying these tempeh sticks twice makes them extra crispy.

INGREDIENTS | SERVES 2

1 8-ounce package tempeh
½ teaspoon salt
½ teaspoon garlic powder
Oil for frying
Seasoning salt, to taste

Simmering Tempeh

Most tempeh recipes will turn out better if your tempeh is simmered in a bit of water or vegetable broth first. This improves the digestibility of the tempeh, softens it up, and decreases the cooking time. And if you add some seasonings such as soy sauce, garlic powder, or herbs, it will increase the flavor as well.

1. Slice tempeh into thin strips. Simmer tempeh, covered, in 1 inch of water for 10 minutes. Drain.

2. While tempeh is still moist, sprinkle with salt and garlic powder.

3. Heat oil and fry tempeh for 5–6 minutes until crispy and browned. Place tempeh on paper towels and allow to cool for at least 30 minutes.

4. Reheat oil and fry again for another 4–5 minutes. Season lightly with seasoning salt while still warm.

PER SERVING Calories: 256 | Fat: 17g | Sodium: 591mg | Fiber: 0g | Protein: 21g

Basic Baked Tempeh Patties

Baked tempeh is a simple entrée, or use as a patty to make veggie burgers or sandwiches. Slice your tempeh into cubes to add to fried rice, noodles, or stir-fries.

INGREDIENTS | SERVES 2

1 8-ounce package tempeh

1 cup + 2 tablespoons water or vegetable broth

3 tablespoons soy sauce

2 tablespoons apple cider vinegar

3 cloves garlic, minced

2 teaspoons sesame oil

What Is Tempeh?

Long a staple food in the Indonesian islands, tempeh sounds a bit odd when described: it's made from cultured (that is, fermented) cooked soybeans. Don't let that turn you off though, as tempeh is chewy, textured, meaty, and super tasty! Look for tempeh in the refrigerator section of natural-foods stores. Several different kinds are usually available, but they're all interchangeable, so try them all!

1. If your tempeh is thicker than ¾ inch, slice in half through the center to make two thinner pieces, then slice into desired shape.

2. Simmer tempeh in 1 cup water or vegetable broth for 10 minutes; drain well.

3. Whisk together remaining ingredients, including 2 tablespoons of water or vegetable broth, and marinate tempeh for at least 1 hour or overnight.

4. Preheat oven to 375°F and transfer tempeh to a lightly greased baking sheet.

5. Bake for 10–12 minutes on each side.

PER SERVING Calories: 278 | Fat: 17g | Sodium: 1,365mg | Fiber: 0g | Protein: 23g

Sinless Chili Cheese Fries

Chili cheese fries sin carne *(without meat) are almost healthy enough to eat as an entrée. Almost. But go ahead and eat them for dinner; you deserve it, and no one will ever know.*

INGREDIENTS | SERVES 4

1 20-ounce bag frozen French fries
½ onion, chopped
1 tablespoon oil
1 15-ounce can kidney beans
1½ cups TVP, rehydrated in water
1⅓ cups tomato paste
2 tablespoons chili powder
½ teaspoon cumin
½ teaspoon cayenne pepper, or to taste
2 tablespoons vegan margarine
2 tablespoons flour
1½ cups soy milk
2 tablespoons prepared mustard
½ teaspoon garlic powder
½ teaspoon salt
½ cup grated vegan cheese

1. Prepare French fries according to package instructions.

2. Sauté onion in oil until soft. Reduce heat and add beans, TVP, tomato paste, chili powder, cumin, and cayenne pepper. Cover and simmer for 8–10 minutes.

3. In a separate pot, melt the vegan margarine and flour together until thick and pasty, then stir in soy milk, mustard, garlic powder, and salt. Add vegan cheese and heat just until melted and mixture has thickened.

4. Smother French fries with TVP chili, and top with cheese sauce.

PER SERVING Calories: 680 | Fat: 21g | Sodium: 1,500mg | Fiber: 20g | Protein: 36g

TVP, Mushroom, and White Wine Stroganoff

Vegetable broth may be used in place of the white wine.
Serve this stroganoff over noodles, rice, pasta, or baked potatoes.

INGREDIENTS | SERVES 4

¾ cup TVP
¾ cup hot water or vegetable broth
1½ cups sliced mushrooms
1 onion, diced
2 tablespoons vegan margarine
½ cup white wine
½ teaspoon sage
½ teaspoon parsley
½ teaspoon garlic powder
1 tablespoon flour
2 cups soy milk
½ cup nondairy sour cream
2 teaspoons Dijon mustard
Salt and pepper, to taste

1. Rehydrate TVP in hot water or vegetable broth and drain any excess moisture.

2. Heat the mushrooms and onions in vegan margarine for just a minute or 2, then add white wine, sage, parsley, and garlic powder and simmer until soft, about 3–4 more minutes, over medium-low heat.

3. Add flour and stir constantly until pasty and thick. Slowly add soy milk, whisking to combine. Heat until thick and creamy.

4. Stir in sour cream and Dijon mustard, and season generously with salt and pepper.

PER SERVING Calories: 293 | Fat: 64g | Sodium: 334mg | Fiber: 4g | Protein: 15g

Mix and Match

Instead of plain TVP, make a batch of Italian "meatballs" from the recipe on p. 170 to smother in stroganoff sauce and top off a plate of noodles.

TVP Stuffed Peppers

This is a great way to use up any leftover rice.
Top with a bit of grated vegan cheese, if you'd like.

INGREDIENTS | SERVES 6

6 bell peppers, any color
¾ cup TVP
¾ cup hot vegetable broth
1 onion, chopped
2 ribs celery, diced
⅔ cup mushrooms, chopped small
2 tablespoons olive oil
1½ cups rice, cooked
1 teaspoon parsley
½ teaspoon oregano
½ teaspoon salt
2 cups tomato or marinara sauce, divided

1. Preheat oven to 325°F.

2. Slice tops off bell peppers and remove inner seeds.

3. Combine TVP and vegetable broth, and allow to sit for 6–7 minutes to rehydrate. Drain.

4. In a large skillet, sauté onion, celery, and mushrooms in oil until onions are soft and mushrooms are browned, about 5 minutes. Reduce heat to medium low and add cooked rice, TVP, parsley, oregano, salt, and tomato sauce, reserving about ½ cup sauce. Heat just until combined.

5. Stuff mixture into bell peppers, place in a baking pan or casserole dish, and spoon a bit of the remaining sauce on top of each. Place "lids" back on bell peppers (optional).

6. Bake for 30 minutes, or until peppers are cooked.

PER SERVING Calories: 145 | Fat: 1g | Sodium: 757mg | Fiber: 6g | Protein: 10g

Chapter 13

Delicious Desserts

Pumpkin Maple Pie

Make a Vegan Cookie Pie Crust (p. 284) with gingerbread cookies to complement the fall spices in this classic American treat.

INGREDIENTS | SERVES 8

1 16-ounce can pumpkin purée
½ cup maple syrup
1 12-ounce block silken tofu
¼ cup sugar
1½ teaspoons cinnamon
½ teaspoon ginger powder
½ teaspoon nutmeg
¼ teaspoon ground cloves (optional)
½ teaspoon salt
1 vegan pie crust

1. Preheat oven to 400°F.

2. Process together the pumpkin, maple syrup, and tofu until smooth and creamy. Add sugar and spices and pour into pie crust.

3. Bake for 1 hour, or until done. Allow to cool before slicing and serving, as pie will set and firm as it cools.

PER SERVING Calories: 266 | Fat: 9g | Sodium: 381mg | Fiber: 2g | Protein: 3g

For a Sweet, Buttery, Candied Pecan Topping

Chop ½ cup or so of pecan halves and mix with a couple tablespoons of maple syrup, a tablespoon or 2 of melted vegan margarine, and a sprinkle of cloves, nutmeg, or cinnamon. Add to the top of the pie about halfway through the baking time.

Chocolate Mocha Ice Cream

*If you have an ice-cream maker, you can skip the stirring and freezing
and just add the blended ingredients to your machine.*

INGREDIENTS | SERVES 6

1 cup vegan chocolate chips
1 cup soy milk
1 12-ounce block silken tofu
⅓ cup sugar
2 tablespoons instant coffee
2 teaspoons vanilla
¼ teaspoon salt

1. Using a double boiler, or over very low heat, melt chocolate chips until smooth and creamy. Allow to cool slightly.

2. In a blender or food processor, blend together the soy milk, tofu, sugar, instant coffee, vanilla, and salt until very smooth and creamy, at least 2 minutes. Add melted chocolate chips, and process until smooth.

3. Transfer mixture to a large freezer-proof baking or casserole dish and freeze.

4. Stir every 30 minutes until a smooth ice cream forms, about 4 hours. If mixture gets too firm, transfer to a blender, process until smooth, then return to freezer.

PER SERVING Calories: 150 | Fat: 8g | Sodium: 120mg | Fiber: 0g | Protein: 5g

Foolproof Vegan Fudge

Vegan fudge is much easier to make than nonvegan fudge, so don't worry about a thing when making this fudge. Regular soy milk will work just fine, but the soy cream has a richer taste.

INGREDIENTS | YIELDS 24 1-INCH PIECES

⅓ cup vegan margarine
⅓ cup cocoa
⅓ cup soy cream
½ teaspoon vanilla
2 tablespoons peanut butter
3–3½ cups powdered sugar
¾ cup nuts, finely chopped

Mint Fudge? Almond Fudge?
For a variation, halve the vanilla extract and add ¼ teaspoon of flavored extract: almond, mint, or whatever you enjoy.

1. Lightly grease a small baking dish or square cake pan.

2. Using a double boiler, or over very low heat, melt the vegan margarine with the cocoa, soy cream, vanilla, and peanut butter.

3. Slowly incorporate powdered sugar until mixture is smooth, creamy, and thick. Stir in nuts.

4. Immediately transfer to pan and chill until completely firm, at least 2 hours.

PER 2-PIECE SERVING Calories: 237 | Fat: 12g | Sodium: 89mg | Fiber: 1g | Protein: 2g

Coconut Rice Pudding

The combination of juicy soft mango with tropical coconut milk is simply heavenly, but if mangos are unavailable, pineapples or strawberries would add a delicious touch to this refined sugar–free dessert.

INGREDIENTS | SERVES 4

1½ cups cooked white rice
1½ cups vanilla soy milk
1½ cups coconut milk
3 tablespoons brown rice syrup or maple syrup
2 tablespoons agave nectar
4–5 dates, chopped
Dash cinnamon or nutmeg
2 mangos, chopped

1. Combine rice, soy milk, and coconut milk over low heat. Bring to a very low simmer for 10 minutes, or until mixture starts to thicken.

2. Stir in brown rice syrup, agave nectar, and dates and heat for another 2–3 minutes.

3. Allow to cool slightly before serving, to allow pudding to thicken slightly. Garnish with a dash of cinnamon or nutmeg and fresh fruit just before serving.

PER SERVING Calories: 448 | Fat: 20g | Sodium: 51mg | Fiber: 3g | Protein: 6g

Maple Date Carrot Cake

Free of refined sugar and with applesauce for moisture and just a touch of oil, this is a cake you can feel good about eating for breakfast. Leave out the dates if you want even less natural sugar.

INGREDIENTS | SERVES 8

1½ cups raisins
1⅓ cups pineapple juice
6 dates, diced
2¼ cups grated carrot
½ cup maple syrup
¼ cup applesauce
2 tablespoons oil
3 cups flour
1½ teaspoons baking soda
½ teaspoon salt
1 teaspoon cinnamon
½ teaspoon allspice or nutmeg
Egg replacer for 2 eggs

Egg Substitutes

Commercial egg replacers are convenient, but ground flax meal works just as well. Whisk together 1 tablespoon of flax meal with 2 tablespoons of water for each "egg." Let it sit for a few minutes and you'll see why it makes such a great binder, as it quickly becomes gooey and gelatinous.

1. Preheat oven to 375°F and grease and flour a cake pan.

2. Combine the raisins with pineapple juice and allow to sit for 5–10 minutes to soften. In a separate small bowl, cover the dates with water until soft, about 10 minutes. Drain water from dates.

3. In a large mixing bowl, combine the raisins and pineapple juice, carrot, maple syrup, applesauce, oil, and dates. In a separate large bowl, combine the flour, baking soda, salt, cinnamon, and allspice or nutmeg.

4. Combine the dry ingredients with the wet ingredients, and add prepared egg replacer. Mix well.

5. Pour batter into prepared cake pan, and bake for 30 minutes or until a toothpick inserted in the center comes out clean.

PER SERVING Calories: 394 | Fat: 4g | Sodium: 406mg | Fiber: 4g | Protein: 6g

Sugar-Free Tofu Chocolate Pudding

Whoever was the genius who first combined chocolate and peanut butter deserves a Nobel Prize. Or at least a MacArthur genius award. Check your peanut butter brand for added sugar.

INGREDIENTS | SERVES 2

1 12-ounce block silken tofu
¼ cup cocoa powder
½ teaspoon vanilla
¼ cup peanut butter or other nut butter
¼ cup maple syrup or brown rice syrup

Process all ingredients together until smooth and creamy.

PER SERVING Calories: 390 | Fat: 21g | Sodium: 160mg | Fiber: 2g | Protein: 16g

Vegan Cookie Pie Crust

Use any kind of store-bought vegan cookie you like for this one: gingersnaps for pumpkin pies, chocolate or peanut butter sandwich cookies for cheesecakes, or wafers for a neutral flavor.

INGREDIENTS | SERVES 8

25 small vegan cookies
¼ cup vegan margarine, melted
½ teaspoon vanilla

It's a Garnish, Too
Plan on having a few extra tablespoons of this crumbly cookie mix to sprinkle on top of your vegan pie or cheesecake for a sweet topping.

1. Process cookies in a food processor until finely ground. Or, working in batches, seal cookies in a ziplock bag and crumble using a rolling pin until fine.

2. Add margarine and vanilla a bit at a time until mixture is sticky.

3. Press evenly into pie tin, spreading about ¼ inch thick. No prebaking is needed.

PER SERVING Calories: 144 | Fat: 7g | Sodium: 228mg | Fiber: 0g | Protein: 1g

Cocoa-Nut-Coconut No-Bake Cookies

*Have the kids help you shape these into little balls,
and try not to eat them all along the way!*

**INGREDIENTS | YIELDS 2 DOZEN
COOKIES**

¼ cup vegan margarine

½ cup soy milk

2 cups sugar

⅓ cup cocoa

½ cup peanut butter (or other nut
butter)

½ teaspoon vanilla

3 cups quick-cooking oats

½ cup walnuts or cashews, finely
chopped

½ cup coconut flakes

1. Line a baking sheet with wax paper.

2. Melt the vegan margarine and soy milk together and
add sugar and cocoa. Bring to a quick boil to dissolve
sugar, then reduce heat to low and stir in peanut butter,
just until melted.

3. Remove from heat and stir in remaining ingredients.
Allow to cool slightly.

4. Spoon about 3 tablespoon of mixture at a time onto
wax paper and press lightly to form a cookie shape.
Chill until firm.

PER 1 COOKIE Calories: 181 | Fat: 8g | Sodium: 55mg |
Fiber: 2g | Protein: 4g

Cheater's Pumpkin Pie Cupcakes

*Add a handful of raisins or chopped walnuts if you'd like a little texture,
or frost and garnish with fall-colored vegan candies.*

**INGREDIENTS | YIELDS 1 DOZEN
CUPCAKES**

1 box vegan spice cake or yellow
cake mix

1 16-ounce can pumpkin purée

¼ cup soy milk

½ teaspoon pumpkin pie spice (if using
yellow cake mix only)

1. Preheat oven according to instructions on cake mix
package and lightly grease or line a muffin tin.

2. Combine all ingredients in a large bowl.

3. Fill each muffin cup about ⅔ full and bake according to
instructions on cake mix.

PER SERVING Calories: 195 | Fat: 3g | Sodium: 284mg |
Fiber: 1g | Protein: 3g

Cheater's Chocolate Cupcakes

Use a vegan chocolate cake mix and
add 1½ tablespoons of cocoa powder.
Kick it up a notch with a handful of vegan
chocolate chips.

Strawberry Coconut Ice Cream

Rich and creamy, this is the most decadent dairy-free strawberry ice cream you'll ever taste.

INGREDIENTS | SERVES 6

2 cups coconut cream
1¾ cups frozen strawberries
¾ cup sugar
2 teaspoons vanilla
¼ teaspoon salt

1. Purée together all ingredients until smooth and creamy.

2. Transfer mixture to a large freezer-proof baking or casserole dish and freeze.

3. Stir every 30 minutes until a smooth ice cream forms, about 4 hours. If mixture gets too firm, transfer to a blender, process until smooth, then return to freezer.

PER SERVING Calories: 475 | Fat: 16g | Sodium: 134mg | Fiber: 2g | Protein: 1g

"Secret Ingredient" Cake Mix Cake

This is another one of those unbelievable recipes that only vegans seem to know about. You just have to try it to believe it! As an added bonus, your vegan cake is virtually fat free!

INGREDIENTS | SERVES 8

1 box vegan cake mix
1 12-ounce can full-sugar soda (no diet)

Flavor Combos

Experiment with different flavor combinations just for fun! Try a lemon-lime or orange soda with a yellow cake mix, a cherry soda with chocolate cake mix, and a grape or strawberry soda with a vanilla cake mix.

1. Grease your cake pan well, as the reduced fat in this cake makes it a bit "stickier."

2. Preheat oven according to package instructions.

3. Mix together cake mix and soda, pour into a cake pan, and bake immediately according to package instructions.

PER SERVING Calories: 289 | Fat: 5g | Sodium: 425mg | Fiber: 0g | Protein: 3g

Vegan Peanut Butter Frosting

Kids will love this creamy frosting, and it's a nice change from the usual flavors, especially when paired with a chocolate cake.

INGREDIENTS | SERVES 8

1 cup peanut butter, softened
⅓ cup vegan margarine, softened
2 tablespoons maple syrup
½ teaspoon vanilla
2 tablespoons soy milk
2 cups powdered sugar

1. Whisk together the peanut butter, margarine, maple syrup, vanilla, and soy milk.

2. Slowly incorporate the powdered sugar, using a little bit more or less to get the desired consistency.

PER SERVING Calories: 388 | Fat: 24g | Sodium: 257mg | Fiber: 2g | Protein: 8g

Chocolate Peanut Butter Explosion Pie

You can pretend it's healthy because it's made with tofu, or toss all your troubles to the wind and just enjoy it. You'll feel like a kid again.

INGREDIENTS | SERVES 8

¾ cup vegan chocolate chips
1 12-ounce block silken tofu
½ cup + ¾ cup peanut butter
2 tablespoons + ⅔ cup soy milk
1 prepared Vegan Cookie Pie Crust (p. 284)
2–2½ cups powdered sugar

Make It a Little Less Intense

This really is a rich chocolate and peanut butter flavor explosion, but if you want to tame it down a bit, it's still delicious without the peanut butter topping. Shop for sugar-free vegan chocolate chips at your health-food store, or try it with carob chips to make it even "healthier."

1. Over very low heat or in a double boiler, melt the chocolate chips.

2. In a blender, purée tofu, ½ cup peanut butter, and 2 tablespoons of soy milk until combined, then add melted chocolate chips until smooth and creamy.

3. Pour into pie crust and chill for 1 hour, or until firm.

4. Over low heat, melt together ¾ cup peanut butter, ⅔ cup soy milk, and powdered sugar until smooth and creamy. You may need a little more or less than 2 cups of sugar.

5. Spread peanut butter mixture over cooled pie, and return to refrigerator. Chill until firm.

PER SERVING Calories: 561 | Fat: 32g | Sodium: 428mg | Fiber: 3g | Protein: 14g

Pineapple Cherry "Dump" Cake

Just dump it all in! Who said vegan baking was hard?

INGREDIENTS | SERVES 8

1 20-ounce can crushed pineapple, undrained

1 20-ounce can cherry pie filling

1 box vegan vanilla or yellow cake mix

½ cup vegan margarine, melted

How to Grease and Flour a Cake Pan

Especially with lower-fat cake recipes such as this one, you'll want a well-greased and floured pan, to prevent the cake from sticking. A nonstick spray works just as well as a tablespoon or so of melted margarine or cooking oil. Coat the pan well, including the sides. Then, coat with a light dusting of flour, shaking the pan to cover all the edges.

1. Preheat oven according to directions on cake mix box and lightly grease and flour a large cake pan.

2. Dump the pineapple into the cake pan, then dump the pie filling, then the powdered cake mix on top.

3. Drizzle the cake mix with vegan margarine.

4. Bake according to instructions on cake mix package.

PER SERVING Calories: 498 | Fat: 16g | Sodium: 594mg | Fiber: 1g | Protein: 4g

No Egg-Replacer Chocolate Cake

Applesauce helps keep this chocolate cake moist without eggs or egg replacer and cuts down on the fat, too, and the vinegar helps to lighten it up a bit.

INGREDIENTS | SERVES 8

1½ cups flour
¾ cup sugar
⅓ cup cocoa powder
1 teaspoon baking soda
1 cup soy milk
1 teaspoon vanilla
¼ cup applesauce
2 tablespoons oil
1 tablespoon vinegar

For the Perfect Vegan Cake . . .

Vegan cakes tend to be heavier and denser than regular cakes. Here's a few ways to compensate: Step one: really beat the margarine and sugar together, and make sure all the sugar is incorporated, even those pesky little bits on the side of the bowl. A well-aerated margarine and sugar mix means a fluffier cake. To make sure your cake rises to perfection, get it in the oven right away to take advantage of the leavening ingredients. And of course, allow your cake to cool completely before frosting. Patience, patience!

1. Preheat oven to 350°F and lightly grease and flour a large cake pan.

2. In a large bowl, combine the flour, sugar, cocoa, and baking soda. In a separate small bowl, mix together the soy milk, vanilla, applesauce, oil, and vinegar.

3. Quickly mix together the dry ingredients with the wet ingredients, combining just until smooth.

4. Pour into prepared cake pan and bake for 26–28 minutes, or until toothpick or fork inserted comes out clean.

PER SERVING Calories: 213 | Fat: 5g | Sodium: 170mg | Fiber: 2g | Protein: 4g

Easy Banana Date Cookies

The daily fast during Ramadan is traditionally broken with a date at sunset, and a version of these simple, refined sugar–free cookies is popular in Islamic communities in northern Africa, though almonds are traditionally added.

INGREDIENTS | YIELDS 1 DOZEN COOKIES

1 cup chopped pitted dates
1 banana (medium ripe)
¼ teaspoon vanilla
1¾ cups coconut flakes

1. Preheat oven to 375°F. Cover dates in water and soak for about 10 minutes until softened. Drain.

2. Process together the dates, banana, and vanilla until almost smooth. Stir in coconut flakes by hand until thick. You may need a little more or less than 1¾ cups.

3. Drop by generous tablespoonfuls onto a cookie sheet. Bake 10–12 minutes, or until done. Cookies will be soft and chewy.

PER 1 COOKIE Calories: 111 | Fat: 6g | Sodium: 4mg | Fiber: 3g | Protein: 1g

Chocolate Graham Cracker Candy Bars

Have the kids help out by spreading the peanut butter while you do the dipping. Matzo, saltines, or any cracker will work, really, and because half of them will disappear before you're finished making them, you may want to make a double—or even triple—batch!

INGREDIENTS | YIELDS 16 BARS

1 cup peanut butter or other nut butter
8 vegan graham crackers, quartered, or any vegan cracker
1 cup vegan chocolate chips
¼ cup vegan margarine
Optional toppings: vegan sprinkles, coconut flakes, chopped nuts

Half and Half

For a fancier presentation, shop for vegan white chocolate. Dip only half the cracker into the chocolate, then chill, and dip the other half into melted white chocolate. Beautiful and delicious.

1. Line a baking pan with wax paper.

2. Spread about 1 tablespoon of peanut butter on a cracker, then top with another to make a "sandwich."

3. In a double boiler or over very low heat, melt together the chocolate chips and margarine until smooth and creamy.

4. Using tongs, dip each cracker sandwich into the chocolate and lightly coat. Pick up with the tongs and allow excess chocolate to drip off, then transfer to lined baking sheet.

5. Top with any additional toppings, and chill until firm.

PER 1 BAR Calories: 169 | Fat: 14g | Sodium: 156mg | Fiber: 1g | Protein: 5g

Classic Chocolate Chip Cookies

Just like mom used to make, only with a bit of applesauce to cut down on the fat a bit.

INGREDIENTS | YIELDS ABOUT 2 DOZEN COOKIES

⅔ cup vegan margarine
⅔ cup sugar
⅔ cup brown sugar
⅓ cup applesauce
1½ teaspoons vanilla
Egg replacer for 2 eggs
2½ cups flour
1 teaspoon baking soda
½ teaspoon baking powder
1 teaspoon salt
⅔ cup quick-cooking oats
1½ cups chocolate chips

Add Some Zing

Want to impress your friends? Shop for vegan white chocolate chips to substitute for regular chocolate, and add about ⅔ cup chopped macadamia nuts. Voilà! White chocolate chip–macadamia nut cookies! Just saying it sounds heavenly.

1. Preheat oven to 375°F.

2. In a large mixing bowl, cream together the vegan margarine and white sugar, then mix in brown sugar, applesauce, vanilla, and egg replacer.

3. In a separate bowl, combine the flour, baking soda, baking powder, and salt, then combine with the wet ingredients. Mix well.

4. Stir in oats and chocolate chips just until combined.

5. Drop by generous spoonfuls onto a baking sheet, and bake for 10–12 minutes. For a chewy cookie, don't be tempted to overbake them!

PER 1 COOKIE Calories: 161 | Fat: 7g | Sodium: 232mg | Fiber: 1g | Protein: 2g

Sugar-Free Ginger Spice Cookies

A delicious holiday cookie sweetened with maple syrup and molasses instead of refined sugar.
Adjust the seasonings to your taste—add cloves if you like, or omit the allspice and add extra ginger.

INGREDIENTS | YIELDS 1½ DOZEN COOKIES

⅓ cup vegan margarine, softened
½ cup maple syrup
⅓ cup molasses
¼ cup soy milk
2¼ cups flour
1 teaspoon baking powder
½ teaspoon baking soda
½ teaspoon cinnamon
½ teaspoon ginger
¼ teaspoon allspice or nutmeg
½ teaspoon salt

1. In a large mixing bowl, cream together the vegan margarine, maple syrup, molasses, and soy milk. In a separate bowl, sift together the flour, baking powder, baking soda, cinnamon, ginger, allspice, and salt.

2. Mix the flour and spices in with the wet ingredients until combined. Chill for 30 minutes.

3. Preheat oven to 375°F.

4. Roll dough into 1½-inch balls and place on cookie sheet. Flatten slightly, then bake 10–12 minutes, or until done.

PER 1 COOKIE Calories: 136 | Fat: 4g | Sodium: 178mg | Fiber: 1g | Protein: 2g

Basic Vegan Vanilla Icing

A simple and basic vegan frosting recipe.
Add a few drops of a flavoring extract, food coloring, or just enjoy it as is.

INGREDIENTS | SERVES 8

¼ cup soy milk
⅓ cup vegan margarine, softened
2 teaspoons vanilla
3–3½ cups powdered sugar

1. Mix together the soy milk, margarine, and vanilla until smooth.

2. Slowly incorporate powdered sugar until desired consistency is reached. You may need a bit more or less than 3 cups.

PER SERVING Calories: 248 | Fat: 7g | Sodium: 111mg | Fiber: 0g | Protein: 0g

Frosting Tips

Use an electric or hand mixer to get it super light and creamy. Frosting will firm as it cools, which means also only frost cakes and cupcakes that are cooled already, otherwise the heat will melt the icing.

Chewy Oatmeal Raisin Cookies

The addition of applesauce keeps these classic nostalgic cookies super chewy.
No egg replacer needed.

INGREDIENTS | YIELDS 1½ DOZEN COOKIES

⅓ cup vegan margarine, softened
½ cup brown sugar
¼ cup sugar
⅓ cup applesauce
1 teaspoon vanilla
2 tablespoons soy milk
¾ cup whole wheat flour
½ teaspoon baking soda
½ teaspoon cinnamon
½ teaspoon ginger
1¾ cups quick-cooking oats
⅔ cup raisins

1. Preheat oven to 350°F.

2. Beat the margarine and sugars together until smooth and creamy. Add applesauce, vanilla, and soy milk.

3. Sift together the flour, baking soda, cinnamon, and ginger, then add to wet ingredients.

4. Stir in oats, then raisins. Drop by generous spoonfuls onto a cookie sheet.

5. Bake for 10–12 minutes, or until done.

PER 1 COOKIE Calories: 122 | Fat: 4g | Sodium: 85mg | Fiber: 2g | Protein: 2g

Sweetheart Raspberry Lemon Cupcakes

Add ½ teaspoon of lemon extract for extra lemony goodness in these sweet and tart cupcakes. Or omit the raspberries and add 3 tablespoons of poppy seeds for lemon poppy seed cupcakes. Sweet and tart—sweetheart! Get it?

INGREDIENTS | YIELDS 18 CUPCAKES

½ cup vegan margarine, softened
1 cup sugar
½ teaspoon vanilla
⅔ cup soy milk
3 tablespoons lemon juice
Zest from 2 lemons
1¾ cups flour
1½ teaspoons baking powder
½ teaspoon baking soda
¼ teaspoon salt
¾ cup diced raspberries, fresh or frozen

Raspberry Cream Cheese Frosting

Combine a half container vegan cream cheese with ½ cup raspberry jam and 6 tablespoons of softened vegan margarine. Beat until smooth, then add powdered sugar until a creamy frosting forms. You'll need about 2½ cups. Pile it high and garnish your cupcakes with fresh strawberry slices or pink vegan candies.

1. Preheat oven to 350°F and grease or line a cupcake tin.

2. Beat together the margarine and sugar until light and fluffy, then add vanilla, soy milk, lemon juice, and zest.

3. In a separate bowl, sift together the flour, baking powder, baking soda, and salt.

4. Combine flour mixture with wet ingredients just until mixed. Do not overmix. Gently fold in diced raspberries.

5. Fill each cupcake tin about ⅔ full with batter and bake immediately for 16–18 minutes or until done.

PER 1 CUPCAKE Calories: 139 | Fat: 5g | Sodium: 182mg | Fiber: 1g | Protein: 2g

Apricot Ginger Sorbet

Made with real fruit and without dairy, this is a nearly fat-free treat that you can add to smoothies or just enjoy outside on a hot summer day.

INGREDIENTS | SERVES 6

⅔ cup water
⅔ cup sugar
2 teaspoons fresh minced ginger
5 cups chopped apricots, fresh or frozen
3 tablespoons lemon juice

1. Bring the water, sugar, and ginger to a boil, then reduce to a slow simmer. Heat for 3–4 more minutes until sugar is dissolved and a syrup forms. Allow to cool.

2. Purée the sugar syrup, apricots, and lemon juice until smooth.

3. Transfer mixture to a large freezer-proof baking or casserole dish and freeze.

4. Stir every 30 minutes until a smooth sorbet forms, about 4 hours. If mixture gets too firm, transfer to a blender, process until smooth, then return to freezer.

PER SERVING Calories: 154 | Fat: 1g | Sodium: 2mg | Fiber: 3g | Protein: 2g

Chocolate Mocha Frosting

The combination of chocolate and coffee in a frosting adds an exquisite touch to even a simple cake-mix cake.

INGREDIENTS | SERVES 8

¼ cup strong coffee or espresso, cooled
⅓ cup vegan margarine, softened
2 teaspoons vanilla
⅓ cup cocoa powder
3 cups powdered sugar

1. Mix together the coffee, margarine, and vanilla until smooth, then add cocoa powder.

2. Slowly incorporate powdered sugar until desired consistency is reached. You may need a bit more or less than 3 cups.

PER SERVING Calories: 253 | Fat: 8g | Sodium: 109mg | Fiber: 1g | Protein: 1g

Cookies and Cream Cheesecake

Vegan cheesecake is a great way to dispel those stereotypes about granola-munching wheatgrass-sipping vegan hippies.

INGREDIENTS | SERVES 6

¼ cup soy milk
1 tablespoon cornstarch
1 8-ounce container vegan cream cheese
1 12-ounce block silken tofu
2 tablespoons lemon juice
2 teaspoons vanilla
¼ cup powdered sugar
¼ cup maple syrup
¼ cup oil
8–10 vegan chocolate sandwich cookies
1 Vegan Cookie Pie Crust (p. 284)

That Extra Finishing Touch

Drizzle the top of your vegan cheesecake with some chocolate sauce or vegan hot fudge sauce and some extra crumbled cookies.

1. Preheat oven to 350°F.

2. Whisk together the soy milk and cornstarch in a small bowl. In a blender, combine the soy milk with the cream cheese, tofu, lemon juice, vanilla, powdered sugar, and maple syrup and blend until completely smooth. Slowly add oil on high speed until combined.

3. Stir in crumbled cookies by hand and pour into prepared crust.

4. Bake 40–45 minutes. Allow to cool slightly, then chill. Cheesecake will firm up more as it cools, so avoid the temptation to overbake.

PER SERVING Calories: 566 | Fat: 30g | Sodium: 597mg | Fiber: 1g | Protein: 6g

Sugar-Free No-Bake Cocoa Balls

Craving a healthy chocolate snack? Try these fudgy little cocoa balls, similar to a soft no-bake cookie, but with no refined sugar. Much better than a pint of rocky road on chick-flick night.

INGREDIENTS | SERVES 4

1 cup chopped pitted dates
1 cup walnuts or cashews
¼ cup cocoa powder
1 tablespoon peanut butter
¼ cup coconut flakes

Variations

Roll these little balls in extra coconut flakes for a sweet presentation, or try them with carob powder instead of cocoa—they're just as satisfying. Don't have fresh dates on hand? Raisins may be substituted, but skip the soaking. Even with raisins, you really won't believe they're sugar-free.

1. Cover dates in water and soak for about 10 minutes until softened. Drain.

2. Process dates, nuts, cocoa powder, and peanut butter in a food processor until combined and sticky. Add coconut flakes and process until coarse.

3. Shape into balls and chill.

4. If mixture is too wet, add more nuts and coconut, or add just a touch of water if the mixture is dry and crumbly.

PER SERVING Calories: 348 | Fat: 22g | Sodium: 23mg | Fiber: 8g | Protein: 7g

Appendix A

Protein Comparison Tables

SOURCES OF VEGAN PROTEIN

Food	Serving Size	Protein (grams)
Edamame	1 cup	22.2
Morningstar Farms burger crumbles	1 cup	21.2
Vital wheat gluten	1 ounce	21.0
Tempeh	4 ounces (½ block)	20.4
Canned white beans	1 cup	19.0
Cooked lentils	1 cup	17.9
Chickpeas	1 cup	14.5
Tofu	½ block	13.3
Pumpkin seeds	1 ounce	9.4
Quinoa, cooked	1 cup	8.1
Soy milk	1 cup	8.0
Peanut butter	2 tablespoons	8.0
Frozen spinach	1 cup	7.6
Whole-wheat pasta, cooked	1 cup	7.5
Wild rice, cooked	1 cup	6.4

Extracted from the USDA National Nutrient Database and NutritionData.com.
Recommended dietary allowance is 56 grams for men, 46 grams for women.

NONVEGAN SOURCES OF PROTEIN

Food	Serving Size	Protein (grams)
Low-fat cottage cheese	1 cup	31.0
Chicken	½ breast	22.2
Cooked ground beef	3 ounces	21.7
Canned tuna fish	3 ounces	21.7
Fast food hamburger	1 sandwich	13.9
Canned chicken soup	1 cup	12.3
Low-fat yogurt	8 ounces	9.9
2% milk	1 cup	8.1
Mozzarella cheese	1 ounce	7.4
Cooked bacon	3 slices	7.0
Egg	1 medium	5.5

Appendix B

Recommended Online Resources

Vegan Shopping

Vegan Essentials
Whether you're looking for a nonleather belt, a T-shirt proclaiming your love of tofu, or just some nondairy cheese, you'll find it here. Check out the excellent selection of vegan baking mixes and chocolates.
veganessentials.com

Food Fight
Vegan shopping with a sense of humor. With a storefront location in Portland, Oregon, this is not your average vegan shop. The emphasis is on fun and hard-to-source foods, with a heavy bias toward junk food. If you're looking to try vegan haggis or vegan s'mores, this is the place to look.
foodfightgrocery.com

Bob's Red Mill
For those living in rural areas without access to a natural-foods store, Bob's Red Mill has just about everything you need, including whole grains, egg replacer, vital wheat gluten, TVP, and, most important, nutritional yeast.
bobsredmill.com

Advice and Support

Veggie Boards
With membership in the tens of thousands, the VeggieBoards are an active place to discuss everything from urban composting to the best-tasting veggie burgers.
veggieboards.com

Health and Nutrition

Physicians Committee for Responsible Medicine (PCRM)
PCRM is a leader in the field of preventive medicine, presenting cutting-edge research into the benefits of a plant-based diet and providing reliable and comprehensive nutritional information for vegans.
pcrm.org

The Vegetarian Resource Group
Just about everything you need to know about plant-based nutrition is available online from the Vegetarian Resource Group.
vrg.org

Vegan Restaurants

Happy Cow
Find out where to get a vegan meal across the planet, from Toledo to Timbuktu. This comprehensive Internet directory includes contact information and brief reviews of natural-foods stores, vegan restaurants, and vegan-friendly establishments across the globe.
www.happycow.net

Index

Image Credits